the person in dementia

the person in dementia

A STUDY OF NURSING HOME CARE IN THE US

Athena McLean

BROADVIEW ETHNOGRAPHIES AND CASE STUDIES

broadview press

To my mother, Isabel Barthelmess,
whose agency never faltered.

"From instrument to agent in dementia care."

Library and Archives Canada Cataloguing in Publication

McLean, Athena, 1948-
   The person in dementia : a study in nursing home care in the US / Athena McLean.

(Broadview ethnographies & case studies)
Includes bibliographical references and index.
ISBN-13: 978-1-55111-606-8
ISBN-10: 1-55111-606-5

   1. Alzheimer's disease--Patients--Long-term care--United States.
2. Alzheimer's disease--Patients--Long-term care--United States--Case studies. 3. Medical personnel and patient--United States. I. Title. II. Series.

RC523.M45 2006   362.198'97683100973   C2006-904845-2

Broadview Press is an independent, international publishing house, incorporated in 1985. Broadview believes in shared ownership, both with its employees and with the general public; since the year 2000 Broadview shares have traded publicly on the Toronto Venture Exchange under the symbol BDP.

We welcome comments and suggestions regarding any aspect of our publications—please feel free to contact us at the addresses below or at broadview@broadviewpress.com.

North America
PO Box 1243, Peterborough, Ontario, Canada K9J 7H5
PO Box 1015, 3576 California Road, Orchard Park, NY, USA 14127
Tel: (705) 743-8990; Fax: (705) 743-8353
email: customerservice@broadviewpress.com

UK, Ireland, and continental Europe
NBN International, Estover Road, Plymouth, UK PL6 7PY
Tel: 44 (0) 1752 202300; Fax: 44 (0) 1752 202330
Email: enquiries@nbninternational.com

Australia and New Zealand
UNIREPS, University of New South Wales
Sydney, NSW, Australia 2052
Tel: 61 2 9664 0999; Fax: 61 2 9664 5420
email: info.press@unsw.edu.au

www.broadviewpress.com

Typesetting by Aldo Fierro.

PRINTED IN CANADA

Contents

Foreword

This book is a stellar achievement. It documents the social and cultural factors that create or extend behavioral disturbances by elders with Alzheimer's disease and other dementias who reside in a nursing home. In addition, it is an ethnography of that nursing home. Further, it is the only book I know of that applies recent advances in social and critical theory to better understanding the nursing home as a constructed, power-based system.

What is also exceptional about the book are its portraits of individuals, most of whom are demented, who live in the nursing home. These persons emerge clearly as having distinctive characters, motivations, and selfhoods that are visible despite the disease process. Given the focus on personhood that this book supplies, the behavioral "disturbances" enacted by residents become understandable, given the sometimes restricted linguistic codes that are being utilized, due to the disease process. The author suggests that we cannot understand what people who live in the nursing home think they are doing, without reference to a detailed knowledge of that person's life course, biography, and history, and therefore their unique motivations. A "generic" response to the dementia or a treatment program for the demented does not go far enough in tailoring materials for the individual.

In addition, *The Person in Dementia*, unlike so much other research literature in aging, does not treat nursing home workers as passive agents, without their own personal histories, predilections, and issues. Indeed, so much of the "treatment" of behavioral disturbances involves the nuances of workers' situations, personalities, pressures, and professional needs.

One other feature that makes this book exceptional is the close tracing of the politics and personalities of the nursing home and how these *directly* affect the lives of the residents, the nature of any disturbed behavior, and how this behavior is handled by the staff. In this area, two things are of note. First, the book clearly demonstrates how two head nurses' distinctive philosophies of care, directly tied to their personal and professional histories, are responsible for quite unique programs of care and thus the distinctive ways in which behavioral disturbances are treated. Second, this book documents how an aggressive, combative nursing home administration directly and indirectly affects the quality of life of residents. This occurs in several ways and includes such factors as staffing levels, administrative pressures on the head nurses, tolerance for exceptions to strongly promulgated rules, and the general need to control others.

I am so impressed with this work because it tells the truth about what goes on in nursing homes.

Robert L. Rubinstein

Preface

This book is long overdue. It is based on research I conducted at a nursing home on the east coast of the United States from 1992 to 1994. Robert Rubinstein, then Director of the Polisher Research Institute, along with other researchers, had received a grant from the Alzheimer's Association to conduct an innovative ethnographic study of communication in dementia. The study focused on the "disturbed behaviors" of elders diagnosed with some form of senile dementia. They wanted to explore the possibility that these behaviors represented efforts on the part of the elders to communicate and function in their cognitively altered world. I was invited to conduct the research. At the time I was unaware of just how progressive this project was. A few bold articles had suggested that what appeared as disturbed behaviors to others, was actually nonverbal communication (Bartol 1979) or expressions of purposeful activity (Shomaker 1987: 372). But no one had attempted to qualitatively study this before.

Since that time, there has been a literal explosion of writing on caregiving for the demented elder, based to a great extent on the writing and pioneering care practices of the late British psychologist, Thomas Kitwood. Kitwood pushed researchers and caregivers to see, and work to preserve, the person in dementia when others argued that no person remained. His ideas have slowly been imported into North America.

Meanwhile, home-born approaches, like the Eden Alternative, and the grassroots Pioneer Network, have challenged the belief that little can be done to help elders with dementia, and begun to transform practices in many long-term care facilities. New medications beyond tacrine, the only available medication when I was conducting my research, have also been developed. Unfortunately, they have only postponed deterioration, not cured the dementia.

After discovering the changes which had transpired during the last ten years, I was encouraged, only to be disheartened to discover that they are still very cutting edge. They represent only a trickling of actual nursing home caregiving practices that remain far from desirable for the most part. There is now good research suggesting that the sense of hopelessness that had previously surrounded long-term dementia caregiving with "behaviorally disruptive" elders was overly pessimistic. My own research reported here certainly attests to that as it also morally challenges us to examine the unfortunate consequences that a hopeless approach to care can produce. I hope that my research will add fuel to the incipient movement to improve the way in which elders with dementia are regarded and to bring them the kind of dignified care that supports them as persons in their final years.

Acknowledgements

I wish to acknowledge Dr. Robert Rubinstein, Professor of Anthropology at the University of Maryland, Baltimore County, Baltimore, Maryland for the opportunity to conduct this study; he wrote the initial grant that made this project possible and was a very generous mentor who made himself available to discuss ideas and offer guidance. Bob's early recognition of the importance of the *person* in dementia got me thinking along those lines. I also cannot thank enough the staff (both administrative and clinical), residents, and family of the special care units I studied for sharing so fully of themselves. A special thanks go to the charge and head nurses who patiently answered my incessant questions without complaint, and to the nursing assistants who allowed me to accompany them during care routines and responded to my continual inquiries. Many families went out of their way to help me understand the unique history and situation of their relative. Special gratitude goes to the residents who welcomed or endured my company in a world that was already very invasive. I also wish to acknowledge Tula, a resident and the "poet" of Snow 1 for her many apt comments, which got me thinking about life on the unit; some of her comments introduce the case studies. A grant from the Alzheimer's Association (#11RG-92-076) made the research possible. And a Research Professorship Award 2003-2004 from Central Michigan University enabled me to complete this project.

Mark Royer, Barbara Frankenfeld, Sandy Schmunk, and Cathy Hackney kept me informed about the latest developments in nursing home care, while generously sharing their own wisdom about these. Miriam Moss kindly kept me abreast of developments at the research site. Critical comments from Judith Barker and Maria Vesperi on my original draft were invaluable for rethinking how to make my manuscript widely accessible. A special thanks also goes to Trevor and Thea McLean, who offered keen readings of my introduction and provided encouragement and helpful suggestions throughout, and to Thomas McLean, who helped me to find language when my mind refused to cooperate. I appreciate Judy Somerville's permission to reprint her painting for the front cover.[1] The woman on the cover was struggling, like so many persons I have seen with dementia. She did not have dementia, however; she was struggling to hold back a smile. Finally, thanks go to Judith Brand for helping to shape the final form of this manuscript, to Judith Earnshaw for putting it all together so well, and to Anne Brackenbury for all her support and editorial wisdom.

---

[1] "Sometimes Broadway, Sometimes the Catskills," artist's copyright 1980, is a painting by Judy Somerville in acrylic on canvas, 79 in. by 57 in. It is one of an extended series of paintings of older persons whom she has encountered on her many travels. Her works, have been exhibited in the US, Germany, France, Belgium, the UAE and Japan, can be found on her websites <gallerydir.com/judysomerville> and <newyorkartists.net/somerville/judy>.

Introduction

In 1990, Janet Adkins, a 53-year-old woman, devastated by her diagnosis of early Alzheimer's disease and the horrifying prospect of becoming a "nonperson," decided to end her life (Au 2000: 215). She became Dr. Jack Kevorkian's first case of assisted suicide (Potter 1999: 2).

Called the "disease of the century,"[1] Alzheimer's disease, the most common type of senile[2] dementia—a cognitive, functional, and behavioral disorder affecting millions, has likely become the most dreaded disease of old age. Estimates suggesting that close to one half of the population over 85 is affected by Alzheimer's disease (AD) have convinced the public that few elders can escape the disease. By 2050, the number of cases is expected to triple to 12 million, pressing toward a "crisis in caring for the aged," according to a recent White House Commission on Aging (Zwillich 2005). In addition, popularized discourse about the loss of self[3]

---

[1] According to the Alzheimer's Disease and Related Disorders Association (1982), cited by Gubrium (1986b). See also Lock (2005: 200).
[2] "Senile" refers to old age.
[3] As popularized in a volume of that title by Cohen and Eisdorfer (1986).

has led many people to fear losing control over their minds and bodies and to anticipate ending up behind the locked doors of a nursing home. Janet Adkins's story illustrates the loss of human worth that can be felt by persons diagnosed with AD and the extremes to which fear of the disease has carried us.

This was not always the case. Alzheimer's disease, prior to the 1970s, was viewed not as a disease at all, but as an uncommon, pre-senile (i.e., not related to old age) form of dementia, mainly affecting persons between the ages of 30 and 50. During the 1970s, senility—a gradual physical and mental deterioration believed to be *normal* to old age—was biomedically reframed as an *abnormal* condition, Alzheimer's disease, in response to a combination of political, social, and scientific pressures and considerations. The reframing occurred in order to bring attention to the problems of senility and to dispel the notion that decline was an inevitable (and normal) feature of old age (Fox 2000: 212). This redefinition resulted in an explosive number of declared cases of Alzheimer's disease—an "apocalyptic demography" (Robertson 1991: 135)—and a public terror over a disorder that had always been with us.

The biomedical redefinition of senility as a disease has seriously frightened and incapacitated many elders and family members who, according to one caregiver, would have been able "more or less to handle senility."[4] While the impairments of senility cannot be denied, the popular imagination is now consumed with terror about impending Alzheimer's disease. Even minimal evidence of memory loss—a possible sign of eventual dementia—brings panic, often masked as humor, to ordinary conversation.

Because of its pervasive impacts on behavior and identity, Alzheimer's disease (which I shall use interchangeably with "dementia" for purposes of general discussion)[5] can be called a "disease of the person." This is because the person with dementia is often seen as not only *having* the disease, but also as *being* the disease (c.f., Estroff 1993: 251).[6] It is not enough that one *has* dementia; once labeled, the person becomes *identified with* the dementia. After senility was redefined as a disease, heavy research expenditures became directed at discovering cures. As of yet, neither definitive cause nor cure has been found (Wysocki 2002: A16), denying benefits to patients despite its biomedical reframing. This has left a now savvy public

---

[4] As quoted in Gubrium (1986a: 46).

[5] In general discussions, the concern is more about the impacts of the disorder, whatever the cause. I will distinguish among Alzheimer's disease (AD), vascular dementias (VaD), and mixed dementias (MD) when I discuss more technical issues later.

[6] Estroff, however, is referring to mental illness.

frustrated, fearful of "losing their minds" and of eventual nursing home placement, and in cases like Janet Adkins, calling for death hastening.

The explosion of cases of dementia that were identified with its new disease label and the panic this entailed led to the opening of *special care units* by the early 1980s. These units were devoted to providing specially designed nursing home care to accommodate the needs of cognitively impaired elders with *behavioral disturbances* (BDs) like agitation, repetitiveness, wandering, hitting, and screaming (Wagner, Terio, and Orr-Rainey 1995). Although many innovative models have been tried in units like these, with some positive findings, their approaches in working with "behaviorally disturbed" elders have been extremely varied and their success doubtful (Henderson 2003). Too often, the reality for elders has been locked units and warehousing of elders in homes with inadequate staff to provide ethical care—a condition that threatens to worsen with the shortage of qualified caregivers (Zwillich 2005). Treatment of "difficult" behaviors often has been confined to control by physical and chemical (pharmacological) restraints. At the 2005 White House Commission on Aging, ethicist Leon Kass warned against euthanasia and assisted suicide as "an increasing temptation ... we have to guard against" (Zwillich 2005). Until a cure is found, the picture remains grim.

In the absence of a cure, we are left with a sense of nihilism, that is, that "nothing can be done" to help the person. Disturbed behaviors that may indicate legitimate problems or concerns demanding attention are seen instead as unintentional disease artifacts that can be ignored (or should be suppressed), and affected elders are often seen as empty shells of their former selves. It is thus easy for a caregiver to disregard the statements and actions (the *agency*) of someone with dementia under the assumption that the actual *person* is gone and that it is the disease that is meaninglessly acting or uttering. To dismiss an elder's actions and words as meaningless, however, is to render the elder invisible and powerless. As one chronically ill person declared, "I am fundamentally denied."[7]

To deny a failing elder also raises serious moral and ethical concerns. Those in a society who are more capable—and hence more powerful—must take responsibility for those who are more vulnerable and less powerful. How an individual carries out the responsibility of caring for vulnerable individuals says much about that person, and how a society handles the problems of its failing elders says much about the

---

[7]   As quoted in Corbin and Strauss (1987: 249) cited in Estroff (1993: 251).

society as well. Thus Alzheimer's disease presents as much a social and moral challenge as it does a medical one, and decisions concerning "what to do" with affected elders are inextricably tied to the moral foundation of a society.

INTENTION OF THIS BOOK

This book is about elders who were diagnosed with AD or related dementias and who resided in one of two special care units of a nursing home. It is also about the *caregivers* (mostly direct ones like *nurses and nursing assistants*, but also clinicians who directed the care), their approaches to providing care, and the consequences of their caregiving for the elders. I will present my findings and conclusions from an 18-month ethnographic (in-depth observational) study conducted from late in 1992 into July 1994. The elders were living in a large urban nursing home in two special care units designed specifically for persons with more advanced dementia. The units, part of an innovative nursing home complex on the East Coast,[8] were among the first special care units in the United States. Residents were admitted to the units because of disruptive behaviors—*behavioral disturbances* (*BDs*)—believed to have been associated with an advanced stage of their disease.

Although senile dementia is now popularly accepted as a disease to be treated medically, I focus on the way in which mainly *nonmedical* interventions impacted the BDs and affected the lives of particular residents in each unit. The study was guided by a *communications perspective* that took into account the possible problems BDs may have signaled and their meanings for the elder.

Although the two units were identical in floor plan, they differed in the length of tenure of their staff and residents and in their philosophical and organizational approach to dementia care. One unit had adopted a *biomedical and instrumental* approach to understanding and treating dementia by *controlling* disturbed behaviors, which were regarded primarily as *artifacts of the disease process*. At that unit, treatment for disturbed

---

[8]   Although some professionals in the field may recognize the institution and the units, I deliberately have not identified it and have changed the names of the units and residents, staff, and families to respect the confidentiality of those who shared their stories and information with me.

behaviors was confined to physical or pharmacological restraint, and the perspectives of the patients as *persons* were largely disregarded as irrelevant. The other unit assumed a *person-oriented* philosophy of care that paid attention to what the person may have been *communicating* (e.g., pain or hunger) through the behaviors and to the context in which they occurred (such as during bathing). The staff of the second unit tried to understand the underlying *meaning* communicated by the elder through his/her behavior in order to see why it occurred. They then tried to address the source of the problem rather than simply try to eliminate or control the behavior.

I found consistent differences in the outcomes of elders from the two units. Residents on the biomedically oriented care unit showed evidence of decline (often precipitous), whereas those on the person-oriented unit remained stable or even improved. These findings provide promising evidence that the ways in which the person with dementia is regarded and her behaviors are interpreted and treated will profoundly impact her outcome *even in the absence of medical interventions*. Now that cure is still beyond reach, we owe it to our elders to carefully examine the elements of care practices that are the most effective in sustaining them.

This book documents the unfortunate consequences for those elders whose actions, comments, and requests—their *agency*—were *pathologized* as the products of hopelessly diseased brains, and ignored. It also tells the more hopeful story of those who were fortunate enough to be regarded as persons with legitimate feelings, needs, and intentions that needed attention. These differences at the *internal* level of caregiving practices speak powerfully for embracing nonpathologizing person-supporting dementia care. However, even though promising models are being developed both here and abroad that promote such care, multiple *external* barriers (historical, organizational, regulatory, economic, and cultural) have impeded their adoption. That is why an internal level analysis that points to the superiority of person-centered caregiving is not enough. A historical and political and moral economy perspective is also needed to unravel some of those external barriers in order to understand the obstacles that must be confronted to improve the quality of life and care for our elders with dementia.

ORGANIZATION AND DESCRIPTION OF CHAPTERS

Alan Lerner and Robert Friedland (1996: 213) aptly note that, "The concept of Alzheimer's disease has broadened ... as a complex of complicated interactions among a diseased brain, an aging individual, and her genetics, family networks, and community resources." This book addresses aspects of this complexity that are often forgotten or not recognized. It begins with a description of the disorder and behavioral problems that often occur. Then it introduces competing perspectives for understanding and treating dementia and BDs and considers their implications for the person. The remainder of the book discusses my research findings and their implications for dementia caregiving.

This book hopes to reach a broad audience of professionals (academics, clinicians, and policy-makers), undergraduate and graduate students, and lay readers. To accomplish this, I present my main arguments, which set the stage for the research, in the first three chapters of the book. Throughout the text, I include footnotes or direct readers to appendices. This is done to accommodate both readers requiring basic background information (e.g., demographics) and others desiring greater elaboration on particular topics. This should also give instructors flexibility in assigning material of varying relevance to their courses.

Part One (Chapters 1, 2, 3, and 4):
Theoretical and Methodological Considerations in Dementia Care

Part One provides the theoretical and historical background to the study of dementia caregiving, describes the methodology, population and setting, and offers a glimpse of the nursing home environment. Chapter 1 discusses possible organic sources that explain differences among dementing disorders and describes their associated signs (medically termed, *symptoms*), their varied clinical course, and the problematic notion of progressive stages of decline. It then introduces the central problem of behavioral disturbances (BDs) that often accompany dementia and are of concern in a rapidly aging society. How these BDs are interpreted and the types of interventions institutional caregiving staff use to address them have major consequences for the elder and are central concerns of this book.

Chapter 2 introduces core theoretical concepts for analyzing dementia care. It briefly examines how AD came to be socially constructed as a biomedical condition (cf. Gubrium 1987). Then it contrasts the more dominant biomedical perspective with the communications perspective for framing how caregivers might regard the person with dementia and treat her BDs. The chapter goes on to examine some of the ongoing debates on personhood associated with these perspectives and considers their implication for the person. It ends by differentiating three types of self and three types of identity, used later in the book's analyses.

Chapter 3 reviews the history of dementia caregiving in the United States up through the development of special care units like the ones I studied. It then discusses the particular value of ethnography as a method for studying nursing homes and describes the comparative framework and methodology for the study.

Chapter 4 examines the research setting, power structure of the nursing home, and the resident population. Given the historic design of the special care units that were years in the making, this chapter elaborately details their unique physical layout and features, the history and conceptualization behind their design, and changes and erosion in their utilization over time. It also discusses various roles of the units' clinical staff and their differential power in the home. Finally, it offers a glimpse of the living and working environment of the units.

Part Two (Chapters 5, 6, 7, and 8): Ethnographic Case Studies and Analyses

Part Two forms the heart of the study of the *internal* unit-level caregiving practices. Chapter 5 examines three case studies of elders from Snow I, and chapter 6 presents three from Snow 2. Each set was selected for vividly representing the caregiving approach developed by each head nurse. Chapters 5 and 6 each begins by discussing the history and "culture"[9] of each unit, taking into account characteristics of residents and staff, the philosophy and organization of care, caregiver teamwork, and relations between families and staff. The case studies offer detailed descriptions of residents' severe behavioral disturbances (BDs), staff

---

[9] Although the term "culture" can have many meanings and is even contested as having its beginnings in an oppressive colonial history (cf. Pandian 1985; Asad 1979; Abu-Lughod 1991), I restrict it in this usage to the characteristics and ways of interacting among the key players in the nursing home unit, especially the staff, residents, and their families. This includes unit-specific rules and their understanding and acceptance or violation among the various actors.

and family interventions, and the outcomes for the elders. These contrasts provided the opportunity to examine the impact of nonmedical differences on outcome between the two units. Chapter 7 thus compares characteristics that differentiated caregiving and outcome on the two units. Residents of Snow 2, with its stronger person orientation and communications perspective to BDs, fared remarkably better than did those from Snow 1, with its instrumental and stronger biomedical orientation. The chapter identifies, however, factors that prevented Snow 2 from being even more successful.

Chapter 8 briefly summarizes the differences between caregiving on the two units and offers 10 main conclusions and a final comprehensive conclusion, along with recommendations for future dementia caregiving. The chapter argues that dementia caregiving is necessarily a *moral enterprise* that involves *mutual accountability* by a spectrum of stakeholders, not only caregivers and receivers. The chapter identifies these stakeholders and offers concrete recommendations for each of them.

Part Three (Chapters 9 and 10): Looking Ahead in Dementia Care

The recommendations from chapter 8 for promoting quality dementia care point to the need to look beyond the *internal* caregiving practices of a given facility to the larger political and moral economy within which "reciprocal obligations" and competing values and political and economic interests interact. These interactions shape the relative distribution of a nation's social goods (Minkler and Cole 1999: 40), like access to quality long-term care.

Part Three is therefore concerned with looking ahead to consider how to improve dementia caregiving in the future. Toward that end, chapter 9 examines *external* barriers that have impeded the provision of quality dementia care. These include factors that have favored an institutional model and instrumental bias to dementia care, legislative regulations that have further encouraged instrumental approaches, and the *political economy* of nursing home care that has favored a for-profit industry that has not always delivered. The popular view of dementia as a dismal disease for which little can be done also contributes a cultural barrier to quality care. The fragmentation and lack of community in the United States is an additional problem that must be addressed.

Chapter 10 discusses the move toward community options and pioneering approaches that demand radical "culture change" in long-term dementia caregiving. It examines older models and aspects of recent models that are compatible with my research findings. Given the impending increase in the elderly population and the anticipated caregiving preferences of these baby boomers, some of the models are calling for homelike community alternatives and forecasting the end of the nursing home era. The chapter suggests drawing on these models and on humane and economically viable designs from other countries to make person-supporting long-term care accessible to everyone. This calls for a *moral economy* of care that is sensitive to the deleterious outcomes resulting from irresponsible regulatory and funding policies. More knowledge is available today than ever before to provide humane person-preserving care, but it may be ignored because of political and economic reasons. The book ends by considering the moral consequences of this dilemma.

SUGGESTIONS FOR READING THIS BOOK

I encourage new readers to this subject to read this volume in its entirety. Clinicians and casual readers should read at least the case material in chapters 5 and 6 and the conclusions offered in chapters 8 through 10. I recommend that advanced readers review the material in chapter 1 on behavioral disturbances (BDs) and in chapter 2 on perspectives on dementia and the person since these lay out the theoretical and bioethical issues relevant to the case studies and analyses in the book. Undergraduate students and anyone interested in the history of long-term care should also be sure to read the beginning of chapter 3, which covers that history. Students of ethnographic research are likely to find the sections on ethnography in chapter 3 also of interest. Those who are interested in design and planning of dementia units should find material in chapter 4 of historical relevance. Policy-makers should find chapters 8 and 9 of particular relevance since they offer recommendations for improving dementia care and also identify barriers to that care.

A NOTE ON LANGUAGE

I wish to call attention to certain terms and my deliberate use of language. Since I believe that our older population—including persons with dementing disorders—deserve respect for having negotiated their lives and worlds, I refer to them as "elders." I avoid using terms such as "the demented," that identify persons with their impairment, given its negative connotations in a hypercognitive society (Post 2000a: 245).[10] However, I do occasionally, use "demented" as a modifying term (e.g., "the demented elder") to emphasize the disability.

When I place "management" of the elder or his behaviors in quotation marks it is to convey the problematic concept of "managing" another person. This concept suggests an instrumental orientation to care because it emphasizes "control over" another person. The perspective underlying this book, supported by my research findings, is that genuine "care" needs should focus on the *person* with dementia, not attempt simply to eliminate behaviors deemed as problems by others. This involves trying to interpret those problems as signs of distress and to correct the source of distress, not to "manage" or eliminate them solely for the convenience of the caregiver.

Similarly, "treatment" is a potentially problematic term in an era where we still have very modest, and short-lived, treatments for dementia. There has been some success in treating *secondary disabilities* (like hearing or vision problems, which may worsen cognitive problems of dementia), but efforts focused on rehabilitation have often given way to preservative measures. The caveat here is to remain honest about what can actually be done and to not mistake measures directed at eliminating behaviors that are troublesome to *others* (by using, for example, antipsychotic medication) as actually "treating" the patient.

The staff at the units I studied referred to elders living at the home as "residents," the current convention in the nursing home industry (Vesperi and Henderson 1995: 3). As the head of one unit told me, "This is their home, and that is why we call them 'residents' and not 'patients.'" Indeed, because many of the elders lacked or had only mild medical conditions, they were not exactly patients; it was their dementia that brought them to the unit. Yet I found this sensitivity with terminology puzzling because the facility was very medicalized: staff were dressed in medical garb, and the residents were placed on a regimented hospital-like schedule, far from the casual flow one might have at home. As

---

[10] Thus, while calling someone "a diabetic" similarly reduces the person to his/her disease, it does not carry the same negative connotations that occur when calling someone with a cognitive disorder "the demented," or someone with a psychiatric disorder, "a schizophrenic."

Stafford notes (1995: ix–x), euphemisms serve to mask uncomfortable recognitions of power and control. In fact, the continued use of the term "resident" often obscures the reality of actual practices (Vesperi and Henderson 1995: 3). Nonetheless, I retain the term "resident" not to obscure this reality, but to emphasize that the unit is primarily a living quarter. Implicit in this is the expectation that visitors and staff *should* honor the elders' privacy, space, wishes, and so on, however inadequately this may in fact be accomplished.

Finally, I want to clarify the various ways I use the term "institution" throughout this book. Foremost, I talk about the particular nursing home as an "institution." Similarly, when referring to the institutionalization of an elder, I mean his admission to the nursing home. I also mention the more formal social structural "institutions" like medicine, health care, or the economic "institution" of the nursing home industry, but may also use the term for less formal societal institutions like the "institution" of the family.

FURTHER READING

Maslow, K. (1994). Current knowledge about special care units: Findings of a study by the US Office of Technology Assessment. *Alzheimer's Disease and Associated Disorders*, 8, Supplement 1, S14–40.

PART ONE

theoretical and methodological considerations in dementia care

CHAPTER 1

Organic Sources, Signs, and Course of Dementia

Dementia is a cognitive and behavioral disorder that poses serious problems both for the affected person and her caregiver. Much has been written already about dementia as a personal problem for the family trying to provide care for the elder (e.g., Mace and Rabins 2001). This chapter examines symptoms and their possible organic sources and introduces the problem of behavioral disturbances (BDs) that affect both the elder with dementia and her caregiver.

POSSIBLE ORGANIC SOURCES OF DEMENTIA

Senile dementia is characterized by progressive cognitive deterioration in persons 65 and older as the result of neuropathological changes in the brain. Only 3 per cent of cases are believed to be fully reversible by removing brain tumors or correcting metabolic disorders (Binstock 1993: 134). Although dementia has been attributed to 7 reversible diseases and some 70 diagnoses or causes, Alzheimer's disease (AD) and vascular dementia (VaD) are the two primary sources of neurological impairment associated with dementia. AD is the principal degenerative dementia; vascular, metabolic, and traumatic dementias are produced by nondegenerative organic processes (Gimzal and Yazgan 2004). Estimates have attributed about 50 to 60 per cent of dementia cases to AD and 10 to 20 per cent to VaD (Beghi, Logroscino, and Korczyn 2004); 5 to 20 per cent was due to their mix (MD) and 10 to 15 per cent to other causes. Recent studies suggest, however, that there is considerably more overlap between the two forms, and fewer cases of VaD alone. The relation among these various types is poorly understood (Norris, MacNeil, and Haines 2003: 177, 181), and there is evidence that some types of vascular dementias may magnify the effects of AD damage (Roman 2003: 160). Despite this confusion, about two million cases of dementia remain linked to VaD (half to post-stroke VaD and half to damage caused by congestive heart failure) and another four million to AD, totaling six million cases.

In *Alzheimer's disease* brain damage is believed to result from brain cell atrophy or from death of brain cells due to abnormal accumulation of plaques[1] and neurofibrillary tangles[2] in the nerve cell. The resulting loss of synapses between neurons leads to declines in cognitive functioning (thinking, perception, and organizational ability) and performance. *Vascular* dementia (VaD) is associated with brain injury due to cerebrovascular and cardiovascular disease (Román 2003: 149–150). Stroke is believed to be the proximal cause of VaD (Norris, MacNeil, and Haines 2003: 173). Stroke kills off brain cells by interrupting the blood flow to the brain and halting the supply of oxygen and nutrients to it. VaD may be the result of multiple smaller strokes or a profound singular stroke.

Plaques and tangles are expected to accumulate with age. However, the postmortem differentiation of AD from normal aging, on the basis of the

---

[1] Plaques are dense, clumped fragments of the beta-amyloid protein together with other molecular and cellular deposits around the nerve cells in the brain, particularly in regions involved with memory. It is unknown whether the plaques are causative or a byproduct of disease process. For more information, see *Alzheimer's Disease: Unraveling the Mysteries*, National Institute on Aging (NIA) (2003: 20–23).

[2] Neurofibrillary tangles are twisted fibers of the *tau* protein that lead to the disintegration of the neuronic support structure and, hence, the collapse of its transport system. See NIA (2003: 20–23) for additional information.

amount of accumulated plaques and tangles, is a judgment call. Post-mortem investigators have had even greater difficulty in agreeing on the diagnosis of VaD because the judgments about the necessary degree of vascular damage are subjective (Norris, MacNeil, and Haines 2003: 184). Thus postmortem diagnosis becomes a negotiated process, rather than a clear-cut determination. Clinically, manifestations of symptoms are similar, making it difficult to distinguish dementia due to AD from that due to VaD. In fact, upon autopsy, most cases identified clinically as VaD appear to be mixed or even AD (Norris, MacNeil, and Haines 2003: 173). The absence of uniformity in the patterns of designated symptoms and course of dementia is striking and calls into question whether we are, in fact, dealing with discrete disease entities (Gubrium 1986a: 1). The frequent discrepancy between clinical diagnosis of symptoms and post-mortem findings raises further questions. (For further discussion of the scientific problem of linking dementia neuropathology to specific diseases, see Appendix A.)

SIGNS (SYMPTOMS) OF DEMENTIA AND CLINICAL COURSE

While questions persist about the organic bases of dementia, clinicians depend on the behavioral signs (medically called "symptoms") that an elder presents during examination in order to diagnose it. In fact, clinicians regard AD and VaD as clinical *syndromes* (Richter and Richter 2002: 19), a set of co-occurring signs that together characterize an abnormality.

Dementia affects the cognition, functioning ability, mood, and behavior of the elder. Clinicians typically view senile dementia as a progressive, debilitating, and ultimately terminal disorder. However, there is a continuum of cognitive and functional impairments in the elderly that vary from more benign conditions associated with normal aging to more serious conditions like AD. "Benign senescent forgetfulness" (Kral 1962), for example, refers to memory losses associated with normal aging and depression (Rabins 2004: 291). "Age-associated-memory impairments," a somewhat broader category, include age-related memory impairments of healthy adults 50 and older with subjective complaints of memory difficulties and evidence of somewhat poorer performance than young adults (McEntee and Larrabee 2000). "Mild Cognitive Impairment" (MCI) requires additional corroboration of impaired memory function (and possibly other cognitive impairments, e.g., planning) for a given age and education level, but without dementia (Rabins 2004: 292). Recently, MCI has come to be seen as a precursor of dementia, even though it is not currently possible to predict whether MCI will in fact worsen (Rabins 2004), or even improve. For this reason, it remains a controversial concept, particularly for clinical application (Whitehouse and Moody 2006: 11). Similarly, differentiating depression from dementia can be quite complicated. Generally with depression, the only cognitive impairment is with memory, and new learning is not impaired as it is in dementia (Blackmun 1998). Finally, delirium, a functional impairment of oxidative metabolism in the brain is also often mistaken for dementia since both indicate "brain failure" (Richter and Richter 2002: 22). Hallucinations and fluctuating levels of awareness often accompany delirium. However, delirium may also coincide with or be a sign that dementia is developing (Richter and Richter 2002: 22–23).

In progressive dementia, people typically early on tend to experience problems with cognitive abilities. The first possible sign of dementia is difficulty with short-term memory. Affected persons may also have difficulty recalling material they previously knew well and may be impaired in their ability to learn new things. They may also have trouble concentrating and with executive activities, like organizing or planning. Along with these, affected elders may begin to show problems carrying out *instrumental activities of daily living* (IADLS), such as balancing a checkbook or keeping an appointment. Subtle personality changes may develop, perhaps out of the person's recognition and frustration that something is wrong, or in response to the growing annoyance of family members. At this point some elders may be self-conscious of their impairments and try to compensate, for example, by making lists as memory aids to prevent others from realizing that something is wrong.

If the disorder worsens, language disturbances (aphasia), comprehension and abstract thinking, and orientation to time and place may be affected. Wandering may also begin. Driving may be particularly risky because of disorientation and increasing difficulty in reading and immediately understanding the meaning of traffic signs. The person may also have problems in daily functioning and need assistance with personal care *activities of daily living* (ADLs), such as dressing, bathing, and toileting. Some persons may begin to experience sleep disturbances and/or psychotic symptoms, like delusional thinking or hallucinations. Behavioral symptoms, such as repetitive questioning, agitation, crying out, arguing, and fighting (discussed below), may also occur. Mood changes, such as fearfulness or depression, may also develop since the symptoms become prominent and the person's awareness of impairment is most acute now. These combined changes place enormous demands on the family, and it is in this period, perhaps after exhausting existing community services, when families often seek nursing home placement.

If the dementia advances still further, the person may lose complete orientation to time and place, become incontinent, forget the names of close family members, and begin to have difficulty walking without help. Further deterioration is evidenced by the need for total care in feeding, hygiene, and mobility. She/he may lose complete recognition of family members and become mute and unresponsive, a state that too often carries the dehumanizing label "vegetative" (Kayser-Jones 2003: 59).

Onset may appear more gradual in cases of persons diagnosed with AD and more abrupt with those believed to have VaD, perhaps because VaD is a post-stroke event. For similar reasons the course of decline may be gradual in AD and present a stepwise progression in VaD. Also, those diagnosed with AD may show a more rapid initial deterioration of memory, but this decline evens out as decline continues among all groups. A greater degree of motor impairment is apparent in persons with VaD or mixed dementias (MD). However, rates of cognitive decline, mood, and behavioral symptoms and, worsening of behavioral symptoms do not seem markedly different among diagnostic groups (Norris, MacNeil, and Haines 2003: 185–187), perhaps because they already vary so widely within groups. The difficulty in making clear diagnoses in the first place makes it difficult to distinguish clear symptom patterns.

Variation of Course and Behaviors

Dementia varies greatly both in course and behavioral presentation. According to clinicians, time between the onset of symptoms and death can vary remarkably anywhere from 3 to 20 years, although average time to death (for reasons not necessarily related to late disease stage) is 8 to 10 years (Richter and Richter 2002: 35). What abilities are retained or lost and when also vary. Some elders can walk, talk, and recognize family members many years after the first signs of the disorder; others may lose these capacities within a few years. For example, one woman may recognize and remember the names of family members late into her illness, but show early difficulty in finding her room. Another person may lack difficulty with orientation but lose memory for family members much earlier.

Finally, there is striking irregularity in memory and symptomatic behaviors *even in the same person* from day to day or even from hour to hour. In the book *Old Friends* (Kidder 1993), for example, Martha may wander away from the nursing home to head for "home" in order to prepare dinner for her husband, who is deceased, only to remember and mourn his death later that day. Some people have consistent times of day when they are agitated, such as at bedtime. Many others become anxious late in the afternoon, when they begin to wander, a condition frequently called "sundowning," which is now thought to be delirium rather than dementia per se, by at least some geriatricians.[3]

According to some writers, the impairments seem particularly selective early on perhaps because only certain parts of the brain, which control specific functions, such as language, are affected (Richter and Richter 2002: 34). Thus, one would expect a similar course and common development of symptoms in patients as the disease progresses and more parts of the brain are affected, but this is not the case. Explanations for variations in clinical course and symptoms have often attributed these to differences in underlying disease pathology. However, discrepancies between the presence and degree of dementia in live patients and the presence and degree of pathology found at autopsy indicate the inadequacy of this conclusion. These findings have led researchers to believe that there are a variety of organic conditions and other nonbiological factors (such as environment, relations with caregivers, or quality of care) that may influence both the development of dementia symptoms and their progression.

The Problematic Concept of Stages

Despite this wide variation in course among persons diagnosed with dementia, it is surprising that some writers have identified a course that follows discrete stages of decline. There seems to be something compelling about referring to a rational stage model of gradual inevitable decline, even when the stage model contradicts the clinical evidence. Even writers who have acknowledged the problems of this model continue using it.[4] It may be that the enormous variety of cognitive and behavioral phenomena that present in dementia leads clinicians and researchers to seek some order to make sense of it all.[5]

While perhaps helping the clinician or family feel more in control of events to come, such models may also lead them to anticipate decline

---

[3] I thank Judith Barker (Professor in Residence, Medical Anthropology Program, Department of Anthropology, History and Social Medicine, University of California, San Francisco) for bringing this to my attention.

[4] For example, Mace (1987), as cited in Lyman (1989: 601).

[5] This is the very argument that Gubrium (1987) proposed to explain how Alzheimer's disease became differentiated from normal aging: to create order from the chaotic quality of living with dementia.

prematurely, and to attribute the problems an elder may be experiencing on a particularly rough day to the "fact" that she is moving to a more advanced stage. This assumption moves some clinicians to limit expectations or opportunities for the elder. For example, an activity specialist at a special care unit told one family member that her mother could no longer remain in a skills program because she wasn't able to keep up with her other "fives" (people identified by a particular stage).[6] Applying the problematic concept of stages in this way limits opportunities for the labeled elder to participate in programs that encourage social engagement or skill development, thus fulfilling the prophecy of inevitable decline.

The Question of Rementia

Some persons who manifest memory difficulties never decline into a dementing pattern. Others plateau for over a year at the same level before they show signs of deteriorating. Still others may even show unexpected improvement in the absence of any pharmacological intervention. However, when these appear, most clinicians expect them to be short-lived (Richter and Richter 2002: 34) since they expect decline is inevitable. This notion of inevitable and progressive decline has come into question as evidence from some studies suggest *rementia*, or the improvement or restoration of some cognitive and functional abilities, especially, but not exclusively, to a restoration of continence and anxiety reduction (Kitwood 1989: 5). These improvements occurred not as a result of biomedical interventions, but by changes in the social and care context and heightened attentiveness by caregivers.

The idea of rementia is beginning to gain credibility by clinicians who have witnessed improvements that they previously believed were impossible. However, the biomedical view of inevitable decline has remained dominant.

DEMENTIA AND THE PROBLEM OF BEHAVIORAL DISTURBANCES (BDS)

A significant problem of dementia—and the central focus of this book—is that of *behavioral "disturbances"* (BDs), also called "disturbed" or even

---

6   She used the model not only to label stages of the disease, but also to label and identify people according to those stages.

"disturbing" behaviors of the person with dementia. To label a behavior as a "disturbance" is to make a social and even political judgment (Lawton and Rubinstein 2000: xiv–xv). Behavior that might be regarded as "disturbing" by one person in one environment might not be similarly regarded by another person in another environment. For example, an elder wandering around a village in Turkey would not only be known by almost everyone, but be taken in stride by all the members of the community, who would likely be unruffled by "grandma's" visits. In contrast, the wandering away from home by an elder in an urban area, where she is unknown to most people and could get lost or hurt, would be seen as disturbing. The judgment at the same time is politically tinged because it is a judgment by a more powerful person over a vulnerable elder that could justify relocating the elder to an institutional setting, even against his/her will, or restraining the elder to "manage" her behaviors.

In general, behaviors seen as problematic include those that may cause harm to the person with dementia or others, that overly stress or tire out the caregiver, and that may be regarded as socially unacceptable (Mace 1990: 75). Such behaviors would include both aggressive and nonagressive verbal, vocal, and motor activity (Cohen-Mansfield 2000: 42). Examples include repetitive questioning about the same subject, screaming or yelling for no apparent reason, agitation, wandering, inappropriate sexual behaviors, destructive or self-destructive behavior (e.g., repeatedly scratching one's own arm until the skin is damaged), or physical aggressiveness (such as hitting, scratching, or biting a caregiver during hygienic care). BDs have been labeled *catastrophic reactions* (Mace 1990: 83) when stressors that seem minor to others provoke unexplainably extreme reactions (such as rejection, crying, pacing, and even lashing out) in the elder.

These behaviors provide evidence that something is amiss or disturbing to the elder—something that she may not otherwise be able to communicate. BDs are troubling to family members who feel they must constantly attend to the elder to prevent harm. If the behavior cannot be corrected at home, it becomes a familial problem when it results in the family's needing to decide whether they must relocate the elder to an institutional setting, often against both the family's and the elder's own preference. For institutional caregivers these behaviors are difficult to handle, frustrating, and time-consuming. In the busy, often inadequately staffed world of nursing home care, this can lead to the use of restraints (physical or chemical) to "manage" or control them, rather than finding more challenging, yet less invasive, solutions. Finally, BDs are socially costly since they lead to expensive, largely publicly supported nursing home care that might be avoidable, or at least delayed, if they could be corrected at home.

Although not everyone with dementia displays these kinds of behaviors, their prevalence among elders in the community tends to be high, and in cases where they occur, they tend to worsen as the dementia itself worsens. Difficult behaviors are a principal reason why families seek nursing home placement. While figures vary, well over half of the residents of nursing homes and over 90 per cent of persons in special care units, designed specifically for persons with dementia, manifest seriously disturbed behaviors (Wagner et al. 1995).

Increasingly, researchers have been curious about the causes and/ or meaning of the disturbed behavior as a possible clue to correcting them. Beyond damage in the brain itself, other causes for BDs have included mood or psychiatric conditions secondary to the dementia that produce paranoia or other psychosis-like states that upset the elder. Other potential causes may include the continuation of the elder's premorbid personality or patterns of coping in a new context (Shomaker 1987: 370), other bodily conditions (such as the urge to urinate or pain) that are disturbing the elder, and disturbances in overly stimulating physical, social, or emotional environments (Mace 1990: 78). Some researchers have also attributed the behavior to correctable *excess disabilities* that are not related to the dementia itself, such as hearing or vision impairments, that can stimulate or exacerbate delusions or hallucinations (Kovach 1997: 138–39). Still others have found that the problematic behaviors are actually strategies of the elder to avoid embarrassing situations (Sabat and Harré 1992: 453, 457–58). Still other researchers have associated aggressive behavior towards institutional caregivers with the elder's sense of invasion of her personal sphere (Graneheim, Norberg, and Jansson 2001: 257); they have encouraged caregivers to work with the elders to support their autonomy as a way of avoiding such responses (p. 263).

In any case, considerable work needs to be done. From her study of research on BDs, Christine Kovach concludes that behavioral problems in dementia "are not problems in and of themselves," but communicate another need, feeling (such as pain or a perceived threat), or attempt to cope (Kovach 1997: 140). The BDs may signal an effort of the elder to respond to an internal stressor (such as sadness) or an external stressor (such as hurried pressure from the institutional caregiver to get groomed in the morning). In fact, she argues that most "problem" behaviors are actually the elder's effort to cope with caregivers' own problematic actions (or inaction) or with some environmental stressor (p. 127). She suggests that many of these behaviors can be prevented by satisfying basic needs of the elder (like getting her to the bathroom for an imminent bowel movement), increasing the quality of social interaction with staff, and decreasing environmental stress (p. 128). Sadly, she admits that these suggestions are for "better care than that which is now provided in many settings" (p. xv).

In trying to determine the meaning of different kinds of BDs, Cohen-Mansfield (2000) found that most BDs, and especially verbal/vocal agitation, are evidence of discomfort or pain. Physically nonaggressive BDs, such as repetitious mannerisms, may offer stimulation to make up for its absence in the nursing home environment. Physically aggressive behaviors are associated with severe cognitive impairments and may result from the elder's frustration at not being able to communicate needs (Cohen-Mansfield 2000: 46). Those with more advanced dementia are more likely to express aggression when facing unpleasant conditions (like cold or being pressured to get groomed) or when feeling threatened (e.g., through invasion of their personal space by caregivers or other residents) (p. 48).

Among the most common problems triggering BDs are hunger, pain, and lack of stimulation. BDs occurred most often when residents were physically restrained, during periods of inactivity, during low staffing levels, and when it was cold at night. Thus Cohen-Mansfield suggests that treatment for these BDs should consist of determining the unmet need and trying to correct it (p. 49). This strategy could correct the source of the disturbance and eliminate the need for physical or pharmacological restraints to suppress the behavior itself. Cohen-Mansfield also encourages caregivers to be flexible in adjusting the typical routine (such as meal times, wake-up and grooming times, and type of bath) to better accommodate the individual needs, moods, and habits of the elder.

Given the considerable personal and societal impacts of behavioral problems in dementia and the impending growth of the elderly population, the suggestions of these researchers and of future research that will interpret BDs at their source should help minimize their occurrence and improve the quality of life for millions of elders. They could also eliminate serious side effects of medications as well as reduce the cost of treatment considerably. By 2030 the number of persons 65 and older is expected to double from current figures to 71.5 million persons; almost 10 million are likely to be 85 or older

(Moody 2002: 41).[7] Currently 1.6 million persons reside in nursing homes (over half of them suffering from severe dementia with BDs) (Wagner et al. 1995), exceeding $100 billion dollars in expenditures, half of which supports those with dementia. In fact, treatment of all sorts for dementia has already passed the $100 billion annual mark (Richter and Richter 2000: 10). BDs are a major reason for nursing home placement of the elder with dementia. Given the mounting costs of nursing home care and the increasing growth of our elderly population, persons with dementia and BDs are posing a serious demographic and social problem as well. (See Appendix B for a fuller discussion of the demographic dimensions and social, economic, and policy implications of this problem.)

---

[7] Since age is a major risk factor for dementia, and the population is aging, the number of cases is expected to climb, together with the costs of care. Alzheimer's disease affects 2 to 3 per cent of persons by age 65, increasing in *incidence* (number of new cases) with age. It doubles every five years so that by age 85 almost one of every two persons is affected (Turner 2003: 2). Four million persons in the United States have been affected by AD alone, and eight million with a milder form that possibly places them at risk of developing AD (Wysocki 2002). If these figures continue to increase proportionally with the elderly population, the number of persons diagnosed with some degree of AD could triple to 36 million by mid-century (Zwillich 2005). In Canada, the number of diagnosed cases is expected to increase threefold to 800,000 cases by 2030. Vascular dementia (VaD)—the second most common form after AD—adds at least two million additional cases in the United States. As with AD, age is a major factor in the *incidence* (number of new cases), which also doubles every five years (Román 2003: 149, 153).

CHAPTER 2

Perspectives on Dementia and the Person

This chapter discusses two contrasting perspectives on dementia—the *biomedical* perspective and the *communications* perspective—as these affect the way the *person* with dementia and her behavioral disturbances (BDs) are viewed and treated. It then considers what it means to be a person with dementia. The first section focuses on the *biomedical model* that has shaped the dominant understanding of dementia. It begins by reviewing the social processes by which senile dementia came to be constructed as a biomedical disorder. It then examines features of the biomedical model and their implications for dementia caregiving. Last it considers limitations in the biomedical shaping of institutional care, and some efforts to move beyond those limitations. The second section examines an alternative *communications perspective* on dementia, which has informed my approach to studying BDs. Since dementia can also have devastating subjective, legal, and material consequences for the affected person, a third section of this chapter examines two alternative concepts of *personhood*—cognitive and noncognitive—and considers their relation to the two perspectives on dementia and their implications for the person and her care. A final section examines the concepts of self, identity, and agency as they relate to the person with dementia. It also differentiates three types of self (s^1, s^2, and s^3) and three types of identity (i^1, i^2, and i^3) that will be used in subsequent analyses.

THE BIOMEDICAL PERSPECTIVE ON DEMENTIA AND BDS

Alzheimer's disease and related dementias have come to be defined as biomedical in nature, shaped by the assumptions of scientific medicine. The biomedical model has provided a cultural lens for organizing and interpreting observable phenomena related to dementia. As scientists press onward to find cures, this lens continues to dominate our views about dementia and the care of those affected by the disorder (Downs 2000: 369). Still, as seen in chapter 1, biomedicine has not offered a clear-cut understanding of dementia. In addition, there have been questions about where to draw the line between healthy and diseased persons. Below we will see how this line was drawn when senility was relabeled (that is, socially "constructed") as AD.

The Social Construction of Alzheimer's Disease (AD) as a Biomedicalized Disorder

The clinical phenomena we call Alzheimer's disease (AD) (and related dementias) did not always fall under the purview of biomedicine because they were not always regarded as abnormal. The "discovery" of Alzheimer's disease in elders reveals a complex history of negotiation among scientists that "involved a political process more than simply biomedical discovery" (Lyman 1989: 597). This is documented in many places[1] and will not be repeated here. However, because the biomedicalization of AD and other dementias has had serious impacts on the institutional caregiving of affected persons, I will briefly describe how AD came to be socially constructed as a biomedical disorder and then consider some of its consequences for the elder.

---

[1] For more information about the history of conceptualization of Alzheimer's disease and the shift from senility to AD, see Gubrium (1986a, 1987), Fox (1989), Robertson (1991), Whitehouse, Maurer, and Ballenger (2000), and Beard 2005.

Social scientists do not understand disease in the same way that biomedical scientists and practitioners do. For example, they do not accept that disease entities exist in nature only to be discovered (Freund and McGuire 1995: 192). Rather, they understand that the professional and lay *ideas* about phenomena that are deviant (or "abnormal") are *constructed* in particular ways, for example through biomedical explanations suggesting organic causation of pathology or disease. Through the biomedical model, deviant phenomena are biomedically redefined as *natural* disease entities, such as AD. Whatever the ideas, they are based on the constraints of language and cultural assumptions at the time of their development, and are subject to social, political, and economic influences as they are produced. Thus medical ideas, like any other ideas, are always delimited by the ways in which they capture and represent the natural world.

In the case of AD, biomedical scientists were finding that plaques and tangles, like the ones found in the postmortem brains of younger persons diagnosed with Alzheimer's, also existed in the brains of senile elders. What was *political* was the researchers' *decision* to relabel "disease," patterns of senility previously regarded as "normal" for an older population. This act created the "apocalyptic demography" that stimulated a research industry and filtered government funds into finding a cure for AD, thus improving the position of researchers. As Gubrium (1986a; see also Cohen 1999) describes, this redefinition also produced some sense of order and predictability to senility, which enabled family caregivers to gain some sense of control over it. This was very important to them, and many families embraced the ideas presented by the researchers, further promoting support for their research.

Because of these deliberate actions to extend the diagnosis of Alzheimer's disease to the elderly, AD has been called a *social construction* (Gubrium 1987). Calling it a social construction, however, does not negate the existence or importance of underlying natural (that is, organic or biological) processes. Rather it draws attention to the *deliberate social processes* by which professionals redefined senility as pathology and placed it within biomedical jurisdiction.

Features of the Biomedical Model and Their Implications for Dementia Caregiving

Although the biomedical model deals with natural phenomena, it does not provide a direct reflection of the *natural* world. Rather, it is a *cultural* model that provides a particular scientific way of organizing and understanding observable phenomena. At its most basic, the biomedical model of disease encompasses the following features.[2]

First, it is a mechanical model grounded in a materialist philosophy in which the *laws of nature* are seen as determining how matter must behave. Given that matter is subject to natural laws, there is a prescriptive quality of inevitability and predictability to behavior. This view encourages nihilism—the sense that nothing can be done—because nature requires it to be a certain way. Natural phenomena must conform to certain laws; once gone astray, the phenomena must be controlled in order to conform once again to those laws. In fact, as a positivist science, its goal is to predict phenomena in order to be able to control them. Thus it operates instrumentally to impose a particular order—natural order—even where this order may not naturally occur. In this scheme of things, physical dimensions, like the body, which can be objectively measured, take priority over subjective impressions, such as a person's emotions and cognitions, which are less likely to conform to natural law.

For dementia, the emphasis on natural processes directs attention to organic phenomena, which provide the primary source for understanding *deviant* clinical behavior. The affected person and the troubled behaviors he displays are seen as the result of natural processes; both are diseased. Thus the *behaviors* (and the person) must be *managed or controlled* to restore some semblance of *normality*. In addition, because nature necessarily follows laws, the disease processes underlying dementia are also expected to result in predictable patterns of decline. Unless the disease process is somehow stopped, the outcome is seen as unavoidable. In the constructs of AD and clinical stages of dementia, the processes of progressive decline are prescribed by nature, thus leading to the conclusion that they are inevitable. At the same time, these constructs impose a sense of order and predictability over natural and clinical phenomena gone astray (Gubrium 1986a). Scientists are viewed as able to correct the clinical phenomena of dementia by somehow adjusting the underlying disorderly organic processes.

Second, the biomedical model is *reductive* in its focus, applying scientific approaches to understanding causality. This requires that phenomena be reduced to their component parts, each analyzed separately from the others (Longino and Murphy 1995: 42–43) in order to establish linear causal links. Disease is located foremost in the *individual* and his/her body, which is further broken down into its ever-reducible parts. The cause or causes

---

[2]   See McLean (1990: 977).

of dementia lie strictly within the body, most likely the brain, which is reduced still further to neuronal cells, molecules, and ultimately, to genes.

The clinical symptoms presented in dementia are seen as the ultimate product of a finite physical cause. This eliminates consideration of any contributing factors outside the body (e.g., historical factors or the social environment in which that individual lives, acts, and engages with others). As Zucker notes, "The presupposition of reduction in medicine is that all disease is physiology gone astray. Where there is truly no physiological problem, there is no disease,"[3] even when the patient experiences illness (Young 1992). Thus the biomedical model directs its attention to these finite processes, and *away from the patient who is experiencing them.* The focus is on physical evidence of *disease*, not the *illness* experienced by the elder, or its social acknowledgment as *sickness* by others (cf. Frankenberg 1980; Young 1992).

Third, some of these distinctions derive from biomedicine's adoption of *Cartesian dualism*—the separation of body from mind (feelings, cognition, and emotion), as conceptualized by René Descartes in the 1600s. *Cartesian mind/body dualism* similarly separates *subject from object*, and *value from fact.* However, only *body, object, and fact* are relevant to its concerns. *Experiential, biographical, and social phenomena do not factor into this scheme of things.* Complex behavioral phenomena must be reduced to organic principles in order to be understood or must be ignored. This challenges theories that illness affects *the whole person* (body and mind) and can never be seen apart from human *agency* (the subject) of the person, moral evaluation (value), and cultural interpretation (cf. Turner 1984).[4]

In dementia, Cartesian dualism conceptualizes deviant behavior and cognition of demented elders as strict deviation from normal biological functioning. Thus it locates the problem in the body (or brain) of the elder, and ignores the elder's subjective states and deviant behaviors as simply *artifacts of disease processes.* Similarly, it dismisses the relevance of the human subject as an *agent* whose disordered behaviors may be intentional acts in light of other psychological, physical, or environmental conditions to which he is responding. Changes in mood and behavior are seen as stemming strictly from the disease, so social and environmental conditions, which may affect the elder's condition, are ignored. The elder's evaluative account—even when it is not distorted in its expression—is

---

[3] A. Zucker, as cited in Longino and Murphy (1995: 43–44).

[4] As cited in Robertson (1991: 138).

disregarded as irrelevant to understanding the disease process that is seen at bottom to be responsible (cf. Cohen 1999: 303).

Fourth, biomedicine adopts the assumption that there is one *specific cause* for every disease. The role of medicine is to determine that cause and to counteract it so as to eliminate the disease. This has worked well in *acute* illnesses (like those caused by bacterial infections),[5] which can be corrected by specific biomedical interventions (like antibiotics). Indeed the biomedical approach has had some marvelous successes of *cure* in this area. However, it has been less successful in, and perhaps is less well suited to, handling *chronic* conditions, which persist and require ongoing *care*. These conditions cannot be treated by isolating and targeting a singular unitary pathophysiological cause.

For AD, VaD, and other diseases of dementia, the hope is to isolate a specific cause for which treatment will be possible. With dementia, hope has been placed on developing a medication (such as the acetylcholinesterase inhibitors like donepezil or new medications like Nemenda®) that will stop, if not reverse, the disease process and prevent further organic damage and clinical decline. The deviant behaviors of dementia are seen strictly as symptoms of a disease process with a unitary cause. Thus they can be corrected *only* by determining that cause. The day-to-day *personal* problems and concerns stemming from dementia are outside of the scope of concern in finding a cause.

Fifth, in order to isolate disease phenomena and to evaluate them, biomedicine encourages a *neutral stance* on the part of the physician or scientist who is examining the body. Personal or emotional attachment is seen as only interfering with this evaluative process. This encourages detachment or *disengagement* by the physician or caregiver from the patient.

Last, the biomedical model attempts to universalize phenomena and causation and generalize to everyone. This leads to ignoring vital biographical data that can explain behavioral phenomena and fosters standardized caregiving that discourages unique individualized attention to personal care needs.

---

[5]　But even in infectious diseases, social conditions (such as poverty) can play an immense role in making a person more or less vulnerable to disease, by affecting exposure to lethal agents and variously impacting immunity. This is why everyone who is exposed to disease agents does not get sick. See Farmer (1999).

Limitations in the Biomedicalized Shaping of Institutional Care

At medically oriented facilities, like nursing homes, the biomedical perspective dominates the way in which caregivers regard bodies and persons, and shape institutional priorities, especially in larger nursing homes. Fashioned after other medical facilities, like hospitals, which are structured to accommodate doctors' costly time, they are regimented, operating according to a time schedule that must accommodate needs of the entire facility (Henderson 1995: 42). However, unless the elder with dementia is also suffering from an acute condition, which requires medical attention, most of the contact elders have in nursing homes is with nursing assistants (NAs) who provide ongoing hygienic body care at various levels of need.

As *total institutions*,[6] nursing homes must provide for all basic care needs. The NAs, who provide the bulk of hands-on care, are often overworked (Diamond 1992; Foner 1994; Gubrium 1975). Medical facilities impose strict time demands and task expectations on their staffs. In order to complete their requisite body maintenance tasks, they themselves must be regimented, tied to a clock. Time is a precious commodity that must not be wasted (Henderson 1995: 42). Residents must be awakened, cleaned, and groomed in time to eat their meals, which arrive on a regular schedule, while they are still hot. Since feeding residents is regarded as a priority, there is little opportunity during meals to respond to extraordinary requests (e.g., assistance in getting to the bathroom) or to deal with disturbed behaviors. Under such conditions, NAs have little motivation or desire to satisfy personal requests and needs of the demented patient, especially when, from a medicalized perspective, they are seen as pointless.

When a person enters a hospital for an acute condition, she stays for a short time, receives help with the condition, and moves on toward recovery. The elder who enters the nursing home with a chronic condition like dementia does not come for a short stay, but to live out her final years. She expects to receive care for fundamental needs. *How* those needs are understood and defined determines how that care is delivered and can dramatically shape the quality of the rest of her life.

For an elder with dementia, who is losing her faculties, is confused, forgetful, and confined to a new location away from the familiar markers of home and family, her confusion and pre-existing problems may temporarily worsen, and she may appear to decline. NAs, who have the most

---

6   See for example, Goffman (1961: 4–124).

direct and frequent contact with the elders, are best positioned to support them amidst the stress of relocation. They can do this by acknowledging them as *biographical persons* with particular histories of engagement with the world. However, institutional pressures encourage caregivers to remain *disengaged* from the elders and to regard any decline as a "natural" and inevitable feature of a progressive disease for which nothing can be done. This fosters a nihilistic attitude that dismisses as pointless efforts to improve the elder's condition by addressing personalized needs; attention is often directed instead to custodial care—body hygiene and physical maintenance—as a more achievable goal. By diverting attention from personal needs, opportunities to enhance the person's well-being—and even to prevent further decline (Kitwood and Bredin 1992)—are lost. The pessimism of a biomedicalized view of dementia, however, relieves them and their institution of the moral obligation even to try (Kitwood 1997: 115).

In addition, neutral detachment is seen as vital to promoting cure and to avoiding preferential treatment of one patient over another, so it is promoted in medical settings. However, it is not well suited to *care*, which entails ongoing interactions between the care-receiver and the caregiver. Whereas the clinician's personal involvement with a patient may impede cure, the caregiver's personal involvement with an elder becomes the vehicle of sustenance. The culture of institutional caregiving, with its premium on time and its biomedicalized emphasis on the body, however, supports a caregiving culture that is attentive to body task-centered care over person-centered care (Williams 1990).

Biomedically oriented caregiving thus assumes a model of dementia care that prioritizes the body over the person's experience, attempts to control or suppress disturbed behaviors rather than try to understand them, and objectifies the person in order to carry out care tasks. By suppressing troubling behaviors, it denies her the right to express distress. Such care promotes neither security nor well-being in an elder already confused by dementia. While directed at preserving the body, it invalidates the person. Dementia, however, affects not only objective *diseased* states, but also the *person* subjected to these states. Since dementia alters a person's cognition and functioning, it affects her psychological state and social interactions with others. Biomedicalized nursing home care, which focuses on "diseased" behavior and the body, is unable to adequately accommodate the subjective experience of the affected person. Nor can it address nonobjective conditions (e.g., psychological, social, or environmental) or invisible nonmeasurable sources of discomfort that may be contributing to the elder's condition. As Lawrence Cohen poignantly notes, biomedicine ignores both suffering and "the meaning of a mindful body facing its decline" (Cohen 1999: 303).

Caregivers who regard disturbed behaviors as "disease artifacts" discount the validity of elders' subjective states and agency. They may even ignore disturbed behaviors that stem from pain unless these can be substantiated by objective evidence. Once labeled "disease," behaviors that may express legitimate needs, discomforts, and concerns are either disregarded or are marked as "symptoms" and targeted for "treatment" by chemical or physical restraints.[7] Significantly, Cohen-Mansfield cautions that if the underlying need persists, medicating the behavior eliminates the "final means of communicating" it (2000: 51), *effectively denying the person the very right to express it.*

Beyond the Limitations of the Biomedical Model for Dementia Caregiving

Despite these serious drawbacks for dementia care, however, the biomedical perspective can be mediated by the way it is interpreted in practice (cf. Barker, Mitteness, and Wolfsen 1994: 323–24).

It is possible to believe that a person's actions are the result of a diseased brain, but to accept, nonetheless, that there is more going on with the person than simply disease.[8] The limitations presented earlier would result only from a full embracing of the reductionist and objectifying assumptions of this model. Caregivers vary, however, in the extent to which they can or want to disengage and objectify the people for whom they provide care. They also vary in their energy and desire to support the persons under their charge beyond the necessary body tasks and in the extent to which they feel personally motivated to do so. The biomedical model aside, some may even feel personally or spiritually compelled to support the person. The danger of relying on a biomedical model is that even those caregivers and administrators who may be inclined to support person-supportive care may be persuaded by its pessimism to better spend their

---

[7] Although this was common during the time of my research, physical restraints are rarely used today.

[8] This certainly characterizes the sensitive work of geriatric physician Peter Rabins (2003–04), whose films for caregivers highlight the need for interpersonal sensitivity when working with elders with dementia.

time accomplishing concrete tasks that are more achievable. Its compat-ibility with routinized care can be a further hindrance to innovative ap-proaches for spending time to reach out to residents.

On the other hand, some clinical circles, particular in Great Britain, have reacted so strongly against biomedical approaches as to be guilty of denying any value that medicine can possibly bring to dementia care-giving. In those circles, alternative notions, which attempt to offer a corrective person-preserving orientation, have come to be accepted as truth (Parker 2001: 333). An uncritical acceptance of person-oriented approaches, however, may prevent examining just how, or under what conditions, they can most benefit elders. What they accept as intuitively correct may have explicit linkages to specific psychological, environ-mental, and social as well as physical conditions that can be better understood. By ignoring these, they may limit the potential for produc-tive partnerships with medicine and other disciplines. Although a criti-cal view is essential, a total rejection of what Kitwood calls neuropathic ideology (1997: 36) could lead to a dogmatic acceptance of a preserva-tionist ideology that might ironically impede the realization of its fullest potential.

Some researchers have called for a holism that embraces psychosocial and environmental approaches without losing sight of valuable medical interventions (Parker 2001: 331). One recent approach that purports a rapprochement of mind/body dualism, however, continues to perpetu-ate reductionistic elements of the biomedical model. This approach ties problematic moods or behaviors to particular parts of the brain, as a way of making them seem more understandable (Zeisel and Raia 2000: 331), even when the evidence is lacking. In these researchers' view, the biomed-icalization of a condition actually serves to identify dementia sufferers as worthy of biomedical attention.

Today many biomedical practitioners also recognize the limitation of the model for helping persons with chronic incurable conditions. Biomed-icine has thus developed many sub-specialties that address the need for more holistic and integrative approaches to care and the need to combine talents with professionals in related fields to address the complex needs that determine well-being in chronic conditions. Some practitioners have looked to experiences in hospice and other palliative care models and car-ried these over in working with different chronic conditions.[9] They have

---

[9] One example is the pilot project of home-based palliative health care being conducted by Mid-Michigan Visiting Nurses' Association in Midland under funding from the Rollin M. Gerstacker Foundation.

even developed innovative, albeit costlier, models that bring expertise to people in their homes, saving impaired people from having to come to them. In short, progressive practitioners in medicine are attempting to improve the quality of the lives they treat, and in many places, biomedicine has moved beyond the limitations presented above.

THE COMMUNICATIONS PERSPECTIVE ON BEHAVIORAL DISTURBANCES

In part, disturbed or unusual behaviors of severely impaired elders result from cognitive impairment due to dementia. However, these behaviors are very likely more than mere artifacts of disease (Shomaker 1987: 370). Many researchers are re-evaluating the assumption that disturbed behaviors are objective symptoms of disease and are beginning to consider the subjective meanings and experiences of persons with dementia (Downs 1997: 597). Some of them are becoming persuaded that at least some of these behaviors may represent the deliberate efforts of elders to communicate needs, maintain their senses of self, or keep their personal stories alive (Sabat and Harré 1992). These views have come to constitute a *communications perspective* that respects the agency of persons with dementia, regarding them as potentially meaningful communicators who negotiate their environment within the limitations of their impairments. It also offers more reasonable explanations for behaviors that had been viewed previously as simply pathological, meaningless, or ill-willed (Shomaker 1987: 374).

As an embodied agent, the elder with dementia is believed to intentionally communicate both verbally and through bodily gesture—a kind of body praxis (Lock and Scheper-Hughes 1996: 65). As Charles Taylor asserts, "Our body is not just the executant of the goals we frame.... Our understanding is itself embodied. That is, our bodily know-how, and the way we act and move, can encode ... our understanding of self and the world."[10] The communications perspective assumes that intentionality continues, even when understanding may be compromised by dementia. "Disturbed behaviors," whether verbal or physical, are part of the continuum of efforts by elders attempting to communicate their needs, feelings, and wishes. When persons can no longer verbalize or adequately organize

---

[10] Quoted in Hughes (2001: 88).

their thoughts or intentions, or when they have difficulty interpreting the intentions of a caregiver or communicating their intentions, they use their bodies to communicate need, distaste, or fear (Mace 1990: 84, 87). The use of body (body praxis) may in addition signal protest or resistance (a subversive reaction) against their conditions of living or perceived relations of power (cf. Rhodes 1992: 54) with caregivers and others. However, when such communications are medicalized as individual pathology, they lose their force.

Communications theory, as applied to elders with dementia, is the basis for a *person-centered* understanding of dementia and its care (cf. Cotrell and Schulz 1993; Harrison 1993: 428; Feldt 1999: 249–50). This theory is a theory of agency (Knuf 2000: 186) that reasserts those with dementia as intentional agents. Communications theory regards disturbed behaviors as the meaningful, if apparently distorted, efforts of elders to communicate needs, feelings or frustrations within the limitations of their impairment, their history, and their current living situation. It also entertains the possibility that aberrant behavior results from the way elders interpret the behavior of others in their environment. Thus aggressive behavior may be an effort by elders to protect themselves from their perception of impending harm or a sense of invasion of their space (Graneheim, Norberg, and Jansson 2001: 257).

Shomaker observes how behaviors that appear disturbed in today's context were reasonable in that of yesterday. For example, a former bus driver may be agitated unless seated in the driver's seat of the family car, or a woman may wander around looking for the bus to take home to cook dinner for her family. In these cases the behaviors are consistent with their past stories; the context of its expression in their current situation of dislocation from their previous one is what makes the behavior appear abnormal (Shomaker 1987: 373). Thus in order to make sense, the behavior must be understood within the relational and social context of its expression, as related to the unique biographical history of the elder.

A communications approach to dementia would evaluate the competencies and behaviors of an elder with dementia within the intersubjective context of care receiver and caregiver, in which mutual understanding must be negotiated (Knuf 2000: 491). This approach brings attention to the predicament of the elder, struggling for control over her life. At the same time, it recognizes the caregiver as an integral part of the communication. For example, if a caregiver misinterprets an elder's behavior as evidence of decline, without addressing the core problem (cf. Sabat and Harré 1992), this can precipitate further withdrawal of the elder.

Even more serious, if the caregiver ignores the communicative content of the problematic behavior, by viewing it strictly as a *symptom* and trying to eliminate it, his/her actions may pose serious clinical risks for the elder and be *ethically contestable* as well. For example, a caregiver may use medication to eliminate a disruptive behavior (such as screaming) that signaled a genuine need (such as pain). Although the disruptive behavior may stop, the suffering continues, leaving the elder unable to communicate it. Interpretations of behaviors as strictly evidence of disease (or denials of their validity) can thus lead to treatments that do not address the actual problem the behavior attempted to communicate (Kovach 1997: 127). By silencing the disturbed behavior, these approaches serve to silence the person as well. A communications approach attempts to avoid this result by seeking the actual source of the problem rather than simply eliminating the problematic behavior.

In contrast to the biomedical perspective that focuses on the objective body and symptom, the communications perspective privileges the subjective *person* with dementia. This raises the important question of what in fact it means for someone with failing mental capacities to be a person in Western cultures. The sections below discuss ongoing debates from Western perspectives on this question and then draw contrasts between cognitive approaches that are typically associated with the biomedical perspective and relational and contextual approaches most often associated with the communications perspective.

THE PERSON IN DEMENTIA

As discussed earlier, dementia can have devastating effects on a person's memory of recent and past events, persons, and experiences. It can dissolve the memories selectively, partially, or entirely. It can also disorder time so that memories are recalled—and sentiments and motivations produced—but without the correct context in which to anchor the memory. Some of this goes on in all of us. However, for the person with severe dementia, places, people, and time can become entirely out of sync. When this happens, her capacity to make decisions also becomes suspect. Eventually the person is no longer regarded as responsible as she may wander off, forgetting her destination. In addition, the elder may no longer be able to consider implications or consequences of her or others' actions. At this

point, she is considered to be no longer *medically competent* to make decisions over her medical treatment, including whether or not to receive it. The
elder by now is also likely to have lost *legal rights* of determination over her
property and may have passed power of attorney over to a family member
(or had a legal guardian appointed) to make major decisions for her, including the power to decide where she will reside. Thus, with cognitive losses
also come severe personal losses, including the loss of rights over oneself
and one's belongings. Such personal and social consequences of dementia
are extremely disempowering and can be frustrating for an elder.

In Western societies, the elder who faces these losses forfeits rights of adult
citizenship. To some extent these are the defining rights of *personhood*. They
are associated with *reason* and one's ability to make responsible decisions.
These rights also relate to *autonomy*, a person's ability to act independently,
on the basis of her presumed *moral authority* that is granted on the condition
that the person can take responsibility for her choices (Smith 1992: 46). This
ability requires rationality. In fact, in Western societies rationality figures
greatly in granting rights to a human being, and in many cases, even the basic right to belong to the category "person." By this way of thinking, extreme
utilitarians could argue that a computer, which is logical, has more right
to personhood than a human being who has lost this ability (Graf 2000:
170–71)! Similarly, in the United States, another nonhuman entity—a corporation—is regarded as a legal person, with relevant rights bestowed.

The very notion about how to define a person varies considerably from
culture to culture, but most agree that only those individuals who are
regarded as *persons*, however they are defined by the culture's members,
preserve full rights in that culture. In Western societies, bioethicists
(professionals from such disciplines as religion, philosophy, psychology,
clinical medicine, anthropology, and sociology) deliberate in difficult
cases on the question of personhood and rights in deciding whether to
provide or withhold medical treatment that may extend life. The field of
bioethics developed after 1970 (Graf 2000: 169–70) with Paul Ramsey's
publication that year of, *The Patient as Person*, that was concerned with
the dignified treatment and protection from exploitation of people
in an increasingly technologized practice of medicine (Doucet 2001:
122–23). Within two years, however, Ramsey's concern with the dignity and rights of persons as "embodied souls" had been diverted to a
concern only for *particular persons* defined solely by their rationality,
self-awareness, and self-control (Fleischer 1999: 315).

Since then, philosophers and bioethicists have continued to argue back
and forth about the essential ingredients of a person. Some would insist

that the ability to reason must be the defining characteristic of person-hood, while others hold a more durable concept of personhood based on one's history as someone who had actively occupied specific social roles (e.g., mother or husband) that endure even when memory does not. Still others have argued that personhood can be maintained only by an ongoing relationship or at least recognition by others; without intersubjective social acknowledgment, they would argue, one cannot be a person. By this way of thinking, a computer, despite its logic, could never constitute a person. This very criterion for defining personhood is precisely what British psychologist Tom Kitwood (1997) considers essential for preserving the well-being and functioning of an elder, what he calls "the preservation of the person."

There has been an explosion of publications on personhood in recent years, as debates rage on preserving life or hastening death across life stages from the fetal to the oldest old. Contemporary debates concerning the person go back to Aristotle and Plato. However, they have been further shaped by medical, legal, and moral concerns, additionally bolstered by modern tech-nological capabilities and the challenges these impose. These debates range from questions about beginning- and end-of-life issues to esoteric subjects, like the rights of scientifically produced anomalies (e.g., entities composed of human and nonhuman genes). In each case, the outcome of debates bear on how a human being (or a genetically mixed creature) and the rights be-stowed on him or her (including right to life) are defined. How—or wheth-er—one defines a human being with dementia as a person, is extremely relevant to the nature and quality of caregiving to which she is entitled. Therefore, below, I will summarize some of the most prominent arguments regarding personhood and their relevance to those with dementia.

On Being a Person

To be a person is not the same as to be human. Being human is a species-specific concept. If one is a member of the *Homo sapiens*, she is regarded as human.[11] To be a person, however, is a technical concept that is more spe-cific. While the concept of a person is common to all cultures, the specific

---

[11] Of course the issues are yet more complex. A human being has a particular set of chromosomes that distinguishes him/her from other creatures. Technically this could mean that a clone of a human being is also human. In addition, while humans are currently born into the world by women, technological innovations may well extend this. Furthermore, the point at which a developing organism with the right set of chromosomes is regarded as fully human is also subject to debate.

criteria each culture uses to define a person (e.g., subjection to particular rituals, demonstration of bravery, or evidence of rationality) vary given the culture's particular history and values. Thus in all cultures, persons are defined by their social recognition by others in that culture. If a human being has attributes or acts in ways that do not match the criteria demanded for being a person, he or she is not bestowed the full rights of personhood in that culture (e.g., the right to marry, to freely choose how to conduct one's life and to select one's companions, or to own property).

For example, cultures associated with European philosophical and legal traditions stemming from the Enlightenment, a historical period that looked to rationality as the value needed for improving the human condition, have tended to define persons strictly in terms of their ability to act as rational individuals. However, contrasting Western definitions of personhood, which stem from Abrahamic[12] (Christian, Jewish, and Muslim) theological traditions and secular humanist ones, place intrinsic worth in all human beings and define persons on the basis of this worth and their relational recognition by others. Thus, like the closely related concepts of the self (Battaglia 1995), both individuated and relational concepts of personhood co-exist in Western cultures.

Debates on Defining a Person

The literature on personhood concerns the defining characteristics of a person and the rights associated with this distinctive category. Perspectives concerning personhood in dementia tend to cluster around two views—those that depend on attributes of the individual as the basis for defining the person and those that draw on larger theological, contextual, or relational considerations. Those arguments that rely on traits of the individual bestow or withdraw the privilege of personhood from the individual as these traits change over time. They provide either a transitory or a permanent status depending on random events that affect the abilities of the individual, beyond his or her control. In contrast, perspectives that

---

[12] Although the nursing home I studied was Jewish, it did not adopt a specifically Jewish ethics in its ethical decision-making regarding the person, although that definitely factored in. However, its practitioners represented a wide range of secular and religious traditions, from which they drew. For this reason, I review both secular and the principal Christian and Abrahamic traditions. I only touch on Islamic bioethics, however, since it is still an emerging field, and the subject of a recent conference. (See http://rockethics.psu.edu/islam_bioethics/cfp.htm.)

look beyond the individual provide a more enduring concept of person-hood and of privileges that accrue with that status.

Individual Attributional Views on Personhood

Perspectives favoring individual attributes rely strictly on the individual's *cognitive* traits, such as rationality and self-consciousness, as the necessary ingredients of personhood. These notions are rooted in the mind/body dualism of seventeenth-century French philosopher René Descartes (1596–1650), who privileged mind (reason) over body, and the moral philosophy of Enlightenment thinker John Locke (1632–1704), who celebrated reason and moral agency. During this "Age of Reason" (late seventeenth through eighteenth centuries), Enlightenment thinkers used the tools of scientific inquiry to break down complex phenomena in order to understand them. Their inquiries have left a lasting imprint on a host of Western traditions from biomedicine to conceptions of human nature. Most importantly, their approaches appealed to reason and tools of scientific objectivity as a preferred substitute to divine creation as the basis for a moral understanding of humankind.

Given their acceptance of perfectibility through scientific progress, the liberal philosophy of Enlightenment writers associated morality with reason. John Locke, for example, defined the person as "a thinking intelligent being that has reason and reflection, and can consider itself the same thinking thing in different times and places."[13] Their impacts have been lasting, as many bioethicists today similarly ground personhood in nonmoral cognitive characteristics such as rationality and self-consciousness and use these traits to draw conclusions about their moral standing and their capacity to act as moral agents (Beauchamp 2001: 59–60). As such, a person is defined as a moral being based on the capacity to make rational choices and to reason about their consequences. The person's rationality alone is used as evidence that she can act as an *autonomous moral agent*, an individual who is free to exercise judicious decisions over herself and her well-being.

By this way of thinking, when one loses this ability to reason, as in dementia, one ceases to be a person and to retain one's rights as a moral agent. This essentialist understanding, which locates personhood as the property of a rational individual, bodes poorly for those with senile dementia, who have been called "arguably the most vulnerable" and least

---

[13] From Locke's *Essay Concerning Human Understanding* (1690) as quoted by John Harris (2001: 106).

powerful members of society (Kunin 2003: 211). The cognitive definition of personhood marginalizes and excludes demented elders from the world of persons, potentially leading to "insensitivity, if not to great wickedness" (Smith 1992: 47). For this reason, this cognitive rule of exclusion has been called "personalism"[14] (Fleischer 1999: 309), just like racism, sexism, and other isms based on exclusion. Excluding cognitively impaired elders from the community of persons imposes a stigma and shame that only compound the elder's sense of impairment. Separating persons from nonpersons on the basis of cognitive capacity, when carried to its logical extreme, can lead to the acceptance of death hastening of those with serious dementia (Graf 2000: 173).

Such are the perils of what bioethicist Stephen Post calls the Western bias of a "hypercognitive culture" (2000a: 245) that places value on "cognitive skills, economic productivity, and self-control to the neglect of emotional, relational, aesthetic, and spiritual aspects of well-being" (p. 247) and the tragic "lived experience" of the elder (Moody 1992: 34). The hypercognitive bias of bioethicists' definition of the person has stemmed in part from their efforts to achieve consensus concerning policies and procedures to determine access to medical treatments. In the end they could agree only on a watered down morality invested in the *nonmoral* principle of moral autonomy; bioethics had abandoned its original roots in religious traditions together with its concern for the profound questions on the meaning of life (Fleischer 1999: 316; Becker 2000: 4).

Noncognitive Approaches to Personhood

Increasingly, however, bioethicists and dementia researchers have been arguing that cognitive approaches to personhood are limited and particularly inappropriate for those with dementia. In response to this inadequacy, they have called for alternative noncognitive approaches to personhood that look to broader human qualities and draw on humanistic,

---

[14] The term "personalism," however, has had other, quite opposite meanings as well, as it was originally developed in reaction to narrow positivist views (Delumeau 2001: 17). That use of the term is defunct, and it is currently rarely used in discussions of the person.

theological, relational,[15] and/or contextual considerations. They seek to combat the reductionism or dualism, fragmentation, and the exclusivity of individual cognitive approaches to personhood.

Both humanistic and religion-based approaches to personhood emphasize the dignity and fundamental worth of all persons. Following Kant (1724-1804), this worth is seen as inhering in all human beings as "ends in themselves," not as means to something else (Novak 2001: 43). Even more forcefully, Kant states, "What has a price can equally be replaced by something else of an equivalent value. What is superior to any price, however, and what, therefore, has no equivalent is what has dignity."[16] By this dignity, humanists define all human beings as persons, worthy of respect (Bernard 2001: 57–58). As an Enlightenment philosopher, however, Kant limited his views to *rational* humans. Still, his comments argued convincingly against a *utilitarian* view of personhood that restricts human worth to economic productivity or usefulness toward some other end. Quite simply, according to thinkers that followed him, "persons are not for use" (Goodman 2001: 20). Catholic social thinkers have further argued that the overvaluing of cognition has led to reducing the body to its "pure materiality" for use (McCann 2000: 162) or *instrumental* value.

Christian-Judaic rejection of utilitarian personhood argues for the unity of personhood through all phases of life, without assigning greater or lesser value to one or another period. According to Jewish law, if less value is placed on the end of one's life, when the person is less capable, human value becomes dependent on its usefulness, productivity, or some other measure; this diminishes the absolute value of human life (Kunin 2003: 211). In Catholicism, personhood unfolds over the entire course of one's life, with no period privileged morally over another; respect for persons and their care remains constant throughout this course (McCann 2000: 165). Protestants also challenge any phasic notion of personhood; the moral person is embedded in a larger life history independent of any limitations that should befall her.

---

[15] Thomas Kitwood has provided the most fully articulated relational formulation of personhood with regard to dementia caregiving. To Kitwood, personhood is not a property of the individual but a human condition nurtured and realized through social interaction. It stems from intersubjectivity and "is provided or guaranteed by the presence of others" (Kitwood and Bredin 1992: 275). Like Downs (1997: 598), he would place ultimate responsibility for maintaining the personhood of those who are cognitively impaired with those who are not. Further, as a proponent of the interconnection of body with mind, Kitwood believed that caregivers who supported the well-being of those with dementia (i.e., their souls or *minds*) could simultaneously preserve their bodies (or *brains*) and avoid further decline (Kitwood 1997: 49–50).

[16] As quoted in Bernard (2001: 58).

Those who believe in a Creator elevate all persons on the basis of their creation in God's image. In Christianity, the very word "person" came to refer to all people as "children of God," like Jesus, the firstborn "Son," and originally contained deep religious significance (McCann 2000: 154). While some theologians have grounded this image in reason, again opening the doors of restriction, Jewish tradition considers all beings born of human parents to be persons, regardless of their limitations (Novak 2001: 47); no human life is seen as more valuable than another (Kunin 2003: 211). For Catholics, persons are those who share in the genomic spectrum of the species. The worth of all persons derives from the fact that they are the "objects of God's concern" (p. 50). According to Protestant theology, the restricted ability of someone to act is no basis for denying that individual the moral status of personhood. Compromised ability is seen within the larger trajectory of the person's history of freedom. As such, moral persons are expected to recognize other human beings as moral persons (Graf 2000: 176–77). Similarly, Jewish thought recognizes all persons as existentially equal, despite empirical differences in their abilities. Indeed, the very fact of these differences among persons "accentuates the underlying sameness of dignity" in all (Goodman 2001: 20; Agich 1993: 17). Islamic ethics also teaches that life is sacred, even if its quality is poor, and encourages respect for all persons (Daar and Khitamy 2001: 60–61). While religious philosophy reinserts an inclusive dignity to personhood, some theorists fear that religious visions, when applied to ethics, can be potentially oppressive (Agich 1993: 30); for this reason, they favor secular humanistic perspectives.

For secular humanists, the moral value of all persons is inherent to human nature itself (McCann 2000: 155). In their dissatisfaction with cognitive approaches to personhood, many have turned to aesthetics for an alternative vision embracing higher human aspirations. Following French philosopher Lucien Sève, the person is a "value-form" equally ascribed to every member of the human race (Plourde 2001: 145). As an aesthetic construct, persons are socially ascribed a dignity and worth. This makes it subject to social change and renders it more tenuous than the intrinsic dignity (Plourde 2001: 147) of religious based views on personhood. The aesthetic vision, however, borrowed from the religious position the view that all humans were created in the image of God (Silberfeld 2001: 313). It thus argues for the commonality of all persons, including the most vulnerable—a human condition to which all are subject.

Both humanist and religious visions of personhood acknowledge the vulnerability to impairment and suffering that all humans share. This recognition of shared human frailty lends an ethical dimension of *inter-subjectivity* to personhood far more profound than cognitive approaches to personhood can offer (Plourde 2001: 140). Weisstub and Thomasma eloquently argue that "at its essence" personhood arises in the "act of honoring the vulnerability of the other ... by righting the imbalance created in that vulnerability" (2001: 330). For secular humanists, the fundamental dignity and worth of vulnerable persons places demands on others to care for them (Harrison 1993: 431). In Jewish thought, by thus responding *relationally* to those who are vulnerable, one participates in God's own concern for those created in God's likeness (Novak 2001: 52).

For elders with dementia in long-term care, this relational concept of persons seems more relevant to their experience of dependence on others than does the personhood of the autonomous individual embraced by modern ethics (ter Meulen 2001: 130, 132). In fact, some writers feel that autonomy is no longer a relevant criterion for the person with dementia in long-term care (e.g., Moody 1992: 86, 90–91; McLean 1993). Others would maintain only a radically modified autonomy for elders who are dependent but can benefit from additional reinforcement in the context of the nursing home (Agich 1993: viii, 12).

Implications of Competing Views of Personhood for Caregiving

The particular view of personhood adopted by caregivers is likely to affect how they will regard the elder with dementia and how they are likely to care for her or him. Given the premises of each view of personhood, cognitive views are more likely to be associated with a biomedical orientation to caregiving, whereas contextual and relational approaches that regard persons with dementia as full persons are philosophically more consistent with communication orientations in caring for the person with BDs. The actual practice of caregiving, of course, places enormous demands on the caregiver. Still, an ethics of caregiving that is based on a particular view of personhood in dementia should impact the way in which the caregiver approaches care.

For example, those who accept a cognitive attributional view of personhood are likely to view cognitively impaired elders as diminished, with neither sense nor rights. They are likely to be seen as bodies who no longer retain the status of persons. The disease construct of dementia fits well with the cognitive view of personhood. As Herskovits describes (1995: 152), the biomedical model encourages the view that "the disease, not the person" is responsible for deviant behavior. It disregards the agency of the elder and reinforces the view that the person has gone and only the body remains. The cognitive view of personhood together with the biomedical model reinforces caregiving oriented toward controlling the body and dismissing the elder's wishes. Thus a cognitive view of personhood encourages an ethics of practice in which the caregiver is detached and objectifies the elder.

In contrast, caregivers who adopt a contextual/relational view of elders would be inclined to render care in a way that supports their dignity[17]— both psyche and soma (Martin and Post 1992: 59). Like Hughes (2001), who developed a situated-embodied-agent view of the person similar to the *communications* perspective, they are likely to see the elder, even in advanced dementia, as retaining some agency, even when actions may appear pathological or bizarre. The person's disturbed behaviors would be seen as embedded in contexts (e.g., historical, environmental, emotional) having personal and emotional significance to the elder. Thus the caregiver would attempt to interpret them as the products of meaningful action by the elder in terms of a larger biographical history (Hughes 2001: 87–88) rather than as evidence of disease pathology.

Such caregivers are likely to treat persons with advanced dementia with consideration comparable to that shown other elders. This may involve protecting them from shame—and further loss of "the public or social self" (Downs 1997: 599)—by removing, for example, traces of excrement from their clothing. They may wish to learn more about the elder's history, background, and life circumstances to better help them cope with disabilities (Downs 2000: 598). For very advanced dementia, it may simply mean being present with the elder regardless of outcome (Martin and Post 1992: 56) and taking steps to eliminate a noxious social environment (Kitwood 1990: 181–85) that could set the vulnerable elder back. The most courageous may work further to "prevent the loss of the patient to the disease" (Martin and Post 1992: 57). These

---

[17] Despite these advances, relational views of personhood in dementia and the responsibility it places on caregivers are not without critics. Trevor Adams, for example, is sympathetic to relational personhood, but questions the adequacy of Kitwood's evidence for preservative dementia care, fearing it could divert attention from other productive approaches (1996: 948–53). Daniel Davis more vehemently argues that relational personhood is unattainable, dishonest, and unrealistically demanding on caregivers (2004: 369–78). In the absence of stronger supporting evidence, he portrays a hopeless, vehemently pessimistic loss of personhood that begins early in dementia. While hoping to free families from guilt and to begin grieving sooner, he prematurely returns us to a dispassionate nihilism.

expansive views of the person encourage an ethics of *intimacy* (Martin and Post 1992: 57) and intersubjective engagement as a fundamental way of being with the failing elder. They thus encourage care *completed with, not delivered to* the elder by directing the caregiver to tune in to the elder's own expressions of need or desire in trying to fulfill care.

Personhood as Related to Self, Identity, and Agency

Personhood thus refers to the formal socially bestowed status of one human being by another (Kitwood 1997: 8); it is determined on the basis of specific criteria or social judgments. As seen above, whether a human being is granted or denied personhood depends on the particular cognitive or noncognitive ethical perspective underlying the applied criteria. Thomas Kitwood urged that we preserve the personhood of elders as a strategy to prevent further deterioration in dementia. The personhood Kitwood hoped to preserve, however, is more than this externally bestowed status; it refers as well to the *interiority*—the *selfhood*—of the person, that is, his or her subjective states.

SELF, IDENTITY, AND AGENCY: KEY CONCEPTS FOR THE PERSON WITH DEMENTIA

There are many aspects of the person with dementia that we will examine in subsequent chapters. These concern the "self" and "identity" of the person. There is considerable confusion and overlap with these terms (Erde 1999: 141), however, and with their relation to the person. Person, self, and identity are all interrelated, but each has separate and one or more distinct meanings. Whereas *person* is a socially bestowed concept, the *self* (or *selves*) emerges in social practices and is an interior, agential,[18] and processual construct that develops over the course of one's life. The related concept of *identity* is the subjective product or social realization of one or more selves. This section will elaborate upon these distinctions with particular relevance to the person with dementia.

---

[18] Several writers, however, argue that the self is only partially self-determined. See, e.g., Marcus (1995), Ginsburg (1995), and Battaglia (1995: 5).

Three Types of Selves and Identities

"Self" and "identity" each have several meanings, some of which overlap. A single writer may apply one or more meanings without necessarily distinguishing among them, adding to the confusion. In addition, the relations between particular kinds of selves and identities are rarely specified.

1. Self[1] (s[1]):The Self of Personal Identity (i[1])

The term "self" commonly refers to one's internal sense of unity or singular inner being ("the being that I am") (Erde 1999: 154) that is independent of sociality (Herskovits 1995: 159). Steve Sabat and Rom Harré (1992) call this *self[1]* (s[1]), the *self of personal identity* (i[1]). This self is the center of initiative (Ewing 1990: 255) and meaningful purpose. It is associated with a sense of *agency* (Sabat and Harré 1992: 445) and personal point of view. One way this self is expressed is through the pronouns "I, me, my" that index statements and actions as uniquely belonging to the person. *Self[1]* is a structural feature of mentality. It lacks content and does not rely on time, memory, or, according to theorists, on other people. In the case of dementia, *this agential self[1] persists deep into the disorder.*

2. Selves[2] (s[2]): Public Self-Representations) and Social Identity (i[2])

Another kind of self (or selves) (s[2]) refers to particular personae or self-representations that are publicly presented.[19] These selves are variously produced during the course of a person's development through interaction with significant others in particular historical contexts (Ewing 1990: 254). For example, an infant acquires an early self and sense of subjectivity when it first learns that its gestures or calls for help produce an immediate response; at this same time the child comes to recognize his/her power or effectiveness as an agent who can elicit a response from others (Kitwood and Bredin 1992: 275). Although *self* (s[1]) is a singular entity, a person has multiple selves (Scheibe 1989: 145–46), such as mother, daughter, wife, scholar, and patient. Once formed, each self may emerge consciously or unconsciously as social circumstances demand.

One's *social identity* (i[2]) *is realized when one or more of these selves are presented to another* person (Scheibe 1989: 145). Because selves

---

[19] See, for example, Erving Goffman, (1963), *The Presentation of Self in Everyday Life*, as cited in Sabat and Harré (1992: 445).

are produced under particular social and historical circumstances and with particular persons, they may contain different facets of who we are. Social identity is related to agency insofar as a particular self acts selectively in revealing itself out of conditions of moral character and circumstance (p. 142).

Each *self² is the author or agent of a particular narrative or story line*, which derives from the way in which that self originally developed in the given social context. The public presentation of one such self is a declaration of one's story. We present facets of ourselves through narratives that we actively construct from our memories; as we have more than one audience, we have more than one narrative (Scheibe 1989: 148). Our self-presentation to selected audiences communicates part of who we are, our selected self or facets of it.

3. The Communal Self³ (s³) and Cultural Identity³ (i³)

Because of the complexity and fragmentation of selves in modern life, some writers have argued that people need to be part of a larger shared cultural narrative. This larger communal narrative reveals yet a different communal self³ (s³), linked not only to narrow circumstances and selves² (s²), but to a broader, more familiar story-line shared by many. Given the extreme fragmentation of individual selves² that occurs in dementia as memory is compromised, a shared cultural identity³ (i³) would link elders with caregivers even when they are not familiar with the elder's particular stories or selves.² Philosopher Charles Taylor[20] argues that cultural identity can be realized only as part of a larger cultural or spiritual tradition that has been lost in Western society. He calls for a "horizon of meaning" about old age that caregivers and elders would both share and that could help to eliminate the fragmentation shared by both.

Continuity and Unity of Self: Reality or an Illusion?

Beginning with Enlightenment philosopher David Hume, there has been considerable debate about the actual unity and continuity experienced by the self. Historically there have been two competing theoretical camps: those who argue that the self is one continuous unified whole (*the essentialist view*) and those who argue in favor of a series of selves that vary

---

[20] As cited in ter Meulen (2001: 134–35).

with context (*contingent or contextual view*). Hume denies the existence of a unified self (Murray 1993: 3). For him, the sensations or ideas that people have are totally disconnected, even though they may seem connected because of a psychological mechanism (pp. 12–15). In reaction, Kant developed the idea of a transcendental subject in order to preserve the notion of the continuity of the self (p. 11).

More recently, psychologist Heinz Kohut, a proponent of the essentialist view, also postulates a cohesive, bounded unified self. In contrast, anthropologist Katherine Ewing argues that the experience of unity or continuity is itself an illusion (Ewing 1990: 265); there is simply no cohesive self at the center of experience (p. 258). Still Ewing understands that individual selves (or self-representations), however fleeting, may be experienced as a timeless whole (p. 252). This enables people to deal with inconsistency in their lives. The contingent/contextual camp has increasingly gained favor, given supportive findings about experiences of people from other cultures. The influence of postmodern thinking, which emphasizes inconsistency, particularism, and the importance of context (Murray 1993: 3), has also challenged the essentialist view.

Some of the confusion here may actually stem from the different ways in which "self" has been used. Kohut's boundless self and Kant's transcendental subject more closely refer to the self[1] who acts as a purposeful agent and serves as an "indescribable core" (Herskovits 1995: 159) of moral being (Scheibe 1989: 152). In contrast, the selves or self-representations described by Ewing are more similar to the selves[2] described by Sabat and Harré.

Can There Be Self or Identity Without Memory?

The Loss of Self (Cohen and Eisdorfer 1986) is the title of a book on dementia that suggests a self can be lost. But is this really possible? It depends on how we define the self. If we agree that the self depends on memory, then once memory is lost so is the self. But there are other approaches to considering this question. Certainly, attributional views of the person, based on the tradition of John Locke, reserve "personhood" for those who have retained cognitive traits like reason or self-consciousness. Continuing in this Lockean tradition, personal identity would also depend on an ongoing self-consciousness (Takala 2001: 92) or psychological continuity that links present with past states. For Locke, as well as contemporary writers of his tradition, a person's identity reaches back only as far as his/her memory (pp. 87–88); without memories, there is no personal identity.

Thus from a Lockean viewpoint, a self can be maintained only when a memory enables continuity of past with present.

In contrast, a number of writers have challenged the reliance on ongoing memory as a primary feature of identity because it ignores the highly selective, constructed, and unreliable aspects of memory, the continued agency of the elder, and the vital role of others in recognizing identity or selves. Ewing, for example, argues that memory provides no guarantee of continuity (1990: 267). The sense of continuity only requires the recall of a few selective memories (some accurate, others not). Different frames of reference, associated with different self-representations, rest on yet different sets of selected memories. Similarly, Sheibe argues that we do not passively recall that which happened, but rather selectively remember, forget, and even possibly fabricate memories as they help us create a meaningful sense of identity or selves (1989: 148). The organizational power of self[1], through the use of the indexical "I," enables the person to select particular content from the internal archive of their biographical selves[2] to present publicly (Sabat and Harré 1992: 450).

The importance of the self as *agent* in recall cannot be underestimated. Scholars have become increasingly interested in the ways in which people actively present themselves through their stories ("the self as narrative"). The identities of those whose limited memories confine them to the present continue to appear in their character, will, "moral being," and ability to develop meaningful relationships in the present (through an implicit semantic memory) (Scheibe 1989: 151–52). Semantic memory allows for the persistence of customs, social niceties, and more importantly, the ability to socially engage with another. Even after social identity can no longer be maintained because memories of others have ceased in time, the capacity for inner, timeless symbolic memories survives through an inner personal identity (identity[1]) (pp. 157–58). The differentiation of social selves[2] from the inner self[1] helps explain how identity survives when continued reference to the past no longer occurs. The self[1] of personal identity depends not on an intact memory, but rather on the continued sense of agency apparent in a person's use of the subjective pronouns, I, me, my (Sabat and Harré 1992: 447). After that verbal ability has been lost, the person's effort to communicate through gestures provides lasting evidence of their agency (Sabat and Harré 1992: 448; Hughes 2001: 90–91).

From a *social constructionist perspective*, like that of Sabat and Harré, the self does not depend on memory for its preservation, but on the way in which others treat the person. When the I is taken seriously, in spite of lost memory, identity is maintained; the self cannot be lost. Similarly, when gesture is acknowledged as an important signal warranting attention, even after both memory and verbal ability are gone, the self as agent remains. Thus from this perspective, as long as a person receives social acknowledgment by others, she/he need not be threatened by the loss of self.

Presentation of the Self[2] in Dementia

Once formed, selves must be maintained through social interaction with others. Unlike *self¹*, one or more *selves²* can be lost if they do not receive acknowledgment from others (Sabat and Harré 1992: 460). Especially in dementia, where the person is more vulnerable to losing self-esteem from faltering abilities, it is other people who are essential for preserving their selves (Parker 2001: 338). Each *self²* can be maintained as long as the story line can be kept alive. Thus the self² as wife will be maintained insofar as she continues to receive the recognition of this story line. The self² as lawyer, however, may be lost if it ceases to be acknowledged. When a person with dementia can no longer verbally express a particular self through narrative, that narrative (and the self with which it is associated) can still be kept alive by those familiar with her story. Even the person's agency can be guaranteed as long as some person acts to preserve it (Gubrium 1986b: 43).

Human beings continue to create new selves or new renditions of older selves in order to protect themselves from risk or hurt (Parker 2001: 336). Persons with dementia may employ creative strategies to adjust to their cognitive impairments and preserve their selves. Social identity can only be guaranteed when others acknowledge their stories. Since social identity (i^2) is realized when the self (s^2) is presented to others, it is subject to being treated with dignity (through acknowledgment or positive attention) or shame (through ridicule or negative assessment) or to being reduced to solitude (from disregard).

In dementia, however, the expression of a particular self² may occur in ways not always understood by caregivers, particularly nonfamily caregivers who lack knowledge of the person's history. In addition, caregivers may misinterpret as symptoms the deliberate efforts of elders to maintain both kinds of selves in accommodating to the limitations imposed by their disorder (Sabat and Harré 1992: 448). Their positioning of persons with dementia as "demented" serves to invalidate their stories as well as their fundamental role in creating them. When caregivers' own storylines explain the elder's behavior strictly in terms of disease, they do violence to the actual motivation of a particular self as agent (Sabat and Harré 1992: 453). Not knowing, or not recognizing the relevance of, a person's history makes it impossible to understand the way in which the person acts and the changes in his/her action over time (Hughes 2001: 88–89). Thus Alisdair MacIntyre (1981) insists: "Histories of individual agents not only are, but *have to be* situated."[21]

Sabat and Harré (1992) describe several cases where staff at an adult daycare center misunderstood behaviors of elders with dementia. One woman who was known for being very helpful in setting tables would avoid situations (like group discussions) that would reveal her difficulty with speaking. She would wander away from the group to avoid losing her standing as a helpful person. Caregivers who interpreted her wandering as evidence of deterioration, due to disease, rather than her intention to save face, did injustice to her as a conscious agent. Similarly, a man who had been a professor found the activities at the center prosaic and boring, so preferred to read, talk with staff, or go for a walk. Staff who lacked knowledge of his background, or discounted it as irrelevant, interpreted his behavior as withdrawal and wandering due to the dementia.

In both cases, the behaviors were not a product of disease, but of deliberate intentional actions, consistent with their stories. This intentionality was lost or misinterpreted by staff who regarded the behaviors as evidence of pathology. As Sabat and Harré remark, "Just because the person A ... is confused about ... the AD sufferer B ... does not mean that person B is confused" (1992: 260). Even though these elders acted in meaningful ways (consistent with their histories and ongoing self-narratives), their agency and the communication it signaled were lost to those who refused to acknowledge it or its possibility.

A person communicates something about herself and history through her narrative. Her identity is revealed by sharing that narrative. How it is received, understood, or misunderstood, or whether it is even countenanced, affects the subjectivity of the teller. When that teller has dementia, and is already insecure about her position, the ways in which others interpret and respond to her words (and actions, as motivated by an understanding of the situation) may profoundly impact her self-concept, stories, and future behavior. Caregivers who attribute her behaviors to

---

[21] As quoted by Hughes (2001: 88), emphasis mine.

disease will discourage any future construction of a self[2]. Thus, a lost or reduced ability to project a self[2] may result from the quality of social interactions rather than the disease itself (Sabat and Harré 1992: 460). For Anthony Giddens, a person's identity can be found "in the capacity to keep a particular narrative going."[22] *Others disable that ability by ignoring or misinterpreting that narrative.* This is why writers such as Kitwood insist that those who are cognitively intact are responsible for maintaining the elder's "self-identity or self-esteem" (Downs 1997: 598).

Sabat and Harré argue that dementia contributes to the loss of selves only indirectly (1992: 448) by leading to a reduced *positioning* of the person as demented (p. 453). This diminished positioning moves caregivers to disregard the elder's behaviors as diseased rather than as part of her continuing life story, retained in the nursing home environment. Part Two of this book will examine the clinical consequences of caregivers' ignoring elders' life stories and communications.

FURTHER READING

Conrad, Peter, and Schneider, Joseph. (1992). *Deviance and Medicalization: From Badness to Sickness*. Philadelphia: Temple University Press.

Gordon, Deborah. (1988). Tenacious assumptions in western medicine. In Margaret Lock and Deborah Gordon (Eds.), *Biomedicine Examined* (pp.19–55). Dordrecht, NLD: Kluwer Academic Press.

Harrison, Christine. (1993). Personhood, dementia and the integrity of a life. *Canadian Journal of Aging, 12*(4), 428–40.

Marshall, Patricia. (1992). Anthropology and bioethics. *Medical Anthropology Quarterly, 6*(1), 49–73.

Moody, Harry. (1992). *Ethics in an Aging Society*. Baltimore: Johns Hopkins University Press.

Murray, D.W. (1993). What is the Western concept of the self? On forgetting David Hume. *Ethos, 21*, 3–23.

The Nun Study. (May 14, 2001). *Time Pacific Magazine, 19*. Retrieved March 5, 2004, from <http://time.com/time/pacific/magazine/20010514/cover3.html.>

Tobin, S.S. (1991). *Personhood in Advanced Old Age*. New York: Springer Press.

---

[22] Quoted in Parker (2001: 337).

CHAPTER 3

Historical Background to Dementia Caregiving and the Ethnographic Research Methodology

This chapter provides the background information for my research. It begins by tracing the evolution of dementia care in the United States up to the development of special care units like those I studied. It then discusses the research methodology for the study, including the value of the ethnographic method in nursing home research, the communications perspective and comparative framework for the study.

HISTORICAL EVOLUTION OF DEMENTIA CAREGIVING IN THE UNITED STATES

As early as the colonial era, structures have been in place for housing frail elderly. Elizabethan Poor Laws brought from England, along with later

American laws, demanded local responsibility through local taxes to care
for the poor, including indigent elders; strangers were shipped off to their
own communities (Quadagno 1999: 119). By Puritan law, adult children
were expected to care for their own parents, while frail elders without children gave up their property to the town treasury in exchange for housing
by local residents; those without property appealed to the public coffers. Institutions for the poor (almshouses), though first established in 1664, were
rare. Through the late 1700s, the majority of the poor who were disabled or
elderly were granted aid or boarded with other community members.

During the first half of the 1800s, the continuous stream of immigra-
tion boosted the urban population by 50 per cent. Periodic depressions led
to a new kind of immigrant pauper who appealed to local authorities for
economic grants. To discourage this, many cities refused, requiring them to
enter almshouses instead. Still, most citizens viewed the elderly as a special
group of deserving poor, and many of them continued to receive aid to keep
them in their homes. By the 1850s, as reformers found almshouses inadequate to meet the needs of the motley population they housed (children,
the insane, deaf and blind, and the elderly), specialized institutions were
developed to address their varied needs, leaving almshouses as long-term
care institutions (Lacey 1999: 205) for the impoverished elderly. By the end
of the 1800s, elderly people constituted one third of almshouse residents;
this figure doubled by the first quarter of the 1900s (Quadagno 1999: 120).
For the most part, however, elders with families remained with them.

By the early 1900s, in addition to almshouses, many religious and fra-
ternal homes for the aged opened their doors, but they were reserved for
white Protestants whose impairments were minimal (Lacey 1999: 104).
As the population of the aged continued to increase to five million, including 300,000 aged 85 and older, the need of the indigent, chronically ill
soared. Charitable homes housed as many as one half of them in urban
areas, but the majority had immense waiting lists. The others were forced
to go to the dreaded almshouses, which were overcrowded, unclean, and
lacked adequate provisions; some were also notorious for abuse. Those
almshouses that started providing chronic care changed their names to
"infirmaries" (Lacey 1999: 105). However, by this point, psychiatric hospitals were increasingly institutionalizing demented elderly persons.

The Social Security Act of 1932 intended to allow elders to avoid the
almshouse by using federal funds to maintain them in the community. In
fact, funding neither from the Social Security retirement program (an en-
titlement program) nor the means-tested Old Age Assistance program for
the indigent poor could be used to pay for almshouse care; this led to the

demise of almshouses. Lacey describes how this provision, however, led unintentionally to a shift of care to psychiatric institutions. While federal dollars could be used for private boarding homes—the predecessors to nursing homes—care in these informal facilities was extremely variable, and there were too few of them willing to support the demented elderly. Thus elderly persons with dementia with no place to go were committed to state mental institutions. By the late 1940s, 40 per cent of their population consisted of people over 65 (Lacey 1999: 107).

With an ever-growing older population, the 1950s continued to face a shortage of needed beds for dependent elderly. Laws encouraged further funding for nursing home care, utilizing a hospital-based model not well suited for those with dementia. Still, by 1955, close to two fifths of nursing home residents had dementia (Lacey 1999: 108). With fewer than half the number of needed nursing home beds, however, elders with dementia continued to be warehoused mainly in state mental hospitals, where they were segregated from other patients and received few services. By the late 1950s, psychiatric professionals began questioning the appropriateness of psychiatric facilities for the care of those with dementia, stimulating gerontologists and government officials to promote reform.

The number of mainly private nursing homes increased significantly during the 1960s due to policies that encouraged private investments (Binney and Swan 1991: 173). With the passing of Medicare (linked to Social Security) and the means-tested Medicaid legislation in 1965, new sources of income became available to nursing homes. In addition, because of political negotiations by both physicians (Estes and Binney 1991: 124) and the nursing home industry, these programs encouraged nursing home placement over community options for elders (Binney and Swan 1991: 173) while offering limited oversight. Enforcement of even minimal standards was weak since existing bed numbers were still inadequate.

By the 1970s the nursing homes industry exploited available public funding to greatly expand the number of available beds. Meanwhile, the social and political movement launched in the 1960s and 1970s to deinstitutionalize patients from state psychiatric hospitals led to massive transfers of elderly patients into nursing homes. However, despite excellent care at some homes, abuses at many others were rampant. Neglect, unsanitary conditions, heavy use of restraints, and needless deaths due to fire and food poisoning alarmed the public and the gerontological community. Still, little regulation occurred, and public funds kept feeding the industry. The stories of horrendous scandals during this decade paved the road for Congressional investigations. During this time the Alzheimer's disease movement became influential. As researchers expanded the category of Alzheimer's disease to include those with senile dementia, doors opened for considerable research funding. Partnerships between researchers and new advocacy organizations like the Alzheimer's Disease and Related Disorders Association (now, the Alzheimer's Association) helped promote nursing home reform.

It was not until 1987, however, with the Omnibus Reconciliation Act (OBRA), that Congress passed a comprehensive nursing home reform bill that set in place major regulations to be implemented over the next several years, and to be fully in place by 1990–91. The law required training and certification of aides, reduction of physical and pharmaceutical restraints (at 40 per cent during the mid-1980s) (Lacey 1999: 119), individualized care plans, and periodic comprehensive assessments of all residents. It also set clear guidelines concerning feeding, sanitation, and expected maintenance tasks and put into place a comprehensive system for documenting all elements of care administered to elders.

Although the Act allows residents to be free of restraint "for reasons of convenience and not required to treat the resident's medical symptoms," this provision is subject to broad interpretation (Binney and Swan 1991: 179). In addition, regulations supported the prescription of biomedically oriented care akin to that provided in hospitals (Lacey 1999: 124), rather than the person-oriented social approaches that were designed in the previous two decades and that residents and their families often preferred. Despite its limitations, OBRA legislation did make major inroads in improving the quality of *custodial* nursing home care, directed at improving hygienic body care. Furthermore, with its demands for restraint reduction, this Act also gave a boost to special care units, many of which shared this goal (Lacey 1999: 121). By 1991 one out of every ten nursing homes claimed to have a special care unit for its residents with dementia (Office of Technology Assessment [OTA] 1992: 22).

Special Care Units and This Research

The research took place on the east coast in the very first special care units in the United States. The earliest special care units were developed during the late 1970s (although a few models had been tried still earlier), but the great majority were established after 1983 (OTA 1992: 1). They were a response to the need for housing a growing population of elders with severe cognitive impairments; many also tried to cash in on a potentially lucrative market (Lacey 1999: 121). Many had developed from the dedicated efforts of clinicians and researchers to provide more humane programs to help those with senile dementia.[1]

Most special care units were physically separate, typically locked, units within an already established nursing home. Some new freestanding facilities dedicated to Alzheimer's care were also established. Others simply used the label to segregate behaviorally difficult elders from others without providing special programs. All claimed to provide for the special needs of persons with dementia, while segregating them from a more coherent population of elders in the home. They shared no common approach, and their quality varied enormously, but overall they marked considerable improvement over the types of care that had historically preceded them.

The research described here took place over 18 months from 1992 to 1994. During that period, early research was being conducted on the value of special care units (Lindeman and Montgomery 1994), following a National Institute on Aging research initiative in 1991 (Ory 1994). By 1999, dementia care had reached a turning point in which innovative and humane models had been developed—building in part from the earlier clinical research—but poorly disseminated (Zarit and Downs 1999). Today, however, there are doubts about their benefits even as special care units persist in popularity (Henderson 2003: 157).

ETHNOGRAPHIC RESEARCH METHODOLOGY

The Challenge of Studying Nursing Homes

A nursing home reflects the society in which it is embedded. It shares and reproduces some of the larger cultural assumptions about aging, the elderly, and their needs; it is thus a product of the social, political, and economic system of which it is a part (Vesperi 1995: 13). A nursing home

---

[1] Some, but by no means all, of those with outstanding contributions include Dorothy Coons and Nancy Mace, Elaine Brody, Powell Lawton, and Miriam Moss.

is at once a home, an institution, workplace, a regulated industry, and most often a business (or nonprofit organization), each with different and often conflicting demands and expectations. Thus, it is also a center of contradiction.

For example, as a home it is expected to provide for comforts and to satisfy basic physical, social, and emotional needs. It is a place where family and friends can come and go freely. Homes are places where people can feel free to be casual and do what they want (for example, eat, sleep, relax, bathe) when they want without concern about outside interference.

As an institution, however, it is a formal organization with multiple parts (e.g., clinical, dietary, laundry, maintenance) that must be coordinated to operate efficiently and systematically to carry out all its functions in order to meet basic needs of the residents. In order to do this, the bureaucracy sets rules and operates within a division of labor that is hierarchical and generally detached, and runs according to a rigid schedule. This is similar to what one would find in a hospital, after which nursing homes have been fashioned, and is most common in the larger nursing home complexes. Smaller nursing homes, however, are not as bound by these institutional constraints and can find creative ways to avoid the rigidity.

As a workplace, it employs people who provide care and services for a wage. The labor is carried out over three eight-hour rotating shifts, and the delivery of care is routinized in order to facilitate its completion. Thus on a given unit, care may be more or less structured in such a way that baths are all given on a particular day, residents must be wakened, washed, and groomed for breakfast by a certain time to eat the meal when it promptly arrives, and residents must be prepared for bed in a timely fashion. In order to accomplish this, work is broken down into tasks (like bathing, toileting, brushing someone's teeth) that a worker (the nursing assistant, or NA) must complete within a certain time frame.

As a regulated industry, the nursing home must follow specific guidelines in order to maintain its licensure and be in legal compliance with OBRA (Walshe 2001). Since OBRA has encouraged a biomedicalized orientation to individual caregiving in correspondence with a hospital model, nursing homes must also shape their care accordingly. In addition, the federal regulation demands documenting all care, charting all notable incidents, and reporting cases of potential abuse. All of these shape the kind of care that is possible.

Finally, the overwhelming majority of nursing homes are privately owned (Walshe and Harrington 2002). Whether these nursing homes are part of large for-profit chains, ever diminishing individual for-profit facilities or a not-for-profit operation, they must try to stay in the black; all must satisfy the goals and priorities of their executive boards. In order to survive, they must at very least comply with regulations. The larger chains especially must also be profitable and satisfy their shareholders in today's competitive economy. This means trimming costs wherever possible, including the direct caregiving staff, one of the costlier items. A smaller staff find it hard, if not impossible, to take care of all the requirements of the job and also satisfy residents' personal requests.

Thus for elder residents, a nursing home is much more than a home. In fact, the provision of "home" is virtually dwarfed by the requirements of bureaucracy, regulation, and business. These result in practices guided by competing priorities, values, and rewards. The product is a nursing home *culture* that is rich with multiple activities and replete with concurrent efforts to satisfy basic resident needs, stay in compliance with regulations, and remain economically viable. These pressures can lead to a provision of care that is dominated by institutional, workplace, and regulatory demands that collide with the ideals of the informal, homelike care expected by the resident and her family. The elder may feel deceived by this new place called "home," dehumanized by routinized care from hurried staff, and frustrated at the staff's lack of attention to her requests. She may feel a dissonance between her idea of what a home should be like and the reality of living in an institutional setting. Families may similarly feel disappointed by the kind of care that is meted out, the lack of flexibility for receiving meals, waking residents up in the morning, and hygienic care, and their sense of being slighted by the staff. Similarly, the staff, in working hard to fulfill their jobs and satisfy their supervisor's demands, may resent residents and family members who pressure them to do something outside of their ordinary routine (Foner 1995: 173). Finally, the administrative bureaucracy may find itself struggling to keep the place running, while trying to satisfy both consumers who want a homelike setting and regulations that favor a hospital model of care (Lacey 1999: 125–56).

Because of the contradictions between the expectations of residents and families seeking the informalities of a "home" and the stark realities and impositions of formal institutional life for its residents, the nursing home is also a place where identities are not only repeatedly threatened (Vesperi 1995: 18), but are even seen as a nuisance to the business at hand. In light of these challenges, ethnographers have long been concerned with the maintenance and erosion of identities in institutionalized settings. The nursing home is an extraordinarily rich cultural setting in which to conduct research because of the endless conflicting expectations, demands, and agendas of its various actors, drawn together for different reasons and co-existing in an artificially created environment. The detailed approach of the ethnographer, which involves prolonged, intensive participation and observation at a particular site attempts to capture this richness. It is no wonder that there is a long history of ethnographic study of nursing homes and similar institutional settings. (For a brief review of some of this work, see Appendix C.)

Ethnography as a Unique Way of Knowing

Ethnography offers a way of knowing the world. Although every ethnographer uses the same tools (prolonged periods in the field site, participant-observation, various forms of interviewing, and heavily detailed in-depth note-taking), the knowledge different ethnographers gain from working in the same field site will never be the same. This is because the methodology of an ethnographer is not a mechanical process. Of course the quality of observations and detailed note-taking are vital, but what each ethnographer sees, hears, is intrigued with, and includes in field notes as noteworthy will vary with the ethnographer. Each brings to the field her own skills, sensibilities, values, openness, socialization, and powers to connect with others; there is no getting around that. These attune her to particular phenomena and divert her from others. These subtly draw her toward certain persons and turn her away from others. They enable her to share more or less of herself at different times with the same and different persons. These particular subjective attributes of any given ethnographer necessarily leads her to make particular interpretations of the transient world she occupies during this part of her life.

   This is quite different from other kinds of researchers whose use of common, objective instruments should yield similar knowledge. The ethnographer, however, is not looking for others to be able to precisely replicate her findings; rather, she hopes to leave the field with a valid understanding of life there (Vesperi 1995: 13–14). Ethnography, during the last 25 years has come a long way toward realizing that such understanding does not mean capturing the whole story.[2] Instead, it involves gaining access to

---

[2] Among the major work to examine this are the now classic edited volumes *Writing Culture* by James Clifford and George Marcus and *Anthropology as Cultural Critique* by George Marcus and Michael Fischer, both published in 1986, which critically examined the authoritative voice of the ethnographer and the ethnography as a total portrayal of the culture. More recent works include Hammersley (1992), Hastrup (1995), Fabian (2001), and the edited volume by Bochner and Ellis (2001).

multiple provisional (Crapanzano 1986: 51) "partial truths" (Clifford 1986: 1) through ongoing subjective engagement of one's selves with multiple changing other selves, and then continually reflecting and revising one's understandings about those limited "truths."

There are many other ways of coming to know about nursing homes or nursing home residents. Residents' functional capacity can be evaluated over time using predetermined criteria. Their sociability can be studied by counting the frequency of their interaction with others or the detail of their social networks. Their cognitive abilities can be measured using valid and reliable scales designed for this population. All of these provide standard information that can be used to compare residents with each other or with themselves over time. What about the nursing home itself? One can look at specific criteria at particular points in time to see if it satisfies measures of quality. One can look at the physical facility, its cleanliness and upkeep, the quality of food, the timeliness of meals, the number of staff, or the availability of quality medical care. The ethnographer would agree that all of these are important as they impinge on the experience of the elder.

However, to gain a closer understanding about life as a nursing home resident, ethnographers try to partake in the life-world of the residents, to experience the care routines to which they are subjected and, insofar as they can, to share in their various joys, sorrows, and tribulations. To penetrate this world, the ethnographer tries to enter their space day in and out for many months at a time. She hears and digests their stories and those of others who also occupy this space (clinical, administrative, custodial and volunteer staff, family, and visitors). She also observes or participates, to the extent possible, in residents' and staff members' daily activities. She observes the mingling of these various actors, each coming from her own history, and each bringing competing needs and personal or professional agendas. To the extent that various actors allow the ethnographer to enter their personal space and embrace her (Hastrup 1995: 156–57), she can capture a sense of what life must be like for those who have revealed parts of themselves.

Ethnography is thus very different from objective approaches to knowing. The power evoked by a bird's-eye view and prolonged intimate engagement with others cannot be approximated by explicitly objective approaches. Thus, ethnography does not aim to present generalities— the "average" case, as might quantitative approaches using statistical analyses. Rather, using the specificity of individual lives, it offers a particular interpretation of "partial truths" about nursing home life.

In contrast to quantitative research methodologies, the *power of ethnographic research* does not lie in the number of sites or cases studied. Its power lies in the validity of its interpretations as convincing[3] and in its implications for others caught in similar structural predicaments. In the case of nursing home research, those structures are the larger shared institutional and bureaucratic features, which generate multiple contradictions and shape the lives of those who lie within. To the extent that a nursing home conforms to these larger features, it provides a legitimate basis for drawing empirically generalizable inferences (Hammersley 1992: 93), despite local differences between them. Those local differences, however, may hold clues to variations in the kinds of care residents receive.

Several works have provided excellent descriptions of the ethnographic process and procedures for conducting an ethnography (e.g. Emerson, Fritz, and Shaw 1995; Kutsche 1998). (For my description of ethnographic research as a kind of journey, see Appendix D.)

The Communications Perspective

The study was informed by a communications perspective, which regarded BDs as potentially understandable or meaningful in light of the context in which they occurred and the limitations imposed by the dementia. Utilizing this communications perspective, the study made several assumptions.[4]

- The nursing home is a social setting where communication and miscommunication regularly occur among its constituent actors—residents, various staff, and family members.
- "Disturbed" behaviors are possible communicative events that should be examined in terms of the biographical person, her history, and the current social context.
- The judgment of a behavior as "disturbed" is itself a communicative act that requires social interpreting and assigning a meaning and intervention to the behaviors and communications of others in their environment (staff, family, and other residents).
- Finally, the behaviors of others are potential triggers to the disturbed behaviors.

---

[3] As suggested by Sanjek (1990: 394), cited in Vesperi (1995: 13).
[4] These assumptions were clearly specified in the original grant by Robert Rubinstein, the Principal Investigator, in conjunction with his other colleagues.

The Comparative Ethnographic Framework for the Study

Despite similarities in the larger structural features that define institutional settings, many local differences can mediate the way in which policies are implemented in individual units. The principal nurse in charge, typically during the day shift, can establish a particular philosophy of care that shapes how NAs provide care. She can negotiate with the administration to accommodate residents in atypical ways. She can exercise license to some extent in interpreting institutional practices. Depending on how she is regarded by the administration, she can also be relieved somewhat of the kind of unrelenting oversight that encourages rigidity. All of these result in local cultural differences among units in the same nursing home that can dramatically vary the quality of caregiving experienced by elders from different units.

The staff from different shifts on a given unit may vary in their willingness to "go that extra mile" depending on their relation with supervisory nurses, the residents and their families, and with other NAs and staff. Individual staff style, unit staff style, and cooperation among staff all affect residents' quality of care. The extent to which staff develop ways of working together may depend on their past experiences working as a team. The prolonged tenure of both staff and residents can also affect the kinds of relationships and expectations that develop over time between them and with the families. All of these contribute to a particular local culture of caregiving, that is, the internally generated, often unspoken, unit-specific rules, staff relations, and ways of working with residents that are unique to each unit.

This study examined these and other *nonmedical* aspects of nursing home life and nonmedical interventions that could affect the behavioral disturbances that were so common among residents with dementia. Given the communications perspective that guided the research on behavioral disturbances, the local cultures of care were seen as creating environments that were variously receptive to interpreting the potentially meaningful communicative content of the disturbed behaviors.

As the research anthropologist for the study, I was given the choice between two special care units as the study site. Since the units were designed identically, and they both took residents with similar impairments, I decided an ethnographic study *comparing* life on *both* units would be preferable. Despite the identical floor plans and the same type of resident population, differences in the tenure of the staff and residents of each unit and of the status and philosophy of their unit heads produced contrasting cultures and living environments. These contrasts were not designed into the research, but gradually developed over the natural life history of each unit. *These contrasts nevertheless provided a unique opportunity to conduct a kind of naturalistic experiment to compare how nonmedical conditions* (like the organization of care, patterns of interaction among staff, residents and families, and staff philosophies about dementia and appropriate caregiving) *could differentially shape the outcome of residents on the two units.*

Methods

The methods I utilized were qualitative and ethnographic, incorporating participant observation and a close relationship with each head nurse as the "key informant" (McLean and Perkinson 1995) who provided my primary understanding about the dominant view of dementia in her unit, her organization and logic for organizing caregiving there, and the larger operations of the nursing facility. I kept detailed recordings of observations of residents and life on the unit, and detailed summaries of both casual conversations and formal interviews with staff members, family members, and, when possible, the residents.[5] I also examined selected residents' current and past medical records for information about their medical and behavioral history, changes over time, the staff's impressions about their behaviors, and interventions or "treatments" that had been tried. In addition, I reconstructed relevant events that may have predated my study by referring to medical records and collecting retrospective accounts of clinical and administrative staff and family members. (For more details about the methods I followed, see Appendix E.) Utilizing the data from these sources, I conducted in-depth qualitative analyses to compare philosophical and organizational aspects of caregiving between the two units and their relation to resident outcome.

---

[5] For an elaborate description of a series of narratives with one woman, see my chapter, "Coherence without facticity in dementia: The Case of Mrs. Fine," in *Thinking About Dementia: Culture, Loss and the Anthropology of Senility*, edited by Annette Leibing and Lawrence Cohen (2006).

FURTHER READING

Butler, Robert. (1975). *Why Survive? Being Old in America*. New York: Harper and Row.

Bohannan, Paul, and Dirk van der Elst. (1998). *Asking and Listening: Ethnography as Person Adaptation*. Prospect Heights, IL: Waveland Press.

Litwak, E. (1985). *Helping the Elderly: the Complementary Roles of Informal Networks and Formal Systems*. New York: Guildford Press.

Stafford, Philip (Ed.). (2003). *Gray Areas: Ethnographic Encounters with Nursing Home Culture*. Santa Fe, NM: School of American Research Press.

CHAPTER 4

The Research Setting and the Residents

THE RESEARCH SETTING:
PHYSICAL SETTING, STAFFING, ENVIRONMENTAL AND
EXPERIENTIAL ASPECTS OF LIFE ON THE UNITS

A setting consists of a *physical* space that various actors occupy and in which they intermingle. It has physical components that are visible and less visible structural components that allow various sets of actors (in this case, e.g., the staff) to exercise power within it. There are also *environmental* aspects to a setting that, quite prominently on the Snow units, are shaped by levels of activity and sound. Finally, there are *experiential* aspects to being embedded in a setting that can best be depicted by those whose lives it most fully penetrates.

The Physical Setting of the Snow Units in the Nursing Home

The study took place on Snow 1 and Snow 2, two historic 40-bed special care units of a 500-bed private nursing home complex on the urban East Coast, but no longer in operation. They were part of a biomedical complex comprised of 10 nursing home units, several comprehensive geriatric clinics, and a limited hospital to accommodate emergency medical crises. The complex was constructed for elderly men and women of primarily Jewish heritage and had a solid reputation in the community for quality care. It drew families of varied socio-economic status because of its biomedically oriented facilities and a medical staff affiliated with a nearby hospital should hospitalization be needed.

History of the Snow Units
The two Snow units, designed as identical special care units, were extremely innovative for their time. They opened late in 1974, after a good decade of research,[1] several years of planning by national experts in gerontology, geriatrics, and architecture, and considerable input from the staff, families, and the more articulate residents.[2] They had been originally designed as residences for persons in the early stages of Alzheimer's disease and other dementias (later classified as Stage 2 or 3)[3] having impairments in memory, time and spatial orientation, functional capacity, and social interaction. The planners hoped to create a unit that could help maintain autonomy and functional capacity of its residents.

Already by the mid-1960s, they had in mind creating an environment that went well beyond the typical custodial care in "surroundings that are totally dehumanized in the name of easing the effort of staff and maintaining cleanliness at all costs" (Liebowitz, Lawton, and Waldman 1979: 59–61). However, by the time of my study, the intended use of the innovative floor plan, with all its special features, had dramatically changed, as had the level of impairment of residents who occupied the units.

Original Intention and Floor Plan of Snow Units
The planners intended to create a physical environment that would facilitate the optimal functioning of residents and that was both prosthetic and

---

[1] Dr. M. Powell Lawton was instrumental in researching and developing the design.

[2] Some NAs complained, however, that they were not part of the planning process and that their lack of input as the persons most involved in hands-on care led to serious omissions in the design, such as bathrooms too small to admit a wheelchair. The NAs were forced to physically move residents to perform daily grooming and hygienic activities—making daily life more difficult both for the resident and NA. At the time of the planning however, none of the residents were in wheelchairs.

[3] This designation was based upon criteria delineated by Reisburg and Borenstein (1986: 50). According to these criteria, Stage 2 involved "very mild cognitive decline," primarily forgetfulness. In Stage 3 ("mild cognitive decline"), there were early signs of confusion as well, including getting lost, showing difficulty in finding words or names, some difficulty concentrating, and reduced retention of new information.

therapeutic to help sustain residents' current level of functioning. They tried to achieve this by an environment that compensated for deficits while offering cognitive and social stimulation. They included visual memory aids and anchors to enable the resident to negotiate the environment with the greatest autonomy and competence. Immediate visibility of daily activities plus involvement in a rich activities program were intended to add meaning to elders' lives and to promote cognitive stimulation viewed as therapeutic (Cohen and Day 1992: 131).

The floor plan was of foremost importance in the planners' design (Liebowitz 1976). It featured a large open core (40 by 100 feet) where most activities would take place. Residents' rooms (15 double and 10 single) surrounded the core on its perimeter on three sides, with the nurses' station on the remaining side. The floor was vinyl and within the perimeter of the core was an eight-foot-wide wandering path, demarcated by a darker color. Within one side of the central core stood a gazebo, decorated with nontoxic plants and designed for activities like music therapy. Next to the gazebo were an exercise rail and steps to be used for physical therapy. At the far right end of the core, beyond the gazebo, was an area intended for formal activities like crafts, games, or therapeutic groups.

There was a kitchen, for "therapeutic" cooking activities by residents, near the gazebo. From the vantage point of the nurses' station, the dining room was to the left of the open core, demarcated by a low rail and divider. Beyond the dining space, at the left end of the floor near the entrance, was a lounge with considerable natural light and a television. The entrance was gated, and a person desiring entry needed to simultaneously push two electronic buttons for access (something more impaired residents could not accomplish).

The unit also offered color-coding using bright primary colors for door seals and bedroom furnishings, and large room numbers and nameplates at eye level (Liebowitz 1976) to help residents locate their rooms. A clock and "reality orientation board" within the core were visible from many vantage points. Light, albeit fluorescent, was adjustable to simulate daytime lighting. Bright colors were used to accent wall graphics and the nurses station. Finally the furniture was given considerable thought. The tables could be arranged to form large octagonal groupings or separate smaller ones. The Skandiform chairs were adjustable and allowed adding wing-like extensions and a table tray.

The floor plan and special features were designed to compensate for cognitive disabilities associated with dementia. The open space in particular allowed residents to view all active areas from anywhere within the core or from outside their rooms. They intended to minimize the effects of memory loss, disorientation, and confusion that result in intense anxiety in elders suffering from dementia. The planners intended the visibility of staff interactions, traffic patterns, and therapeutic activities to provide stimulation and contact with the world. They also hoped that residents would join in activities they observed or experience "passive stimulation" that could have some "increment" of therapeutic benefits (Liebowitz, Lawton, and Waldman 1979).

Visibility of the entire floor allowed ambulatory residents to choose where to go and what activity to select—all with the intention of enhancing autonomy. The planners placed functional areas like the dining room within the sight of residents to help orient them to time by helping them anticipate the next meal. The lighting and special features also added a pleasant warmth that contrasted with the dark, depressing, and isolating features of many other nursing homes.

Usage of Special Features and Floor Plan by the Time of My Study

By the time I began to conduct research on the units, much had changed. Although the structure of the floor remained the same, the use of floor space differed from its original intention, and many of the special features were either no longer present or no longer being utilized. The dining room and large inner core had reversed their functions. Residents objected to sitting together around a few tables in the original small dining area, preferring smaller groupings. As residents became more severely mentally impaired and disruptive, this dissatisfaction increased. The dining room relocated to the larger core, where many smaller tables were arranged. The former dining area then became the center for activities such as music or the religious service.

The gazebo no longer featured plants and was no longer used for resident activities. In fact, it was not used by residents at all, but by the nursing assistants who needed somewhere to sit to document their work. One day as I sat in the gazebo taking notes, I welcomed a resident to come and sit with me as I wrote. A private companion to another resident immediately informed me that the resident must leave as the gazebo was intended only for the staff! (This was particularly ironic since the companion was not even employed by the home.) Given the loss of ambulation of most of the residents, the staircase attached to the gazebo for physical therapy was now used to store supplies and hide wheel chairs. The activities area beyond the gazebo and the "therapeutic kitchen" were also no longer in use.

Many of the special features were also gone or altered. The eight-foot-wide wandering path was gone on one unit and replaced by a much-diminished three-inch black strip on the other. Similarly gone were the bright color-coding for residents' rooms and the bold graphics and color accents elsewhere. The large three-dimensional numbers were still used for rooms, but the lettering of the nameplates on the doors was so small that anyone unfamiliar with the units had difficulty finding rooms. A clock remained for the few residents who still referred to it; the "reality board" now only reported the day's date.

The furniture was also different. Many small square tables that accommodated wheel chairs had replaced the older tables that did not. On Snow 1, some small rectangular tables dominated seating, with rarely more than two at a table. On Snow 2, the staff often placed the little tables next to one another, but residents rarely sat together. The Scandiform chairs were no longer on the units.

With the open core design, noise penetrated everywhere in the unit, and acoustical features were never added to absorb excess sound. As noisier residents moved onto the units, the sound became overwhelming at times when compounded by additional interference from the overhead intercom system, staff and visitor traffic, and maintenance activities like floor polishing. These sounds often triggered verbal outbursts from several residents. The noise also interfered with any focused music therapy session that requires residents' attention. The rich activities programs were now reduced to one 45-minute daily session on Snow 1 and only two a week on Snow 2.

Reasons for the Changes

After all the planning effort in developing the units, I wondered why these special features had been abandoned? It was a response to social, demographic, institutional, administrative, and fiscal changes and governmental regulatory pressures. One major change occurred in the populations of the units. The residents in my study were considerably more cognitively and physically impaired than those who had occupied the units two decades earlier (on one unit, many of the same persons). Residents used to be more ambulatory and needed only supervision to complete activities of daily living (ADL) such as eating, washing themselves, and getting dressed. Even with the locked gate, several of the residents used to leave the unit on their own whenever they pleased. By the time of my study, no more than a dozen residents on each unit were even ambulatory, most were severely demented, and many were referred to the units because of their behaviors, which were seen as disruptive to the more intact residents and staff of other units.

There were several reasons for the changes in residents. First, as alternative living arrangements for less-impaired elders became available in the community, only more-impaired individuals started entering the nursing home. In addition, given the apparent decline that people with dementia often experience over time, the units were witnessing a deteriorating trajectory. Further, many current residents had transferred to the Snow units from other units that had housed less behaviorally disturbed residents. Finally, as the units came to house residents who were more disturbed and became noisier, they became associated with the most severely impaired residents, who then increasingly were routed there.

Fiscal changes also affected the units. When they first opened, most of their residents were designated "skilled." Skilled nursing care is more expensive than regular intermediate care. Fiscal pressures on state budgets led to a changed definition of skilled nursing criteria that resulted in reclassifying most of the Snow residents to an intermediate care status (Brody, Lawton, Liebowitz 1984: 1382). Thus, ironically, as residents who were declining required heavier care, reimbursement changes made accommodating their needs more difficult.

These changes came at a time of rising salaries for nursing staff due to nursing shortages and inflation. Since nursing and custodial needs were perceived as too essential to limit, fiscal cutbacks were directed at reducing activities therapy and social services. In addition, the actual time professionals could spend with residents was further limited by the increased paper work mandated by OBRA.

Because of the decline in the level of functioning of the residents, the color-coding of rooms and furnishings was abandoned by administrators who could no longer justify their additional expense. This was unfortunate for the remaining ambulatory residents who could have benefited from these features. The therapeutic kitchen was also abandoned because so many residents had seriously functionally declined.

The open core design continued to provide contact with the outside world—and an incentive to keep on living, according to several family members. At the same time, this open core, with its acoustical failings, was singularly unsuitable for residents who regularly vocalized their distress. It only disturbed or further confused many of the other residents and provoked verbal and sometimes physical reactions from some of them. It also became distasteful to families and visitors, making it difficult to "sell" the units.

I wondered why there had been no effort to reshuffle nursing home residents into and out of the Snows to maximize the advantages of their design for particular residents who could most benefit from them at different times. Administrators who had been involved in the changes offered several reasons. First, the Snow units house two thirds of the single beds in the 500-bed complex, and those with single rooms were not likely to want to leave. In addition, since the status of cognitively impaired persons is in continuous flux, moving them as they change would have constituted an administrative nightmare in a facility of this size. Finally, as newer buildings with natural lighting and pleasant color schemes became available, families preferred to send their relatives there than to the Snow units, now an institutional beige. Families in fact pressured the administration not to move their family member to the Snow units unless they became very behaviorally disruptive or simply could not manage elsewhere.

These various social, cultural, demographic, fiscal, and institutional factors combined to produce the situation on the special care units when I arrived there. The tragedy is that the vision, energies, and wisdom and hopes of the planners were no longer realized in benefiting elders. Most of the residents, families, and employees knew little of the units' illustrious beginnings.

Staffing of the Units

The Snow units were alive with many different actors—the nursing staff, medical and support staff, social workers, activities therapists, custodial personnel, families, individual companions to particular residents, and the residents themselves; on occasion an administrator or researcher might also appear.

Typically, the principal staff person on the unit was the *head nurse*, a registered nurse (RN), often with advanced degrees. He (more often, she) organized the delivery of care on the unit and so was also called the *care coordinator or CC*. She was also responsible for administering or delegating the dispensing of medication and treatments (such as physician-ordered procedures requiring licensed skills, e.g., catheter care or tending lesions or wounds). The head nurse brought medical concerns to the attention of the medical staff—physicians and physician assistants (PA). She also was required to complete documentation about each resident and her treatment daily. While she worked during the 7:00 a.m. to 3:00 p.m. shift, she was the person responsible for *developing the philosophy of caregiving that*

affected the caregiving practices across all three shifts. She set care priorities
and structured the delivery of care.

During the day shift, the *care manager* (CM), a *licensed practical nurse*
(LPN), was responsible for dispensing medication and in assisting the
nurse in delivering treatments, managing the unit, and completing documentation. There was no RN in charge of the other two shifts (3:00 p.m.
to 11:00 p.m. and 11:00 p.m. to 7:00 a.m.) or on weekends, so the CM who
was solely in charge during those times thus served as the *charge nurse*
during those shifts. This nurse was responsible for delivering medications
and treatments, completing paper work, and supervising the unit. During
the 11:00 p.m. to 7:00 a.m. shift, this nurse was also responsible for completing rounds with four residents, periodically checking them, changing
diapers when needed, and addressing problems. When the head nurse
was absent (e.g., during illnesses or vacations), the care manager on the
7:00 a.m. to 3:00 p.m. shift assumed her responsibilities, sometimes with
the assistance of another LPN.

Nursing assistants (NAs) on all shifts carried out all routine patient
care: assisting residents with dressing, transferring residents from bed
to chair, basic grooming, feeding, changing bed linens, and other assis-
tive tasks. They were required to follow constantly amended care plans
and to adequately plan their time to complete all required care despite
unpredictable events that might interfere. As part of their custodial care
of eight or more residents, they needed to thoroughly inspect their bodies
and bring aberrations to the head nurse's attention, to accurately document procedures and care delivered, to examine toileting patterns, and to
administer enemas when needed.

NAs on the 7:00 a.m. to 3:00 p.m. shift were responsible also for serving
breakfast—a priority—and later, lunch. In addition, they, like NAs from
the other shifts, were required to do their rounds at least twice. This involved systematically toileting (taking them to the bathroom, if continent,
or checking their diapers, when they were not continent) and conducting
any special checks such as vital signs for all the residents in their group. In
between, they would take residents to their rooms for naps, provide snacks
and additional toileting if needed. During this shift, the clinical offices and
labs were open, so NAs were also called upon regularly to transport residents to clinics for appointments. If NAs from the night shift (11:00 p.m.
to 7:00 a.m.), which was less well staffed, did not complete all of their care
tasks (e.g., diapering a resident during their last rounds), this left even more
for the busy morning staff. Although staff from the afternoon shift (3:00
p.m. to 11:00 p.m.) did not have to worry about transporting residents to

clinic appointments, they often had to contend with more active residents and had to prepare them for bed. The number of NAs varied with the needs of the unit and shift. The Snow units, which were better staffed than the other units, had as few as one or two NAs on the night shift to five (and rarely, six) during the morning and afternoon shifts.

A bathing assistant came in one day a week to bath the residents. An activities and music therapist, the social worker, and rabbis who provided religious services also had contact with the residents at least once weekly.

The physician's assistant (PA) came to the unit daily to investigate problems, provide special treatments, write prescriptions, offer recommendations, and make referrals to specialists. Of the medical providers, the PA spent the greatest amount of time dealing with medical concerns. A psychiatrist entered the unit once weekly to check referrals and consider medication changes. This visit could last as long as two or three hours. Finally, a physician came to the unit daily to review charts, the PA's recommendations, and to sign the recommended prescriptions.

Power Structure of the Staff

In general, a staff member's authority and power (i.e., the ability to influence others) related to her amount of time on a unit, level of autonomy in the home, degree of patient contact, visibility, and predictability of appearance. *The less the amount of time, visibility, and degree of patient contact and the greater one's autonomy and unpredictability of appearance on the unit, the greater one's relative power.* Typically, power fell in the traditional gender, race, and class lines representative of the larger society. Virtually all of the nurses, NAs, were female and black, whereas all but one of the medical doctors were male and white. In addition, the PAs and highest-level nurses were white women, except for one nurse who eventually left.

Thus the nursing assistant (NA), who did most of the hands-on care, spent virtually all of her time working on the unit, was heavily supervised, and had the least power among the clinical employees of the nursing home. At the other extreme, the typical physician, whose clinical orders were very influential, would come and go at varied times during each day, review the charts, and be on his way with minimal, if any, patient contact. However, he had to sign off on the minutest orders for care, even when they were not medical, such as a periodic shave, walk, or use of diapers. While every unit had a physician responsible for its residents, this generally accounted for only a part of his professional practice. The organization, amount of time, and extent of patient contact varied with each physician, depending on his investment in this part of his practice.

In contrast to the physician assigned to the unit, the physician's assistant (PA) was invested with less power, had more actual contact with residents, would spend considerably more time diagnosing problems brought to her attention by the nursing staff, and assumed responsibility for recommending treatment. The physician (typically male) would review the prescriptions of the PA (typically female) and provide an authorizing signature as a matter of routine. Thus, it was frustrating to a PA when family members would bypass her or credit the physician for having helped their relative. However, PAs had less influence on units like Snow 2, where the unit physician was centrally involved in treating the residents.

The nursing staff could feel the effects of the physician's power whenever his recommendations seemed to have affected a resident's behavior adversely. Changing or reducing a resident's medication, for example, could render a difficult elder even more disruptive and harder to manage, only increasing the burden of the nursing staff. For their part, family members could wield power by bypassing the nursing staff or PA and appealing to the physician directly to alter, reduce, or eliminate a medication.

Physicians and psychiatrists varied in the extent to which they would consult the nursing staff or PA before signing off or adjusting the latter's recommendations. Some would only consult medical records, which often lacked sufficient detail about subtle changes or day-to-day fluctuations in residents' behaviors. The details reported varied with the recording nurse, how busy she/he was during the shift and how problematic a particular resident might have been during that shift. Often the best people to comment on changes in a resident's behaviors—the nursing assistants, who had daily resident contact—were rarely consulted (Foner 1994: 160).

Personal companions of residents had the least power on the unit. They were not even part of the nursing home staff because they had been hired privately by a resident's family to spend time only with their elder or to help with his/her care. Their place in the hierarchy became clear during a scabies outbreak, in which they were not eligible to receive free medication despite their exposure to the parasite. The nursing home refused to extend medical treatment to them for fear of liability should they develop an adverse reaction. Given their low hourly pay, in comparison to the NAs, and their lack of medical coverage, their further denial of treatment symbolized their low ranking among the unit staff.

The Nursing Hierarchy and Power Within It

Of all the staff in the nursing home, the nursing staff organized themselves under the most striking hierarchical order, beginning with the NAs at the bottom to the Director of Nursing (DON) at the top (cf. Foner 1994: 74–90). This was a classic example of the enduring legacy of Florence Nightingale's hierarchical model of nursing supervision (Reverby 1997: 218–20; Schwartz, deWolf, and Skipper 1994: 267–69; Weitz 1996: 265).

As with other clinical staff, the least powerful nurses (the NAs) spent the most time on the unit, had the greatest amount of patient contact, and the least control in using their time. They were prescribed specific break and lunch times and could not otherwise leave the unit without permission. They also were denied access granted to other staff to use the telephone at the nurses' station. As a nurse moved higher up the hierarchy (from NA to care manager to head nurse), physical contact with the residents diminished, and administrative duties increasingly consumed her time. The NAs were heavily invested with responsibilities that sustained the lives of elders, but as the least formally trained staff, they remained at the bottom of the nursing hierarchy in pay, appreciation, and vulnerability to job loss. They worked in a punitive system and often received little respect from residents, families, and their administration. Like the daycare workers to whom children are entrusted, they were charged with much responsibility but not adequately rewarded.

Next on the hierarchy came the care manager (CM), who was always busy conducting rounds and helping the head nurse manage the unit or serving herself as the charge nurse.

The head nurse, also called care coordinator (CC), typically had the most advanced training among unit nurses and the greatest responsibility and control over the unit. This nurse established rules for caregiving and interacting with family members that extended to all shifts. She also had the most autonomy among the unit nurses.

Above the head nurses were the supervisory nurses, who oversaw operations daily on all units. There were regular supervisory nurses during each shift during weekdays and rotating supervisory nurses on weekends. They were responsible for carrying out the policies their own supervisors had instituted. These supervisory nurses reported to one of four Assistant Directors of Nursing (ADONs), who served in administrative capacities. The ADON assigned to the Snow units would appear every Friday for a briefing with the head nurse; her uncommon presence on other occasions invariably raised concerns. Finally, the Director of Nursing (DON), who was a principal administrator at the nursing home, almost never came to the units. On the rare event of a visit from her, the staff were understandably worried. The DON headed numerous committees in the home and wielded considerable power over residents and staff.

All of the home's highest ranking nurses—the DON and ADONs—were white females, with the exception of a black female ADON, who was replaced by a white woman after she later resigned. At the level of the CCs, only one was black—the nurse who introduced me to Snow 1, but she left just before her six-month trial period had ended. Thus, among many of the NAs and some care managers, there was the distinct impression that the administration was deliberately trying to create a power structure across racial lines. In fact two nurses from the night shift at Snow 1 told me that the professional distinctions at this home were much more drawn along racial lines than anything they had experienced working at nursing homes in the South, particularly in Atlanta. There, they found both African-Americans and whites well represented at all levels of staffing, from NAs to physicians.

Nurses lacked the authority to prescribe medical treatment (except for PRN prescriptions to be prescribed "as needed"); yet they carried considerable influence over the *dispensation* of patients. This influence by the head nurse varied considerably from unit to unit, depending on the perception of her competence and her relationship with the DON and other members of the administrative staff. Patients were moved to different units (as their condition and needs changed) or different rooms based on decisions of a special committee headed by the DON. Residents, their families, and even unit staff did not typically attend these meetings, and their decisions sometimes led to patient transfers even before they had notified families.

The nursing staff believed that some head nurses could mobilize power to move off, or prevent the admission of a resident to their unit. When a resident seemed inappropriately bumped onto Snow 1 (because the elder's condition did not warrant it), the nurses would sometimes jest, "Who does *she* know?" with reference to the head nurse from the referring unit. Some NAs on Snow 1 believed that the head nurse from Snow 2 could refuse to admit extremely disturbed residents to her unit despite its identical admissions criteria with Snow 1.

The Relationship Between the Nurses and the Administration During the Time of the Study

The nursing administration of the home—the DON, the ADONs, and their support staff—had been undergoing changes over the previous dozen years as the institution was expanding. They were experiencing particular turmoil during my period of study. Turnover was so common that two DONs had left, and a third progressive DON who had recently been hired resigned only months after accepting the position. This turmoil in the upper echelons was felt throughout the ranks of the nursing hierarchy.

Over time, the nursing administration had become punitive in its practices. I heard endless reports of administrative staff abusing their power through inconsideration, insensitivity, or going back on their word. Both NAs, who were unionized, and care managers, who were not, felt dispensable and vulnerable to losing their jobs. Even entitlements, like sick pay, were threatened. Administrative staff would look for patterns of absences during reports of sickness, especially for Fridays before and Mondays after a weekend when a nurse was not scheduled to work. The first time the administration detected a possible pattern the NA would be called in for "counseling." The administration would file a grievance the next time this happened, and if this recurred, they would suspend the NA without pay. NAs felt they had to report to work even when they were very sick to avoid facing penalties from a suspected pattern. As one care manager said, "You never know where you stand with the administration."

During a crippling snowstorm, when buses were not in service, workers who did not make it to work had their regular pay docked. Nurses and NAs also complained about reporting for weekend or holiday assignments, only to be told they were no longer needed or worse yet, rudely asked why they had showed up in the first place! NAs, who were at the bottom of the pay scale and had to make special arrangements and payment for babysitters and transportation, felt particular indignation: "It is as if our time doesn't matter at all." Others would agree to work an extra shift if they could remain on their unit, only to find that their requests were not honored. NAs could not make or receive personal calls from the unit floor, even in emergency situations. They could not even take advantage of cost-saving vacation deals, because the ADON could make changes at any time in their schedule, defeating any chance of their planning for more than a local getaway.

Worst of all, they felt that the ADONs were aloof, condescending in their manner, and disengaged from both residents and nurses. Staff from Snow 2 who had worked at the facility over 20 years observed that staff/ administration relations had progressively worsened over the last dozen years as the home had expanded and become less personal. Old-timers remembered the ongoing involvement of administrators during the early days and the meetings they had regularly held to request everyone's input to improve the quality of the working and living environment. They felt valued then. The heavy loss of morale in recent years had left relations with the administration bitter. The old-timers from Snow 2, who had experienced much better conditions in the past, were particularly troubled by the administration.

Daily Life and Environmental Quality of the Snow Units

Anyone who first enters Snow 1 is struck by its level of noise. Snow 2 could also be noisy at times, but it did not have the same quality or prolonged intensity of Snow 1. The NAs on Snow 1 often played loud contemporary music, like rock or rap, whereas the head nurse of Snow 2 played a special selection of music from the 1930s and 1940s to deliberately soften the environment during anticipated noisy periods. Staff who have remained on either unit for some time began tuning out the noise. After being away from the units for several years, I recently replayed an audio-recording of an interview I had conducted with a family member on Snow 1. I could not believe how incredibly loud and distracting the background noise was; it made listening to the interview very difficult. Yet I was not aware of it at the time of recording.

The noise apparently affected residents, however, because many of them regularly told others to keep quiet. Residents who have dementia—especially those who are susceptible to disinhibition (a diminished inclination to hold back comments or actions for reasons of social appropriateness)—seem highly susceptible to powers of suggestion from others.[4] Thus, if one resident yells out, other residents are likely to join, creating a chorus effect.

Residents from both units are typically quiet during the mornings and mealtimes, although some residents would talk loudly with the NA, insisting, "Go away!" or "No!" Immediately after meals, when the residents are sated, the units are also quiet. However, sources other than residents generate noise. The hustle of activity begins during breakfast, when the medication nurse begins to dispense medications. Shortly after breakfast, the units are buzzing with activity. This is when treatments are given, linens are changed, companions arrive, and the cleaner sweeps and mops the floors; the din of the floor polisher adds additional noise. Perhaps worst of all is the blast from the intercom system at any time of day or night, but especially during the day shift.

---

[4]   This was commonly stated by the psychiatrists of both units.

As residents begin to feel hungry again before their next meal or feel the urge to go to the bathroom, the level of agitation and noise rises. Ideally, before each meal, the residents are toileted—taken either to the bathroom if deemed continent and in need of assistance, or to their bed for a diaper change. Before each meal arrives and residents are moved to their various tables, the noise level is extremely elevated. During mealtime, a unit tends to be quiet. Residents who feed themselves are handed their trays. Then one by one, depending on staffing, the "feeders" (those requiring assistance) are fed. This may take a good hour. There is some calming on the unit after lunch is over and the trays have been carted back out. But as the medication nurse begins rounds again and the maintenance staff clean the floors again, noise increases again. Residents tend to be somewhat calmer for about an hour following each meal.

Both family visitors and staff come and go all day long, usually at predictable times. On bath days, residents line up in their wheelchairs or chairs by 7 a.m. before breakfast. The beautician also comes to the floor to give haircuts to those in need in the morning. Throughout the day shift, residents leave and return from various clinics, often with technicians who come to transport them. The pharmacist and clerks regularly visit the nurses' station in the unit to review and update, computerize, or thin out the medical records, while divers others collect data from research or governmental and fiscal reporting. The PA visits twice daily, prescribing medications and treatments, documenting them in the chart, and checking on residents. NAs also frequently visit the nurses' station to complete documenting their ADLs[5] (their regular care routines) and special treatments such as enemas they have administered.

By 3:00 p.m., with shift change, the residents begin to get louder again. The 3:00 p.m. to 11:00 p.m. charge nurse collects her staff and reviews the status of various residents with them. The NAs collect materials (e.g., towels and diapers) as they prepare to begin their rounds, toileting, and checking their residents. The care manager brings around snacks to hungry residents as she dispenses medication and treatment on her rounds. Late afternoon and early evening the physician or psychiatrist do their rounds and are popular times for family visits.

By about 8:00 p.m., the care manager dispenses medications, treatments, and hands out snacks and juice to those who want them. At about 8:30 or 9:00 p.m., the NAs begin to prepare residents for bed. They are

---

5 ADLs refer to basic Activities of Daily Living, such as grooming, eating, and toileting.

given a final toileting or diaper change, are washed and examined, their clothes are changed, and they are put to bed. By 10:00 p.m., the unit is often fairly quiet, with most of the residents in bed.

At 11:00 p.m., the 3:00 p.m. to 11:00 p.m. staff leave the unit and the 11:00 p.m. to 7:00 a.m. staff (the charge nurse and usually two assistants) arrive. The charge nurses review cases and discuss changes in patients' status or special needs; then the new charge nurse updates her staff. On a good day, most of the residents have by now gone to bed, but there may be a couple who want to stay up later. The charge nurse or NA will then escort them to their rooms in preparation for bed. The staff then dim the lights on the unit, contributing to an unusual calm. A few residents, however, remain vocal throughout the night, usually calling for their family members.

By 7:00 a.m., staff switch occurs again, with the 11:00 p.m. to 7:00 a.m. NAs exiting as the new NAs enter. The 11:00 p.m. to 7:00 a.m. charge nurse reviews the cases with the 7:00 a.m. to 3:00 p.m. nurses, who then go over the cases with their nursing assistant staff. And another day begins.

Experiential Aspects of the Snow Setting for Residents and NAs

Early morning wake-up routines in the nursing home represent perhaps the greatest departure from what the resident was accustomed to at home. Depending on which NA is caring for the resident during the typical two-week rotation, this experience can be gentle, and even pleasant, or terribly frightening. It can also set the tone for the day, especially for extremely impaired or agitated elders.

Wake-up times were regulated by the institutional clock, which determined when breakfast would be served. In order to assure that all the residents were awakened, cleaned, toileted, dressed, and groomed by breakfast at 9:00 a.m., the NAs on the 7:00 a.m. to 3:00 p.m. shift started their routines immediately after meeting with their head nurse. In fact, to accommodate all 40 residents, the NAs on the 11:00 p.m. to 7:00 a.m. shift began the care routines for five residents at 6:30 a.m. For NAs, early morning wake-up routines were among the most demanding of their chores, often exhausting them for the rest of the day.

Below I describe two scenarios of wake-up routines, both of which I observed while shadowing the two NAs on Snow 1; based on my observations of both units, these could well have occurred on either unit. I then depict a typical difficult morning in the life of one of the NAs.

A Typical Morning Routine for a Resident (Tula): Scenario 1

Tula was one of the easier residents to care for. Although clearly suffering from cognitive deficits, she could understand what was required of her and was very cooperative. Despite her dementia, she also had an acute sense of relationship and social justice, possibly because of her active involvement in politics during her younger years. She could no longer walk but was light and easy to move. To many NAs, caring for Tula provided a break from dealing with more difficult residents, like her roommate, who was combative.

Jane, Tula's NA for a two-week cycle, quickly entered the room and turned on the lights. Startled, Tula screamed, looking right at Jane, trying to get her attention. Jane showed no recognition that Tula was trying to communicate with her. "Right in her ear, and she didn't even answer me," Tula commented loudly enough for her to hear. Jane appeared completely oblivious to the fact that Tula was even talking to her.

Tula then screamed, "I'm freezing." Her comment registered this time, and Jane, still silent, brought her a towel. Tula responded, "That's warmer, but it's heavy." Again, there was no acknowledgment from Jane.

Then, without a word, Jane grabbed Tula and tried to prop her up in a wheelchair.

"Why are you angry with me?" Tula asked. Again, Jane said nothing. Instead, she wheeled the chair into the bathroom and began washing Tula with a washcloth. Again Tula stated loudly so Jane could hear, "I don't know what she's doing."

Jane made no comment the whole time, except to command with annoyance, "Sit back!" When she was finished washing and dressing her, Jane began to move Tula's geri-chair.

Tula, by now clearly alarmed, heightened her volume and asked earnestly, "Where are you taking me?" Jane did not respond but continued to wheel Tula outside her room, where she left her to wait for her breakfast. Jane then moved on to "prepare" another resident in her group for the morning.

A comment Tula had previously made about another member of the staff is also apt here: "She did not even give me the dignity of recognition."

As obviously pained as she was by this treatment, Tula remained fairly calm. I wondered, though, how someone like her roommate would have reacted, and reflected how an NA's interaction with a resident can affect her, perhaps even stimulating BDs.

A Typical Morning Routine for a Resident (Tula): Scenario 2

Deanna quietly walked into the room and turned on the lights. She had already prepared a small tub of warm water and soap to bring with her and walked right up to Tula. She waited for a moment for Tula to open her eyes and cheerfully said, "Good morning, Tula. It's time to get up." Tula smiled an impish smile, and comically asked, "Oh, am I still alive?"

Deanna smiled, "Well of course." She then explained that she would be washing Tula and would need to turn her over to remove her nightgown, which was buttoned in the back. Tula smiled compliantly, so the NA then turned her, removed her nightgown, carefully covered her with a blanket from the waist down both for warmth and in respect for her modesty (as she explained to me). Deanna then started washing her hands, arms, breasts, and underarms, removing the blanket only as needed. She dried her, placed deodorant under her arms, and dressed her upper body.

Deanna then explained that she needed to remove her diaper, and then moved Tula to her side to slip it off, and washed her bottom and upper legs with the warm soapy water. She quickly dried her, wrapped her in a fresh diaper, and finished dressing her. Since Tula lacked the coordination to brush her teeth, Deanna did that for her and then gave her a cup of water to rinse out her mouth and spit out.

Deanna told Tula that she was now ready for breakfast. She lifted her into her *geri-chair* (a large high-wheeled chair with a locked tray in front that serves as a restraining device) and transferred the chair just outside her room where she could wait for her breakfast. Tula smiled to the NA as she returned to Tula's room to wake up her roommate.

A Typical Morning in the Life of a Nursing Assistant

Very few residents in Deanna's group during this cycle were as easy to care for as Tula. In fact, it was Deanna's turn to work with the residents on Group 4, otherwise the most difficult group on the unit.

Upon entering the unit this morning, Deanna, a young, pleasant, and energetic NA, confirmed her assignment to this group. She next checked the ADL charts of the residents in her group to determine whether there had been any changes in their prescriptions (e.g., an order for a change from diapers to the toileting program). It was essential to check these since changes can occur not only daily but from shift to shift, and she explained that she would not want to miss an important development.

Next she examined each resident's ADL chart, which documented all toileting and bowel movements of the resident to determine if any of them would need an enema. She also checked the chart to see if it was time to take anyone's vital signs (blood pressure, pulse, and temperature).

After taking note of these details, Deanna then met with the head nurse and other NAs to catch up with developments on all of the residents and to learn of any issues not already documented about residents in her own group. At this time, the head nurse might add some duties for a given resident—even if they did not appear on the chart—such as "I'd like you to get vital signs on Arnold" or "Please check to see how those sores are healing on Rebecca."

Then the work began. Deanna quickly secured a cart (there were not enough to go around) and filled it with adequate supplies—towels, diapers of different sizes, and additional cleansing supplies should a resident run out. (NAs must use separate supplies with each resident in keeping with regulations.) Those lacking friends on the team are disadvantaged because in the scramble to get carts and supplies, the NAs look after their own.

After gathering her supplies, Deanna must rush to beat the clock. In facing a group of seven or eight residents, each NA must decide how to approach the task of waking, cleansing, toileting, and dressing all of them in time for breakfast. Deanna, like most of the other NAs, developed a plan to tackle this enormous task. Depending on the group, and her mood, the plan would vary. Group 4, the most difficult group, contained three very combative women; another who was very heavy, difficult to move, and liked to sleep late; one who was loud and somewhat uncooperative; one who was generally quite compliant, but occasionally would bite; and a seventh (Tula) who was sweet, appreciative, and very pleasant; Tula was also the only one who was able to feed herself.

Now, in devising a plan, Deanna kept in mind the floor rules, such as getting residents who can feed themselves up first so that they can begin eating as soon as their food arrives. Other considerations depended on the particularities of a group. In Group 4, Deanna began with Tula, who could feed herself, but turned on the lights in another room of a woman who had difficulty waking up, in order to stimulate her while completing care routines with all the others. Next she tried to complete the three most difficult combative residents, beginning with the one most of the NAs dreaded—Molly, Tula's roommate. She followed this with the noisy uncooperative woman, the generally compliant resident, and finally, the one who likes to sleep late. This plan helped to make her job more manageable, while respecting the preferences of the residents. Occasionally during her two weeks with this group, however, Deanna would be simply too tired to begin with the most difficult residents, so would revise her plan. If possible, she would still attempt to complete her care routines sequentially for both residents from the same room.

Since Tula lacked strength in her legs and could not stand, Deanna did not try to take her to the toilet. For residents with even minimal leg strength, she would walk them there because sitting encouraged elimination in the morning and helped avoid the need to change a messy diaper and cleanup later on. Deanna also learned that it was easier to wash and dress residents when they were seated upright on the toilet.

Molly: Working the NA Hard. Today, Deanna, as usual moved on to Molly after Tula was ready. However, she rarely took Molly to the toilet, even though she was ambulatory, because she was so uncooperative. As soon as Deanna warmly greeted her, Molly jumped up and commanded, "Go away" and then contradicted herself: "Come here, come here, and hurry up!"

Deanna tried to be patient with her and explained everything she was about to do: "Now I'm going to take off your top. Next I'm going to wash you," and so on. After the third comment, Molly yelled, "Just hurry up and do it!" Deanna giggled to herself with embarrassment.

With Molly, every movement was a battle that impeded the process even though she said she wanted to hurry. She was ambivalent about every action, first pushing Deanna away and then telling her to continue. She would then kick, hit, push, and scream and sometimes even spit at the NA when she would try to clean her bottom and get a fresh diaper on her.

When she finished, Deanna remarked "Whew, I'm exhausted and the morning's only begun; you really make me work for my money, Molly."

After managing to finish dressing Molly and walking her to her geri-chair, Deanna moved on to the next person in her group. While not as combative as Molly, this person tried to play with Deanna's clothes, especially with her buttons during morning care. Deanna skillfully just allowed her to do this rather than fighting with her. She found that allowing the resident to engage in an activity would divert her from interfering with the morning care routine. Deanna could then go about her business without too much trouble. She had learned that pushing the resident away only makes her more reluctant to cooperate in finishing the morning routine and leads to her own exhaustion. (Indeed, I had observed another NA screaming at this woman, holding her hands tightly, and fighting with her to complete the morning care.)

Breakfast. After completing morning care with the residents in her group, Deanna had to make sure they got fed. Group 4 had six people who were "feeders," persons unable to feed themselves. Deanna had learned to be resourceful and save time by seating the feeders on either side of her and then alternating feeding them. After feeding one pair, she moved on to another. However, this sounds easier than what I observed.

Molly, for example, demanded full attention. If she did not get it, she would scream, "Come here!" or "Hurry up!" repeatedly as she ravenously ingested her food. If Deanna diverted her attention to the other resident she was feeding, Molly would splash juice on Deanna to let her know she wanted more food.

So by 10:00 a.m., Deanna had well earned her day's wage. However, she still had to check and change wet or soiled diapers on two additional rounds, change soiled clothing and diapers between rounds, take continent residents to the bathroom, administer enemas, and take the vital body signs of selected residents before the next meal.

The demands of the job for a conscientious person can test the patience of even a senior NA. One day, Veronica, an older NA who was very patient, understanding, and skilled in working with residents, was driven close to tears after a rather grueling morning. She was just about to take a much longed-for break when Molly, who she had just finished feeding, threw a big glass of juice at her; her hair and blouse were all wet and sticky. Such are the all too common experiences of NAs on the Snow units. Perhaps this is why some, over the years, had devised strategies to escape or otherwise ease their work burdens.

THE POPULATION OF RESIDENTS IN THE TWO SNOW UNITS

The residents of Snow 1 ranged in age from 66 to 95, with 86.5 as the median age. Twenty-three were in their 80s, 12 in their 90s, and only 5 in their 60s or 70s. Of the 40 residents, 32 (80 per cent) were female, slightly higher than the national average. In Snow 2, the population was slightly older, with more females. Residents ranged from 68 to 98, with 88.5 as the median age. Twenty-one were in their 80s, 14 in their 90s and 5 in their 60s or 70s. There were 34 females, who composed 85 per cent of the 40-bed unit.

Overall, residents of the Snow units represented the most severely impaired elders in the nursing home. *Although virtually all the residents from the Snow units had some dementia, their disturbed behaviors (BDs) are what led to their admission there.* Still, on both units, many of the residents had such severe dementia that they were viewed as being beyond cognitive testing. There were also residents who had reached a state of being mute and nonresponsive.

The admissions criteria and care level of both Snow units were identical. Each unit, however, had a unique character because of the constantly changing conditions in the two groups of residents and in the composition of residents. In addition, since Snow 2 was more stable and had fewer openings,[6] Snow 1 had a larger number of more recent admissions showing seriously disturbed behaviors, a few of them with mild dementia, and one of them with none. Also, because of the stability of Snow 2, many of those who had been ambulatory several years earlier were now in wheelchairs, and some of their disturbed behaviors had softened as their dementia worsened. Thus, the units had evolved so that by the time of my study staff from both units agreed that Snow 1 had somewhat more residents with very disturbed behaviors (especially with combativeness) and more residents who were noisy.

It was rare that elders were admitted to the Snow units from the community. For most of them, admission marked a "demotion" due to advancing dementia or to heightened disturbances in their behaviors that bothered residents or staff on their unit. The demotion tended to occur in steps, whereby a resident might move from a unit where most residents were quite alert and cognitively intact to one where some dementia was present and only later to one of the Snow units. A committee consisting of the Director of Nursing and her assistant, social workers on the units, and possibly, the head nurse from the discharging and admitting units made the dispositions.

Since Snow 1 tended to have somewhat noisier, more visibly disturbed, and more ambulatory residents, it appeared more chaotic to observers.[7] Thus, despite their similarities in unit design and admissions criteria, Snow 2 enjoyed a better reputation in the community, and families often became despondent upon hearing that their relative had been, or would be, transferred to Snow 1.

---

[6] Unit 2 was very stable with regard to resident occupancy because the head nurse was reluctant to refer residents to the hospital unless she was certain their condition could not be handled on the unit. She believed that transfers posed risks for frail elders and preferred to keep them for observation by a staff already familiar with them.

[7] This was certainly my own initial perception. See Appendix C for changes in my perceptions of the residents over time.

PART TWO

ethnographic case studies and analyses

CHAPTER 5

Historical and Cultural Context of Caregiving in Snow 1: Three Case Studies

THE CAREGIVING CULTURE OF SNOW 1

Snow 1 was a unit in flux. Because of the various changes in the unit and residents over its 19-year history, by the time of my study there was some disagreement about its intent. "It's the psych unit of the nursing home," offered one staff member. "It's only for advanced Alzheimer's patients," offered another. "It is the place for persons with severely disturbed behaviors, usually but not always with dementia," the head nurse accurately (according to formal admissions criteria) explained. Family members were more grim in their assessments. "It's the last chance cafe—where you go when no other unit will tolerate you," one daughter said. "It's where you are warehoused, waiting to die," an embittered and resigned husband offered. The disagreement among staff about the unit

evoked as much mystery and ambivalence as did the despairing sentiments from families.

The ongoing turnover among both the staff and residents in Snow 1
shaped the composition of its residents and staff. It also led to shifts in rules
and care priorities that affected staff, residents, and even their families.
Thus it helped to frame the unit's particular culture and to differentiate it
from Snow 2, which was officially supposed to be the same kind of unit for
the same kind of resident—behaviorally disturbed, usually accompanying
severe cognitive impairment.

The staff member with the longest tenure was a nursing assistant (NA)
from the day shift, who had been on the unit for eight years. NAs on the day
shift tended to be young (most in their thirties or late twenties) except for this
senior NA and one other. Most of the other NAs had been there for less than
a year. Many of the residents had come to the unit after residing for years at
units for more highly functioning residents, and had also been there for a
year or less; the longest period of residence was only three years.

All of the NAs and care managers (including the acting head nurse) were
black, and only one male NA worked there, usually on the morning shift.

Hazel, the Acting Head Nurse

Hazel, the acting head nurse of Snow 1, was an African-American woman
in her mid 40s. She was an LPN who had been the charge nurse on the
unit for six years. Her formal training and previous work experience,
however, had been in acute hospital care, rather than long-term care.
Hazel was competent and had a direct but respectful bedside manner that
families appreciated and residents seemed to welcome. As the acting head
nurse, however, she had developed a rather formal style with her staff and
the families, and a rigid approach to structuring care delivery.

Hazel had been trained under a strong head nurse (Mildred) who had
since left the unit. Mildred had instilled in her the importance of "keeping after" her staff and following institutional directives rigorously. Since
Mildred's departure about a year and a half earlier, Hazel held the position of acting head nurse between periods when she would be training
potential successors for the position. Because she was not an RN, she did
not qualify to hold the position permanently as head nurse. However, all
of the trainees had either quit before their six-month training period was
over or were not permanently instated by the administration after this trial period. Such was the fate of the head nurse who had greeted me when I

first visited the unit. Hazel thus once again became the acting head nurse. She continued in this role, except for my last couple of months of study when she began to train yet another nurse for the position.

Although Hazel had all the responsibility of a head nurse, she garnered neither the additional clerical staff granted to other head nurses to handle the paper work demanded by the job nor any additional salary. The reason given by the nursing home administration was that she was not an RN. However, they did provide additional training and workshops to compensate for any potential gaps in her background. Given the temporary, albeit extended, status of her position, however, she lacked the influence that other head nurses enjoyed. With no clerical help for paper work, Hazel was not free to spend time on the floor offering hands-on supervision. Families felt this was unfortunate since this deprived residents of her warm bedside manner. Because she was so pressed for time, Hazel was also less willing than her predecessor to accommodate residents' and families' requests for nonroutine needs. Perhaps for her own protection, given the tentativeness of her position, Hazel tended to interpret the institution's rules quite literally and was rigid in enforcing them. This led her to reject some creative suggestions by the staff or family for helping to deal with residents' agitation or difficult behaviors.

Hazel did not seem to mind the additional responsibility even though she was aware of her constrained authority. Unlike Mildred, who would object to new admissions she deemed were inappropriate for the unit, Hazel never challenged any new admission. She did, however, retain the former head's strong sense of responsibility, institutional obligation, and impatience with incompetence.

Hazel's Relationships with Her NAs

Hazel's previous work history on the unit in a different capacity and with different work relations with the NAs made it difficult to establish herself as a strong authority figure as a head nurse. As a team, Hazel and Mildred had worked well together and managed a tight ship. However, Mildred had served as the "tough parent" who placed demands on the NAs, so Hazel had been freed of the need to oversee or reprimand them. Continuing in this pattern in her new capacity, Hazel typically bit her lip rather than confront an NA directly. There were times, however, that Hazel, perhaps out of frustration, spoke to her staff with a disdainful tone of voice, explaining, for instance, that they were violating the "expectations of their job." The NAs were offended by this and by what they perceived as her depersonalized, sometimes moralistic appeal to authority.

Although Mildred had been demanding, she strongly supported her NAs against the tough administration. Hazel held less clout with the administration, and the NAs did not trust that she would support them adequately if needed. On the few occasions when they asked her for additional staff to help with a higher workload, Hazel discounted their need, arguing that the institution could not afford it, even though other units made similar requests. While they followed her orders, they felt put off by her disengaged managerial style and apologetic attitude toward the administration. This affected their morale and sense of job security and reduced their willingness to help with residents not assigned to them.

The Acting Head Nurse's Care Priorities

> "You swept already. Talk to me, don't sweep; talk to me." (A Snow 1 resident, 3/9/93)

Hazel's tight interpretation of policies and rigid establishment of care priorities provided a clear, if limited, set of expectations for her staff. These priorities emphasized routinized custodial care and medical care ("bed and body work") rather than intersubjective "person-work."[1] This emphasis was based on a set of pessimistic assumptions about dementia as the product of an irreversible and unremitting disease process for which nothing could reasonably be done for the affected person. In addition, her previous training had sensitized her to acute care issues rather than to ongoing long-term care needs. As a result, she established a hierarchy of care priorities that privileged body care over subjective quality of life considerations. Of highest priority were custodial care (e.g., cleaning, feeding, and toileting), protection (e.g., a focus on restraints to prevent injuries), and medical attention to urgent or visible problems (e.g., recovering respiration and attention to new bruises). The second priority was attending to medical complaints voiced by the residents themselves, even though she questioned their credibility given their dementia. Still lower on her list were the use, repair, and/or ordering of prosthetic devices such as hearing aids. For example, one family member complained that six months after he had requested the repair of his father's hearing aid the nurse had still not placed the order. Last on the list were quality of life requests by a resident

---

[1]   This distinction was made famous in Jaber Gubrium's classic work, *Living and Dying in Murray Manor* (1975).

or family member (e.g., requests to change a stained item of clothing or to locate a lost item).

Hazel communicated this set of priorities to her staff through daily staff meetings. She also trained the NAs to refer nonroutine requests from family members directly to her. Thus she socialized family members as to what kinds of requests her staff could or could not satisfy. Limited staffing patterns reinforced the need to establish priorities. In addition, she developed an informal protocol to help the NAs use their time most efficiently to complete necessary care tasks and to determine whether and when to satisfy additional requests. For example, she established the rule that during mealtime it was necessary to feed all the residents on the unit before responding to the urgent pleas of any resident to be taken to the bathroom. Hazel also made it clear that no resident was to receive preferential treatment over any other residents, even when conditions (such as medical problems) may have warranted doing so.[2]

Shift Culture and Cooperation

Hazel's principles of care carried over to the evening (3:00 p.m. to 11:00 p.m.) and night (11:00 p.m. to 7:00 a.m.) shifts. Each shift had its own regular staff that together developed a unique character and working culture. Because of the nature of the unit, nurses from all three shifts had to handle elders who were confused, angry, and unhappy, and who often did not like to be "handled" by NAs who were trying to complete their care routines. These conditions, which were so common on Snow 1, complicated the already intense demands of their job. To help ease some of this intensity, all shifts used a two-week rotation schedule in which each NA received assignments to care for a group of eight residents. This was not structured this way for the benefit of the residents; indeed many residents who grew comfortable with the style of one NA would have preferred not to be passed on to another. Rotation was a way to be fair to the NAs by spreading the responsibility of caring for the most difficult residents.

---

[2] For example, one family member requested that her husband be toileted more frequently than the standard program that allowed for every two hours. He had diabetes and had a need to urinate more frequently. Hazel refused her request as "excessive," insisting no resident should receive "special treatment."

The Day Shift (7:00 a.m. to 3:00 p.m.)
The NAs on the day shift had the most demanding work routines and were known for being hard workers. One NA described her working in terms of "always fighting to beat the clock." NAs on this shift were also known for their strong personalities and limited cooperation amongst themselves. Everyone had to pitch in fully on this shift for the unit to run smoothly; when they did not, tensions emerged. They did not develop a strong sense of cooperation, however, because they felt that Hazel expected too much of them already and did not want to go out of their way to help residents outside of their group, even though they were supposed to. Nonetheless, the NAs never hesitated to follow Hazel's requests, even if they might feel privately resentful.

The day shift had seven regulars from whom five NAs were drawn to allow coverage over the seven-day week. The most senior NA, a hard worker upon whom Hazel heavily depended, exercised influence over the others as to which of the NAs they should help. She encouraged four of the NAs not to assist the other two with their residents since they were not "pulling their weight." This created an undercurrent of resentment that further impeded cooperation and strong teamwork. Despite these problems, the individual NAs overall were quite dedicated and interested in helping their own residents.

The Evening Shift (3:00 p.m. to 11:00 p.m.)
This shift had only four NAs. In addition to completing their rounds, their principal responsibilities included serving dinner and preparing residents for bed. These NAs worked well together and, like their care manager, seemed more relaxed in completing their care routines and working with the residents. Interestingly, a few residents who never talked during the day shift, or only muttered nonsense syllables like "kiki kiki," actually had conversations with members of this staff, perhaps because of the more relaxed atmosphere they fostered.

The Night Shift (11:00 p.m. to 7:00 a.m.)
There were only two NAs during nighttime because this was a generally quiet time when the staff only had to complete their rounds, respond to complaints, and otherwise try to calm agitated elders. In addition, the care manager was responsible for providing routine care for four of the residents, along with her other duties. The small, but cooperative, staff typically could handle the demands of the job, but their resources were pressed when one or more residents was unable to sleep or became highly agitated.

Relations Among Other Staff Members

Hazel worked well with the care manager, who was new to the unit, as well as the care managers on the other shifts. Unlike other units, where NAs from a particular shift developed a pattern of not completing their work, this was not a problem for Snow 1. The few times problems occurred, the charge nurses and Hazel would communicate with each other and with their staff and correct it before it became an issue.

Every week during the day shift, the clinical team—which consisted of the acting head nurse, the care manager, the social worker, the activities specialist, and the nutritionist (all women)—held conferences to discuss the status of a rotating group of residents. This team appeared energetic and cooperative and often spoke in terms of "we." Yet the social worker confided that she had to be careful not to "intrude" upon nurses' territory with requests that they help a resident.

There was considerable tension, however, between the physician assigned to the unit and the physician assistant (PA) and nurses. The PA was the person most involved in diagnosing medical problems, examining patients, and writing prescriptions for the physician to review. The physician, in contrast, spent only about 30 minutes on the unit to read charts and sign off on the PA's prescriptions. He tended to honor family member's requests for changes in prescriptions without first consulting the nurses. He rarely examined an elder directly, even if the elder was in great pain. Yet families idolized him and refused to discuss concerns with the PA, who was much more involved in actual diagnosis and treatment. The nursing staff resented his lack of commitment to residents and false appearance as the "good doctor."

Tensions also existed between the psychiatrist who consulted on Snow 1 and the nursing staff. When asked to review medications, he would make adjustments, based on his observations during his visits to the unit, without ever consulting the nurses. Since residents' behaviors were so variable, such judgments could be misleading, and the nursing staff were left to handle any exacerbation in symptoms resulting from his medication changes. During a private meeting with me, the psychiatrist revealed that he deliberately avoided consulting with nurses because he feared they might exaggerate symptoms in order to try to convince him to prescribe sedating medication for their own benefit, not that of the resident. (While perhaps not *exaggerating* symptoms, nurses from different shifts sometimes coordinated efforts to document every instance of agitation or BD by a resident in order to make the case that the elder needed medication or a change in medication.)

The residents on Snow 1 received a daily 45-minute session with a dy-

namic activities therapist who gave regular input about residents to an appreciative nursing staff. They were fortunate as well to receive two weekly
sessions with a music therapist who was adept in her ability to connect with
withdrawn or agitated residents. She always tried to include as many residents as possible in the activity (e.g., listening to a tape, playing the piano,
or planning a sing-along activity), no matter how behaviorally impaired or
apparently nonresponsive they might have appeared. As a music therapist
she used music as a way of reaching the emotional memories of residents
to stimulate and revive some core meaning. Her supervisor however cautioned her to provide only "activities," not "*therapy*" with "these residents"
in spite of her repeated noticeable success in engaging very impaired persons. Nurses and the activities therapist also looked askance at her efforts to
do more than they felt was "realistically" possible.

Families' Involvement in the Unit

Although institutionalization may appear to mark the end of the family
caregiver's role, a significant proportion of family members continue to remain involved in caregiving even after their relative's admission to a nursing
home (Bowers 1988: 361–62). Those who no longer provide direct care may
still contribute emotional support through their regular visitation and "care
watching" (Perkinson 2003: 171). Such involvement may also alleviate depression in the family member (Bowers 1988: 364). The ways in which families are engaged in caregiving in a nursing home, however, are significantly
limited when compared to their experience at home. In addition, a family
must negotiate their ongoing involvement in the nursing home with the staff
who may either welcome their involvement or reject it as interference.

On Snow 1, the head nurse's rules and priorities for caregiving also applied to families. As with most cultures, family members discovered the rules
whenever they violated them. If a family member made a nonroutine request
(e.g., asking an NA to put a new dress on their elder), the NA would explain
that there was a rule that prevented them from doing this and then refer
them to Hazel for clarification. Hazel would typically offer to accommodate
the family's request "just this once," while letting them know that this was an
exception. Eventually, the family would learn to make requests only to their
relative's NA, not to request a change in their relative's clothing unless it were
wet or soiled, and that requests for particular NAs would not be granted.

Many families found some rules highly restrictive or felt they violated the
dignity of their relative. For example, some family members found the use

of restraints to be inhumane, despite its protective purpose. Others felt that toileting a resident who had the urge to use the bathroom—and who might have an embarrassing accident if she waited—should take priority over feeding residents first. Still others objected to the use of psychotropic medications to control their elder's behaviors, especially when they felt this was done for the benefit of the staff rather than their relative. One man put it this way, "My wife has so little left; I don't want to see the medication take whatever expression of her person is left because of reasons of human dignity."

Such a man would be labeled "an unrealistic" family member, in contrast to "realistic" families who had learned to accept the rules of the unit and ask for nothing exceptional. One "realistic" daughter explained how upset she had been during her mother's first year on the unit to discover that the new nightgowns she had bought her were all gone within six months. She eventually came to be content to see her mother clean and free of any bruises that might suggest rough handling.

Tensions existed on Snow 1 between the nursing staff and families who challenged the treatment of their relative. Hazel distrusted families' ideas because she felt they spent too little time with the elder to know their behavior. Nurses across shifts sometimes collaborated to maintain a common position when dealing with a demanding relative, or chart all incidents to make a case for BDs. Tensions occurred too in the few cases where family members spoke to nurses in a commanding or condescending tone.

Despite OBRA regulations that required nursing homes to inform families if elders would be placed on psychotropic medications, Hazel felt this practice was unnecessarily "conservative." She would inform families when their elder received an order for a physical restraint, but not for chemical restraints (psychiatric medication). Since families signed a form during admission agreeing to having the facility "medically treat" their relative, she thought that freed the institution from having to inform families about medicines. She also refused to share information about medication with a family member unless the PA or a physician was present. Hazel also trained her staff not to share information but to refer all questions to her. Some family members even felt like intruders if they ever went up to the nurses' station to ask about their relative.

While the majority of residents and some head nurses were Jewish and at least middle-class, most of the other nurses and nursing assistants were African American and struggling economically. Many of the residents and their families were disappointed that their caregivers came from a different religious, racial, and cultural background.

Some elders had lived in neighborhoods that had since become largely

African-American. Persisting stereotypes from both sides may have contributed to ongoing tension between the overwhelmingly African-American nursing staff and the mainly Jewish residents and their families. This was especially apparent when families appeared pushy or demanded information or favors. The nursing staff could then choose to withhold or refuse to grant these on the basis that policy did not allow it. Even when families honestly showed curiosity about the unit, the nursing staff tried to limit their access to information. Despite these situations, family members seemed grateful of the nursing staff's efforts to care for their relatives, even though they would have hoped for more input and information about their care.

The following case studies of residents on Snow 1 illustrate the experiences and outcomes of elders with behaviors identified as problematic. Their stories illustrate the types of interventions used by the staff to handle these behaviors. The strategies occurred in the context of the particular unit culture, the expectations of the nursing home facility, and regulatory constraints. The consequences of these strategies, and their meanings for the elders affected by them, varied with each person, her particular biographical history, and the elder's perception of her current situation. Against my own preference, I identify these elders by first name (changed for reasons of confidentiality) in keeping with the custom of the unit.[3]

CASE STUDY I: CARL AND VICKI: A FORBIDDEN ROMANCE[4]

"I'm heartbroken when I think how we came in here, king and queen, and now I'm all the way down the cellar."[5]

"Then that's the end of the dream?"[6]

---

[3] Hazel, the acting head nurse, was the single exception among team members, including the physician, in that she always referred to the person she was addressing as "Mr.," "Mrs.," or "Ms."

[4] Some of this case material overlaps with material I included in Case Study 2 on pp. 243–49 of my article, Power in the nursing home: The case of a special care unit, *Medical Anthropology*, 2001, 19, 223–57.

[5] A spontaneous comment by Tula, the unit poet, whose striking comments often seemed perfectly suited for particular moments in nursing home life. I recorded these regularly as part of my general field notes.

[6] The actual words of a woman on a different unit after the rabbi informed her of the decision that she could not marry the man "of her dreams." The staff felt the woman was too demented to knowingly participate in the ceremony, and the man's children objected to this marriage on the same grounds.

I first learned of Carl and Vicki while exploring the Snow units as possible research sites. The head nurse of Snow 1 at the time—gone when I began my study the following month—was encouraging me to include the unit. As she described different residents from the unit, she paused to tell me about events surrounding a couple who were no longer together. The events she described had transpired during the previous month, so I had no direct observation of them. However, after gaining permission from the families, I reconstructed the following case study from the head nurse's story, medical records, and retrospective accounts from other clinical and administrative staff and family members directly involved in, or knowledgeable about, the case.

Vicki, a woman in her early 70s, was admitted to Snow 1 shortly after the death of her husband with whom she had resided on a different unit. Soon after her arrival, she and Carl, who was in his mid-80s, became drawn to each other. They began walking together around the unit holding hands and soon became inseparable. Occasionally, they would kiss or embrace. Carl was married, but his wife of the past 18 years lived in an apartment and rarely visited him because of prolonged resentment from early in his dementia when he would flirt with other women. According to nurses on her previous unit, Vicki had taken similar walks with her husband before he died, and some of the staff, who feared she was mistaking Carl for him, discouraged the relationship. Any effort to separate them, however, upset Carl.

Carl's History

Carl had arrived at another unit of the nursing home a year and a half before the events reported here. At the time, he lived with his wife from a third marriage in an apartment complex for elderly people. She referred him to the home because his dementia had become more severe; he had started a small fire, and she was receiving pressure from apartment management to move. Various family members had described him as "sweet and hard-working," and his wife described him as "formerly ethical and highly principled." She, however, harbored considerable resentment against him because in their 18 years of marriage, he moved from being a workaholic whom she rarely saw to a socially outgoing person who spent much of his time visiting and flirting with other women in the building. He had shown evidence of dementia about seven years earlier, and the flirtation began about five years before his admission to the home. Although he had always preferred the company of women over men, this open display of affection was out of character for Carl and a likely feature of disinhibition that sometimes accompanies dementia—something his wife did not appreciate.

Despite conflict in their marriage, Carl missed his wife terribly and began to worry about her incessantly at the nursing home. He eventually wrote a suicide note, was admitted to a psychiatric hospital, and upon his return to his unit, attempted to jump off the balcony of his room. At that point, the administration transferred him to Snow 1, which was a locked unit, had a floor plan that allowed for surveillance, and had no balconies. Although Carl was ambulatory and seemed somewhat higher functioning than many of the other residents on Snow 1, his psychological assessments nonetheless indicated that his dementia was severe. Throughout his time at the nursing home, he showed a casual interest in other women, flirting and occasionally fondling them. He indicated that he missed having sexual relations with his wife and wanted to get involved with her again. His wife, however, rebuffed this idea whenever the social worker brought it up to her and indicated she had no interest in such relations. He continued to show interest in other women, although before his encounter with Vicki, he had never shown sustained interest in any one woman other than his wife.

Vicki's History

Vicki arrived at the nursing home with her husband, where they shared a room together for about two and a half years before his death. They had been married for over 40 years and had six children. Her husband had been a retired military officer, and she was a homemaker, with some education in fine arts. The marriage had been rocky due to her husband's drinking problem, and they had separated for several years before their admission to the home. Because of this history, their son, who had arranged for their admission, was worried about their sharing a room together. Indeed, there were times when they would fight verbally or physically, only to walk around the unit hand in hand later in the day. Both suffered from dementia, but Vicki had been taking care of her husband until her own dementia necessitated long-term care for both of them.

By the time of her admission to the nursing home, Vicki's dementia had become more severe, and she had also become depressed. The nursing home environment only worsened her mood, as she would frequently state her annoyance at being stuck at the home. Her medical chart quoted her as saying, "It is an outrage I was brought here, and I'm very depressed." Vicki registered great sadness at her husband's wake and in the following weeks asked where he was; she did not seem to remember or understand that he had died.

At the time of her admission to Snow 1, Vicki's dementia had advanced to the point where she could speak only a couple of sentences at a time, or sing a brief aria,[7] but not in response to actual conversation with another. Her son said that she would sometimes fondle his hair and offer, "I love you darling." He never knew if she intended it for him or his father. Her dementia was so extreme that the clinical staff viewed her to be "beyond testing," that is, too mentally impaired to even begin to understand instructions for taking mental status exams.

The Critical Event

One evening, Mary—another resident's personal companion—caught Vicki and Carl entering Carl's room and shutting the door behind them. Closing doors was not allowed on this unit for fear that the residents might hurt themselves or others. Mary waited a couple of minutes and then entered the room without knocking, as was the custom on this unit. She found Carl with his pants down and Vicki kneeling before him, positioned in preparation for intimate engagement (cf. Shield 1988: 198). Horrified, Mary scolded the couple and ordered Carl to pull up his pants. Carl yelled at her to leave them alone. She then rushed to the nurse's station to report the incident. The nurse in charge separated the two elders, directed them to go to their own rooms (cf. Diamond 1992: 127), and questioned Mary about what had transpired. She then documented the incident in both of the patients' charts, noting, as Mary had described, that Carl had become "highly agitated." The recording of this evaluation in "medicalized" terms had inexorable consequences for Carl and Vicki. Yet, as Diamond argues, medical records "conceal as much as they reveal" (Diamond 1992: 236). What were concealed in this case were the circumstances of this "agitation" and the perspectives of those most affected by their impacts.

The next morning the head nurse called a meeting with the social worker, psychologist, and psychiatrist assigned to the unit and the Assistant Director of Nursing (ADON). The group discussed Carl and Vicki's affectionate displays and their belief that each elder was providing the

---

[7] She had come from an educated family and had studied opera in her youth.

stimulus to agitate the other. Before Vicki arrived in the unit, Carl occasionally would flirt with other females, but never with the consistency or fondness he displayed toward Vicki; he soon called her his wife. In addition to concerns about Carl's marital status, the team feared that he and Vicki were too demented to know what they were doing. They also suspected that Carl was initiating the behavior and that Vicki was too impaired to give her consent, despite her willing participation and apparent enjoyment of the relationship. Since Carl was somewhat less impaired than Vicki was, they also viewed her as a potential victim, vulnerable to sexual exploitation by Carl, who could threaten her "personal rights." The ADON felt the institution had an obligation to report the incident to the state and to "protect" Vicki from further incidents. In this way, the state achieved a broad reach of external control (Diamond 1992: 192) without even realizing its impact.

Because Carl's wife had initially visited him often, the social worker kept her informed about Carl's relationship with Vicki to the finest detail. After the most recent incident, his wife told this social worker to take whatever steps necessary to restrain him—physical or chemical—and to stop calling her. Both Vicki's and Carl's children (from a different marriage), were only given general information about the affair and believed that the relationship should be allowed to continue. They were willing, however, to accept whatever decision the staff, as professionals, would make.

The special team decided to "treat" Carl's behavior with a combination of behavioral therapy and psychotropic medication. The psychologist attempted behavioral modification—directed at addressing the team's realist concerns—by repeatedly showing Carl a picture of his wife, in order to reinforce the fact that *she, not Vicki,* was his *actual* wife. The psychiatrist placed him on Mellaril®, a major tranquilizer and antipsychotic medication, for his "agitation" and on Tegretol®, an anticonvulsant, to minimize his disinhibition.

After several weeks, Carl and Vicki's expressions of affection for each other remained unchanged, and Carl became increasingly upset whenever the staff tried to direct one of them away. Treatment was deemed unsuccessful, and the team decided to separate them permanently.[8] Because Carl was viewed the troublemaker, the staff wanted to keep him on the open unit for better surveillance. In addition, because of his history of

---

[8] This resembled the separation of a mother and daughter at a nursing home that Timothy Diamond studied. There, the daughter would come to her mother's room to cuddle and sleep with her at night. This behavior was viewed "deviant" and charted as "lesbian," and not to be permitted (Diamond 1992: 116).

attempting suicide from a balcony, they refused to transfer him to units that had balconies. Their only alternative was to transfer him to Snow 2, where rooms are rarely available. When a "female bed" became available on Snow 2 two weeks later, they quickly took the opportunity to transfer Vicki there instead. Some of the staff, who continued to blame Carl for the affair, felt she was being unfairly penalized in being forced to move again, after her recent move to Snow 1.[9]

After Vicki left the unit, Carl became increasingly agitated and depressed. He also lost motor control over his tongue, a likely side effect of the Mellaril®, and his ability to speak. On her new unit, Vicki also declined. She became combative with the staff and received Mellaril®, despite protests from her family. She also became socially withdrawn except for her solitary walks around the unit, affectionately addressing some invisible "other." Although Carl eventually restored some sociability with female residents, neither he nor Vicki ever developed another significant relationship again.

When I interviewed the ADON about the incident, she explained how state law required nursing homes to report any incidents of resident-to-resident contact of an abusive or sexual nature that potentially might threaten the rights of either person. The staff viewed Vicki as too demented to offer consent to a relationship, and, according to regulations, her involvement with Carl violated her rights by exposing her to possible sexual abuse. The ADON stated that she would not have reported a similar incident between two residents who were not cognitively impaired.

I wondered whether the staff's decision might have been different if they had not received pressure to view the incident within the paternalistic terms defined by the state. Indeed, other nursing homes that I had visited assumed a more liberal philosophical position on sexual behavior—and received state citations for not having adequately protected their residents. Thus the home's action served to protect themselves as much as, if not more than, Vicki. By taking the more conservative action, they privileged what Shield calls *"life,"* a medically based value that prioritizes protection and treatment over freedom and individual rights, or *"quality of life"* (1988: 67). While well intended, their position is thus not without problems. Bioethicist Arthur Caplan also notes how some residents give less priority to these medically based values (1990: 48). In their paternalistic concerns for protecting Vicki's rights and these medical values,

---

[9] The head nurse of Snow 2 observed that it is very common for elders with dementia to decline following moves or transfers, perhaps because they have greater difficulty in reorienting to a new environment. This may account for why people often appear to deteriorate after being admitted to nursing homes.

the staff in fact violated her *personal right* to pursue a life with quality. Due to their dementia, however, Vicki's and Carl's wishes and values were pathologized as symptoms. Thus they carried no legitimacy and were totally disregarded in the deliberations of the team.

Staff Misgivings about the Decision

After sharing this story with me, the head nurse expressed her own misgivings about the team's decision. She explained that, personally, she believed residents were entitled to the best quality of life possible and, from everything she had observed, that the relationship was mutual. The other NAs and nurses with whom I had spoken entirely agreed, but they did not participate in the decision-making process. As the newest member of the treatment team, the head nurse did not challenge the members who decided on "treating" Carl and eventually moving Vicki because she acknowledged that they were more familiar with the demands of state regulations (cf. Lichtenberg and Strezpek 1990: 117) and concerns about possible malpractice suits from families. Other studies have reported similar ambivalence by nursing home staff who are caught between their feelings for the residents and the pressure to follow government regulations (Glass, Mustian, and Carter 1986: 47; Lichtenberg and Strezpek 1990: 117).

It is in uncomfortable zones like these—the interstices of culture—where conventional practices are unsettling and where the contradictions between doing what *feels right* and acting in socially prescribed ways incite sensibilities. Here is where social control is most poignantly felt—and potentially resisted. Such events and the decisions they necessitate force professionals to pause and consider how they would want events to turn out if it were their case that was receiving deliberation. Those involved in the deliberations over Vicki and Carl, however, were more inclined toward a protective bias, given the dominance of the medical model in the facility and its influence on the particular participants in the team. Nonetheless, situations such as these hold the greatest hope to transform current practices because they disturb sensitivities.

Discussion

Carl and Vicki were the victims of bio-power—French philosopher Michel Foucault's term for power over bodies (Hewitt 1991: 230). Bio-power operates by means of specific disciplinary technologies (like psychiatric medications) designed to create disciplined, "docile bodies" (Hindess 1996: 114–15; Dreyfus and Rabinow 1983: 133–35). By honing in on the individual, the human sciences (such as psychology, psychiatry, and social work) have produced disciplinary knowledges and technologies aimed at controlling and standardizing individual behavior (Hewitt 1991: 243).

The standards or norms developed by disciplinary knowledges and technologies provide a scientific basis for rational administration by institutions like the nursing home in this study. Under the constant visibility afforded by spaces like the open floor plan of the Snow units, deviant behavior (like Carl and Vicki's affair) becomes the target of disciplinary control. "Normalizing judges," experts—like the members of the treatment team on Snow 1—determine normative standards of behavior (e.g., nonsexual behaviors that are *not* disinhibited) and select scientific technologies (such as antipsychotic medication or behavioral therapy) to regulate behavior. Because of their professional expertise and their intent to cure or protect bodies, these "judges" gain public consent from families like Carl's and Vicki's to exercise their judgment as they see fit (Hewitt 1991: 231–32). Bio-power has targeted institutions as much as it has the persons within them. Nursing homes, for example, are subject to legal regulations demanding that they protect their residents. Such laws encourage institutional personnel to adopt paternalizing practices that impose protection at the cost of freedom.

Carl and Vicki's romance was seen as deviant, and a target for disciplinary control because of their diagnoses of dementia. The ADON admitted they would have received different treatment had they been capable of rational judgment. In considering the case, the treatment team emphasized Vicki's inability to offer *informed consent*, that is, to act autonomously as a responsible *moral agent* (Smith 1992: 46) who could make reasonable choices. The team assumed a Lockean perspective that recognized only those persons who retained reason and cognitive competence to act rationally as worthy of retaining human rights. With reason lost, so were personhood and attendant human rights; such was the fate of Carl and Vicki. Although informed consent—and the idea of cognitive competence on which it is based—may be useful for assuring reasonable decision-making about medical procedures, is not well suited for judging one's ability to consent in everyday human relationships (Lidz and Arnold 1990: 65). In fact, psychiatrist Laurence Tancredi (1987: 29) challenges the value of cognitive competence as an indicator of social functioning and as the basis for deciding whether to abrogate an elder's rights. Qualities like human connectedness or the ability to develop relationships, he suggests, are more apt indicators. Ironically, these were the very qualities that the treatment team defined as pathological, and denied Carl and Vicki.

As a substitute to reason, medical ethicists often rely on "authentic" or "precedent" autonomy for making decisions (Collopy 1990: 9; Arras 1987: 65–66). This concept suggests that to be truly autonomous, a person must act in a way that is consistent with the wishes and values of an "authentic moral self," that remains constant over time and shifting contexts. "Out of character" departures from expected behavior, consistent with a person's past, are viewed as "inauthentic" and evidence that the person can no longer exercise moral agency. Inconsistencies with past behavior become attributed to pathology rather than to the person acting as moral agent. Thus having lost his moral agency, Carl's interest in Vicki was deemed pathologically disinhibited, and treated with psychotropic medication. Vicki, as cognitively impaired victim, was also denied agency and choice and was moved to a unit away from Carl. When dubbed pathology, such vital acts and wills are discounted and reframed as meaningless behaviors, devoid of the subjectivity of the actors' own engagement. Ironically, such willful acts are "supercharged" with meaning because they directly challenge the very notion of the person's presumed incompetence.[10]

It is others—like Carl's estranged wife—who decide whether or not a person's actions are "authentic" and can or cannot be allowed to continue; the person's own wishes lose significance. Yet behaviors that may appear alien—or disinhibited—to friends and family may be evidence of new possibilities that can soften the terror of isolation and fragmentation of dementia. Lacking these possibilities, these conditions only worsen.

To proponents of authentic autonomy, the moral agent is a fixed autonomous bounded self. In contrast, Katherine Ewing's research (1990) suggests that each person has multiple selves (or self-representations) (s^2), produced out of identifications with significant persons over the lifelong course of their development. (See chapter 2, pp. 50–51 for further discussion.) Even though they are separate, inconsistent, and context-dependent, these various selves are experienced as a single illusory whole. People experience fragmentation in times of stress when available selves no longer correspond to context and experience. At that point, they may produce new selves (s^2).

In the nursing home, where one is isolated from familiar environments and previously meaningful relationships, the loss of memory and one's selves can intensify the disorientation of being in an alien setting. This may be why elders appear agitated as they experience fragmentation. While people with dementia may lack the *episodic memory* to recall past events, they retain well-established cultural patterns of communication

---

[10] I thank Judith Barker for this insight.

through *semantic memory* to be able to interact meaningfully in the present (Scheibe 1989). They also retain the ability to connect faces with feelings. These abilities enable them to establish relationships, create a new self (s^2) in relation to another person, and restore a current sense of continuity to their lives. Thus, persons like Carl and Vicki can function meaningfully in the present—their only remaining historical locus—long after other selves have been erased from their episodic memories.

A person's social identity (i^2) can only be preserved through acknowledgment by others (Sabat and Harré 1992). (See chapter 2, pp. 54–56) Thus the meaningfulness (or meaninglessness) that others assign to the actions of those with dementia can serve to validate (or invalidate) their personhood and preserve or sever their rights. When the treatment team judged Carl and Vicki's mutual affection to be inauthentic, and therefore meaningless, they deemed them the irrational bi-products of dementia, needing treatment or "normalization." By so doing, they invalidated their moral agency and denied their personhood. The team's Lockean view of human rights, grounded in reason, and biomedical orientation reduced Carl and Vicki's relationship to disease pathology. By relying on reason, professionals blocked their rights to a fundamental human characteristic—their desire for human connectedness. When their agencies—and passions—refused to be tamed medically, Carl and Vicki were forced to part. This ended a relationship that might have prolonged the social being of both of them while adding some measure of hope to lives that had already lost so much.

CASE STUDY II: MARGARET: DISQUIETING NOISE

> "My greatest fear is the inability to take care of myself ever."
> (3/17/1959)[11]

> "They made this lovely place for the people, but it isn't though."
> (12/11/92)

> "Oh, what's happened here is such a misfortune. It was supposed to be a fortunate thing—my placement here—but it's turned out to be a misfortune." (1/15/93)[12]

---

[11] Actual response of Margaret to a question about her greatest fear, written on a questionnaire she completed decades earlier on the date shown.

[12] Actual comments Margaret made during the course of study.

At 89, Margaret was pleasant and socially engaging in spite of her serious cognitive impairment. When I first met her, she would enjoy talking with me at length about her family and interests. Over my nine months on the unit, she had declined so severely that she could no longer converse with me. Then she improved and declined once again.

According to her younger brother, Margaret was childless and had been widowed twice. Still she managed to lead an active life generously helping others and very involved in organizations like the literary group for women that she ran for many years. Margaret had arrived at Snow 1 after spending almost eight years in several other parts of the nursing home complex. Her first few years were in apartment-like settings in the community where she received daily oversight from the clinical staff. This was the first step toward her loss of independence as she depended on her brother for groceries and terminated her involvement in organizational activities. A few years later, after losing her mobility due to severe arthritis and hoping to lighten her brother's burden, she entered a nursing unit. At this point, there was no evidence of cognitive impairment, but she needed considerable help in carrying out daily routines (her ADLs). Moving to a nursing home unit, however, symbolized a total loss of the autonomy she had valued her entire life, and she started to feel depressed.

During her first year in the nursing home, she underwent surgery three times and changed roommates three times. She then moved to a private room in another unit where she remained almost four years. There she broke both hips and, following surgery, began to hallucinate. She remained depressed and began declining cognitively. CAT scans revealed the presence of infarcts, and she was diagnosed with a probable mixed dementia. Margaret had always spoken loudly, and during her last year on the unit she would periodically call out to staff or other residents, especially when she was uncomfortable or hungry. This upset some of the other residents and led to her transfer to Snow 1 just a few months before I arrived.

I encountered Margaret my very first week on the unit. She was anxiously waiting by the locked gate, and when I passed by, asked me, "Can you tell me the way to the trolley station? I want to get home. You know, that's where my family are; I really want to be home." She explained that she would be late for dinner and did not want to upset her mother. (Her concerns, though temporally disordered, are nonetheless reasonable given the importance of these activities earlier in her life, and anguishing to her, given her disorientation to time and place.) I was unsure how to handle her question, so simply indicated that I did not know where the station was. The acting head nurse later told me that I should have oriented her correctly so as not to reinforce her disorientation—a position I later learned was controversial.[13]

Over the next couple of months, Margaret and I continued to carry on pleasant conversations. Her cognition varied remarkably within a week's time, and sometimes even within the same day. Sometimes she would be well aware that an elder brother and sister were deceased, only to ask me if I had been in touch with her father, who had been dead for even longer. She would often talk about her love of books (which, she admitted, she now lacked the patience to read) and the book club where she served as president. At other times, she would reminisce about her parents' beautiful flower garden. Then she would ask me where she could find the #63 streetcar that could take her home. At times, her affect suggested she understood my part of the conversation, but I later realized that sometimes she had not understood at all. While often seemingly lucid, at other times her comments seemed nonsensical in light of her current circumstances.

One unmistakable and consistent theme that regularly came through, however, was one commonly voiced by many residents in the unit—the desire to go home. Margaret would begin to state her desire in the morning and become more intent on leaving by evening, often staying by the locked gate to ask passers-by for help in getting home. While her persistence in trying to leave the unit suggested an inability to understand her permanent placement at *this* "home," she at other times articulated her view of the "misfortune" of her actual placement here.

The staff was amused at our "conversations" because they considered her quite demented. When she would wheel herself over to the nurses' station, where I was reviewing charts, they would ask me to move her away or to talk with her elsewhere. One day she came up to the nurses' station and asked if she could come in. I explained that the nurses preferred that she remain outside. "Everything's closed," she complained. "I can't get in anywhere; I'm so bored. I'm still waiting; I'm tired of waiting." Still, Margaret herself had retained considerable social sensitivity and would frequently observe that I looked busy and apologize for interrupting my work.

---

[13] Reality Orientation was a therapeutic approach developed for veterans diagnosed as having schizophrenia and mental retardation. It insists on orientation to present-day reality as a way of preventing further confusion. When adopted with persons suffering from dementia, it has had mixed results, sometimes making elders argumentative or even more anxious when corrected. In contrast, Validation accepts the reality of the elder as it is and works instead to support them to restore well-being. Their proponents claim that this approach can sometimes lead to better orientation in elders because it alleviates their anxiety (Feil 2002: 126–27).

During her talks with me, she voiced anger at her brother, who she felt did not visit her enough. In fact, he and sometimes his wife visited several times a week and were quite involved with her care, checking regularly with the clinical staff if they noticed any change in her condition. He explained how Margaret had never quite adjusted to losing her independence and that her becoming a burden to her family was the last thing she would ever have wanted. This is what both she and he both found so "painful" about her being here. In his conversations with me, he regularly questioned the ethics of keeping people alive for many years in institutions, even decent ones like this, where the quality of life was inadequate. Yet he felt there were no preferable alternatives.

On her previous unit, about a year earlier, the physician had prescribed a low dosage of an antipsychotic medication to help reduce her noisy vocalizations. It succeeded in doing so, and by the time she arrived at Snow 1, her vocalizations were unremarkable for this unit. Still, she would get loud periodically and sound upset, especially when she wanted to go home. At other times, she would yell at residents who were very noisy, or out of concern, holler at residents for acting in ways she did not understand. "Put your tongue back in," she yelled very loudly to one resident whose tongue hung out, "or you might bite it off." Relative to other residents, however, Margaret did not have markedly "problematic behaviors," so my contact with her gradually diminished over succeeding months as I focused on other residents to study.

One of the things that always had regularly upset Margaret, however, was getting baths. As a modest woman of her generation, she was particularly bothered that the bathing room had a "Men" sign on it and that both men and women lined up to take their baths in the same room. She also disliked getting her hair wet and would often complain about this in a high-pitched voice. Most of all, she was disturbed by the imposing demands of this institutional setting. One morning she told me how an NA had rudely awakened her earlier that morning just to give her a bath she did not even want. When she protested, she was told, "You're going to have it whether you want it or not." Margaret complained, "You get pushed around too much here"—to wake up early, to take baths, to get a haircut, and to get dressed when someone else decides it's time—all concerns she mentioned at one time or another. She told me that she just did not like this place. Her periodic vocalizations had remained fairly constant over the previous year, and although they may have bothered others, her brother was pleased she could articulate her concerns.

The Bathing Bonnet: A Non-medical Intervention

Since Margaret's bath remained a key source of her agitation, her sister-in-law arranged to observe her during a bath. She noticed that Margaret was calm until her hair became wet and that she would really scream when water entered her ears. A couple of weeks later, the sister-in-law brought in a rubber sunbonnet she had seen in a shop during a trip. The sunbonnet fit snugly around Margaret's head and blocked her ears from the water, so she thought it might be a solution to Margaret's problem. She showed it to the nursing home administrator, who was interested in duplicating it, and then brought it to the nurse's station to show Hazel. To her surprise, Hazel thanked her and said she would keep it in Margaret's closet, but could not guarantee that they would use it.

After the woman left, I tried to find out why Hazel did not welcome the device. She explained that she felt it would do little to improve Margaret's condition and that it was simply not economical to use. Hazel regarded Margaret's sister-in-law (who was actually a social worker by training) as "unrealistic" in viewing Margaret's problem as "correctable through immediate and localized environmental accommodation" (McLean and Perkinson 1995: 141). Although feeling sympathetic to the relative's concerns and efforts to help, Hazel felt that Margaret's problems went far beyond these localized concerns to Margaret's more generalized dementia: "It is a much larger problem than the family is willing to admit."

Hazel was reluctant to try the sunbonnet because she was aware of the limited staff time available to her to bathe residents in her unit. The home had hired Rhonda, a special part-time employee, to bathe eight residents a day on Snow 1 within 3¾ hours. During that time, Rhonda had to bathe them, wash their hair, check their skin (an important job that should not be rushed lest she miss some sign of disease), dress them, take their vital signs, and document everything in the charts. She had to accomplish this within the allotted time or the institution would have to pay Rhonda overtime. If she did not complete all the baths in this time, she would receive a poor evaluation and risk losing her job. Under these conditions, Hazel felt it was unfair to add any special requests to Rhonda's responsibilities. It occurred to me, however, that should the device be successful, it could actually facilitate the bathing process, both saving time and making it less of an ordeal.

The next time Margaret had a bath scheduled, I mentioned the device to Rhonda, who out of curiosity retrieved it from the closet and explained its purpose to Margaret, who was willing to try it. Margaret complained as usual about the temperature of the water, first being too hot and then too cold and still did not like getting her hair wet, but Rhonda felt it improved her tolerance of the bath considerably. Though not foolproof, the device sufficiently limited the amount of water that got into Margaret's ears to prevent her usual screaming about her wet ears. Margaret agreed that the bonnet had made the bath tolerable. Despite this improvement, Hazel told Rhonda not to bother with it again since locating the device could cut into her tight schedule. As time went on, Margaret's baths became increasingly problematic and her yelling grew in intensity.

Margaret's Deterioration Following Medication Changes

Several months into my fieldwork, about the time that her baths were becoming more arduous, Margaret's yelling during her bath times became pronounced and began to occur during other times as well. While her screaming could erupt at any time, other sources of noise often provoked it. As her screaming became incessant, Margaret also deteriorated in other ways. She appeared more confused and groggy and lost recognition of her family, the ability to carry on a conversation, and even the coordination necessary to feed herself. She also no longer qualified for a toileting program because she became more wobbly and less aware of her toileting needs.

This decline came on the heels of changes made to her medications following a "very past due" psychiatric consultation. In keeping with the new OBRA regulations, the nursing staff had ordered the consultation to explore the possibility of reducing unnecessary or excessive pharmacological restraints. Margaret had not been seen by a psychiatrist since her admission six months earlier from a different unit and was still receiving an antipsychotic medication. The physician assistant thought it was time that a psychiatrist should decide if it was still needed. At the time of the order, her chart read, "Overall mental and physical condition: alert and verbally responsive with confusion. No episodes in past month, though occasional verbal abuse. *General condition stable.*" The chart also noted that she was participating in a toileting program to remain continent and that she received assistance with bathing, grooming, and ambulation.

As the psychiatric consultant to Snow 1, Dr. Moore made recommendations, which the PA and unit physician generally accepted. Dr. Moore was generally conservative in his approach to using psychotropic medications with demented elders who lacked a psychiatric history because, he explained to me on one occasion, using them was still quite experimental with this population and little was known about their optimal use. He believed that heavy psychotropic medications or high dosages could actually "damage demented brains." During another meeting with me, he further explained that in difficult cases, where an elder's disturbed behaviors were worsening, he preferred to visit the floor repeatedly and see for himself how the elder was faring, rather than simply accept the nursing staff's words on faith. From his experience, he explained, he had come to distrust nurses' requests and recommendations for psychotropic medication because he had seen some nurses use them for punitive reasons or to keep the resident quiet for their own convenience.

Since first coming to the unit, Margaret had been on a small dosage of Mellaril®, a major tranquillizer with antipsychotic and antidepressive properties. Dr. Moore decided to replace the Mellaril® with Buspar®, a less invasive medication. Buspar®, however, took six weeks to take effect, and the dosage needed to be increased gradually. Almost immediately, Margaret complained about dizziness and started yelling incessantly. She could no longer tolerate residents whose behaviors she had previously found annoying. She would shout at them, bang on her table, and sometimes even threaten them. She also cried out for help more frequently and would scream out desperately that she wanted to go "home." The staff on all three shifts were alarmed at the sudden change, as were her family. Meanwhile, the administrative staff were applying pressure on Dr. Moore and the staff to do something to reduce the noisiness on the unit because families of several residents were complaining.

In response, Dr. Moore started adjusting her medication, sometimes on a daily basis. He infuriated the staff by coming in, observing her behavior during a thin slice of time, and on that basis, making changes. They felt he did not give the medication a chance to work. The nursing staff were also disturbed that he never bothered to consult with them since they were familiar with changes in her condition. In response to her heightened noisiness and agitation, he added Haldol®, a fast acting antipsychotic, and an anti-anxiety medication. When she became too lethargic to stay awake during meals and began to hear voices, he withheld the medication. With every change in medication, it seemed as if her condition only worsened.

The Meeting with Margaret's Family

Margaret's brother and his wife remained patient until she lost her depth perception, could no longer feed herself, and stopped eating rather than allow herself to be fed. When she ceased to recognize them, they demanded a meeting with Dr. Moore and the unit staff to discuss her deterioration and their reasons for changing her medication. The PA explained that they changed her to Buspar® because they did not want to use a heavy antipsychotic medication like Mellaril® just to control yelling, especially since it could affect her blood pressure. Dr. Moore added that he prescribed Haldol® to slow her down and calm her on bath days. Margaret's sister-in-law stated that this made her hallucinate and become rigid. Her family requested that she be returned to her previous prescription of 20 mg of Mellaril® daily. Dr. Moore agreed to do so.

It took three and a half months and 29 changes in medication before Margaret began to approach her previous level of stability. However, whatever delicate balance Margaret had previously achieved on 20 mg daily dosage of Mellaril® was upset by the subsequent changes in medication. In the end, it took 175 mg of Mellaril® to achieve her old level of stability; even then she was more impaired than she had previously been.

Further Deterioration

Margaret finally appeared more like her old self, sustained, however, on a much higher level of Mellaril®. She was eating on her own once again, her bouts of yelling had subsided, and she was more conversant again, albeit more confused. While the staff viewed her as calmer, her brother considered her overly sedated. Her ability to recognize and engage with her family had also changed. Sometimes she would enthusiastically greet them by name from a distance; at other times, she did not remember who they were even close up. Despite this, her condition seemed improved over its prior deterioration.

I had by now finished research on this unit and moved on to Snow 2. When I returned for a visit the following month, I was surprised to find Margaret screaming loudly again. This time her eyes appeared tightly shut, closing herself off from her surroundings. When I approached her, she did not respond at all. Nothing I said registered. Even touching her elicited no response; she just kept her eyes tightly shut and continued to scream.

In speaking with her brother, I learned that, about a month earlier, she had been put on a medication (Desyrel®) to which she was allergic; although the allergy had been clearly marked on her chart, the staff ignored it. In the past, this medication triggered acute confusion, which lifted once it was discharged. Her brother brought this to the staff's attention. The medication was terminated, only to be started once again a few days later. Margaret remained on the medicine for over two weeks before he found the error again. He was furious and annoyed to find that no one on the staff, including the physician or PA, was willing to take responsibility for the error. When he confronted the medical staff about the error, they simply noted that the situation "was not really very critical."

Margaret's brother had observed that the precipitous decline coincided with the change of medication. He was surprised to learn that after placing Margaret on the new medication, the medical staff never even consulted with the NAs, who in his view, were best positioned to judge changes in status of a resident. Given their ongoing contact with residents, he thought they should be included in the future.

It had been a couple of weeks since the staff had stopped administering Desyril, and Margaret seemed worse than I had ever before seen her. Dr. Moore was also worried about her low blood pressure on the higher dosage of Mellaril® and was considering reducing or even withdrawing it completely.

Her brother explained that her condition had been quite variable during the last month, from periods of calm to noisiness and refusing to eat. What was new was the tight closing of her eyes while yelling and sometimes singing. He speculated that paradoxically she would act in this "apparently" more disturbed way during those times when she was more aware of her condition, as a means of separating herself from her environment. When she was less aware, her body worked better, she appeared calmer, and she kept her eyes open and ate automatically.

Discussion

The delicate balance Margaret had achieved on her low dosage of Mellaril® was disrupted by Dr. Moore's efforts to minimize psychotropic medications, as mandated by OBRA. Dr. Moore fears that "demented brains" could be damaged by such medications, and his distrust of the nursing staff's input led to continuous modifications that ironically resulted in an eightfold increase in dosage to return Margaret to her previous baseline. After months of working toward this, a prescription for a counter-indicated medication once again upset the balance. Dr. Moore believed that "the demented brain" was vulnerable to damage from heavy psychotropic medications; perhaps it was equally vulnerable to multiple chemical readjustments, even using milder medications.

Margaret was not only victim to medication adjustments; she was also victim to serious communication problems on, and concerning, her unit. Hazel had complained that the Psychiatry Department was "conservative" for informing relatives of any changes they had prescribed. This, in fact, did not occur in Margaret's case. If it had, her brother, who was very involved with her treatment, would have warned the staff about using certain medications. Furthermore, the mischarting—and/or misreading—of a medication to which Margaret was allergic only exacerbated her condition; the lack of accountability by any member of the team for the error underlined the confusion and miscommunication that existed. Finally, the distrust and lack of communication of the psychiatric consultant with the nursing staff and the exclusion of input from the NAs impeded earlier intervention to correct the deterioration and only prolonged Margaret's distress and decline.

At one point, the ADON explained to the staff that, under OBRA, psychotropic medication could only be dispensed for the benefit of the resident, not for reasons of control or staff convenience. Yet at a special meeting exploring noise on the unit, the DON's chief assistant asked if any residents from Snow 1 had been placed on psychotropic medication for "their own benefit." The fact that she would ask this question suggested she entertained the possibility that the staff had actually excluded some residents from Snow 1 from the federal protections, perhaps because of the severity of their behavioral problems. Yet these were the very persons for whom these federal protections had in fact been established. Similarly, it is hard to know whether—and to what extent—adopting the sunbonnet during Margaret's baths might have prevented the pattern of screaming to develop and advance after the psychiatric consultation. It is likely that the original source of her screaming—her dislike of water in her ears—could have been curtailed by using the sunbonnet; Rhonda attested to its success. For the head nurse, however, the bonnet interfered with efficiency, and she preferred to tolerate Margaret's increasingly tortured cries than to slow down her bath and prevent Rhonda from bathing everyone on the schedule. Rather than questioning a system that could not accommodate measures (like the bonnet) that might improve the quality of life of its residents, she seemed more concerned with saving the institution money. Rather than supporting Rhonda for trying to improve care quality—by using more time—she encouraged her to work within a rigid care economy that saved the institution dollars.

Hazel did not view Margaret's screaming as a concern because she saw it as an isolated symptom of her dementia, divorced from any meaning. It is not that Hazel was insensitive to Margaret; she simply did not believe that adjusting a source of localized distress—water in Margaret's ears—could much affect a problem of the magnitude of her disease.

Margaret was assaulted not only by her dementia—and by changes in her brain chemistry brought on by the medication changes—but by environmental stimuli in a setting she could never accept as "home." Whatever changes were triggered by the medication also unleashed expressions on an existential plane. To Hazel, however, Margaret's dementia made it difficult to listen seriously to the content of her complaints or demands—or to those of her family. To this head nurse, Margaret had ceased to retain moral being and had become her disease. Why else would Hazel prioritize care economy over care quality?

The staff had told her brother that Margaret's screaming and singing were no indication that she was suffering, however much this may have bothered the families. In fact, Dr. Moore had asked Margaret during one screaming bout, with her eyes plastered shut, if she were comfortable; she indicated that she was. To the staff, this Cartesian-like disconnect between signs of pain (her screaming) and indications of its absence (her statement of comfort) was simply a reflection of her demented disease. But like her brother, I suspect it was not the physical plane to which her screaming was directed. While her dementia necessitated her current unhappy circumstances, her screaming was directed to these circumstances and the existential state they produced for her.

Margaret had suffered the indignity of placement at a unit about which she could say even in her deteriorated state, "I don't like this place; it's the *whole* thing I don't like." She also experienced repeated invalidations by a staff who disregarded her wishes because of institutional demands and her status as "demented." As a human agent, thus constrained, she was reduced to relying on louder and more pervasive outbursts that changes in her medications helped to unleash. These would ultimately drown out her environment while at the same time articulate her existential condition;[14] that she would resort to such basic means as yelling—her only available vehicle[15]—only intensified their poignancy. Outbursts of this quality were not to be silenced by magic bullets, neither mild nor heavy.

---

[14] I owe this insight to Bob Rubinstein on January 20, 1993.
[15] Similarly, urinary incompetence and food strikes in nursing homes have also been seen as agential acts of rebellion. See, for example, Vesperi (1983).

CASE STUDY 3: BEYOND DEMENTIA: REBECCA'S BATH AND REFUSAL TO CONFORM[16]

"You commit a misdemeanor and you get sent to Snow 1!"

"You can lose your mind here, but I'm not going to let it happen to me."

"How did it all happen that I would end up here?"[17]

Rebecca's Admission: A Penalizing Action?

I was not the only one who was surprised about the new resident on Snow 1. Both the PA and social worker told me that the previous head nurse would never have allowed Rebecca to be admitted to the unit. They also felt that it marked a possible new trend in which difficult residents would be routed directly to the Snow units. The intermediate dementia units, which had taken them in the past, were now reserving space for more cooperative residents to participate in a special research project. Since Snow 2 had few openings, they predicted that most would be coming to Snow 1.

Rebecca was the only person on Snow 1 without dementia. In fact, she was extremely sharp, priding herself, for example, in being the undefeated *Trivia* champion from her previous unit. I had not expected to be following her since she lacked the cognitive impairments typical of those I had selected to study. However, despite her lucidity, both the unit staff and the nursing home administration perceived her as an extreme "problem." I had accumulated abundant information about her through my general field notes on her quarrelsome interactions with others in Snow 1. The administration identified her as a major source of disruption in their concerns about the noisiness of the unit and began to place extreme pressure on her. I decided to include her in my study to learn about the impacts of such institutional pressure on elders, even when they lack dementia. As I saw this strong-willed, cognitively intact woman collapsing under such

---

[16] Some of this material overlaps case material from Case Study 1 on pp. 236–42 of my article, Power in the nursing home: The case of a special care unit, *Medical Anthropology*, 2001, *19*, 223–57.

[17] Statements from the resident herself.

pressure, I wondered how it might affect someone who lacked the cognitive skills to understand it.

Rebecca was confined to a wheelchair and suffered from severe urinary incontinence. She was unable to get herself to a bathroom alone and hated depending on NAs to get there. She refused to bathe and to wear the kind of diapers supplied by the hospital, claiming that they made her itch terribly. She was willing to wear a lighter pad her family provided, but she never seemed to have enough to stay dry. This meant that she often urinated in her chair or sat in a wet pad while her room began to reek. She and her family were not bothered by this, but some residents and their families started to complain about the odor.

For years, the staff on her unit had threatened Rebecca with removal from her unit if she would not cooperate with them. More recently, the clinical team for that unit (the head nurse, social worker, nutritionist, psychologist, and activities specialist) told her that her urinary practices could not continue. Even her psychologist, who had always served as her advocate, warned that if she did not comply with nurses' demands to wear a diaper, she might be "demoted" to Snow 1. One day, not long before her move, a group of eight administrators announced that if she did not soon comply with their demands, she would be forced to move. This authoritative ultimatum followed previous warnings but no efforts were made to negotiate an alternative acceptable to both her and the staff (cf. Aroskar 1990: 187).

Before being pressured to move, Rebecca received a psychiatric consultation that resulted in a list of strict recommendations for the nursing staff to follow. Somehow, they never implemented these recommendations; nevertheless, they wanted her to move. Soon after her confrontation with the administrators, her roommate moved out, and the nursing home was unable to find anyone to replace her because of the odor of urine in the room. While Rebecca's psychologist was on vacation, a private room opened up in Snow 1, and the administrative committee in charge of moves decided it was time to move Rebecca there.

Her psychologist was distraught to learn that these actions had occurred while she was away and unavailable to object and tried unsuccessfully to turn around the order. Moves, as the Director of Nursing (DON) once told me, are not initiated lightly. After a resident leaves a unit, it may be several months before another bed becomes available there. Since Rebecca refused to take the steps needed to leave Snow 1—changing her pads whenever they became wet, cleaning herself, and taking baths—she was stuck there.

"Just a Nasty Old Woman"

At her former unit, Rebecca had developed a reputation for being very unpleasant and verbally abusive to the staff and the other residents. She "just raised hell, swore at people, and tried to run the show there," observed the social worker, who thought that Rebecca was "playing it more conservatively" on Snow 1. On Snow 1, Rebecca talked openly with the staff about her dislike for hot baths and soap. One NA negotiated a sponge bath with her but explained that she would need to use some soap. Rebecca indicated that she hated to do things (like use soap) when she was ordered that she must. The NA was patient and explained how bathing would prevent her from getting sores from the acid in her urine. It seemed for a while that her chances to negotiate her care might be better on this floor since the staff might be responsive to working with a rational resident, a rarity on the unit.

Rebecca and I discussed her difficulty with urinating. She explained that because of a medical condition, she must drink continuously; water was her "lifeline." This resulted in ongoing pressure to urinate, and she was more than happy to wear a light pad. While the Snow 1 staff contended that the itching results from her sitting in wet diapers, Rebecca insisted that she was allergic to them. She also explained that she particularly disliked getting baths on her former unit because the water was always too hot for her, the soap too abundant, and the staff too rough. Later, Rebecca admitted to me that she was no angel, that she swears and gets annoyed, but that she has had no reason to do so yet on Snow 1. She was quite pensive at first about her dilemma, locked in an inappropriate unit without any residents with whom she could converse, yet reluctant to conform to the demands that would allow her to return to her own unit. At her age—eighty-nine—it was not easy to keep moving. Even though she could have conversations and play *Trivia* and *Jeopardy* with residents on her old unit, she despised their materialism, ostentatious styles, and intolerance of her bathing habits. And, although she wanted to return to her unit, she did not want to give in to the staff's pressures. Perhaps, she thought, she could get used to this floor. She did like the increased number of music therapy sessions. Even though the activities therapist was willing to take her off the unit to play *Trivia* and *Jeopardy* with residents from her old unit, she refused, out of embarrassment of constantly needing to go back and forth.

Within a week, her mixed feelings about living on Snow 1 were intensifying. She was missing some of her old friends and realized that she just did not belong on Snow 1. It took about two weeks before Rebecca began to show impatience with other residents. She disdained them as much as she feared some day becoming like them (cf. Macklin 1990: 68). "I'm not as sharp; I'm slipping," she confided in me one day. Rebecca was intolerant and would swear at another resident for making constant demands on the staff. As time passed, she became angrier and angrier. When other residents approached her, she would holler or even kick at them. Both their uncontrolled yelling out and their bizarre behaviors annoyed her. Rebecca came to feel that there was no place for her. She could no longer bear the emptiness on Snow 1, with no one to relate to and activities that were unstimulating, but she dreaded and continued to refuse conditions that would allow her to return to her former unit.

While she had endeared herself at first to the Snow 1 staff, they were growing impatient with her. The new head nurse finally dubbed her "Just a nasty old woman," and the NAs would sometimes encourage another resident to talk to her to get back at her. Although residing on Snow 1 was unpleasant and threatened her intellectual prowess, it did not soften her "stubborn" noncompliance to staff demands. In fact, Rebecca was becoming even more resistant to receiving full baths. She, in short, continued to resist power, an overt expression of dissent perhaps (Lock 1993: 141).

The Bath

As her behaviors became more disruptive, they became the focus of concern and target of control by the administration. One morning, the Director of Nursing suddenly appeared on Snow 1. As I gathered from the puzzled expressions on the faces of most of the staff, this was totally unanticipated by most of them. This occurred toward the end of my nine-month tenure on the unit and was the first time I had seen her come there. Such a rare occurrence forebodes trouble, since someone so high in the power hierarchy does not generally come to the units. She walked up to the head nurse and whispered something. The head nurse then called over to a few NAs who looked as if they had been primed for what was about to follow. Two entered the bathing area while two others approached Rebecca and began to wheel her from her room across the unit floor to the bathing area, against her loud, persistent protests. When they all entered the bathing area, the administrator gave her one last chance to enter the tub willingly. Rebecca refused, and the administrator ordered that she be undressed. Her protests grew louder, turned to screams, then loud sobs, and finally quiet resigned whimpers.

I knew something momentous was about to happen, but I was unsure quite how to capture it, nor terribly enthusiastic about trying. Certainly, I had witnessed baths before—even ones that residents had resisted—but only after receiving formal permission from the families and/or residents to do so. This situation was quite beyond my ordinary protocol. I could have peeked in and seen the entire proceeding, but I would not allow myself this liberty; doing so would have felt like witnessing an execution that I objected to, or worse participating as co-conspirator in the act (cf. Foner 1994: 47). Even permitting myself to witness her inability to resist power felt like a violation. Still, my turning away from that potent scene, distinctly refusing to witness the details of personal violence, and yet not attempting to stop them, consolidated for me at once the contradiction, impotence, and ethical dilemma of my own presence there as observer—an experience, I fear, is all too common in ethnographic research.

Information Management

When the DON entered the Unit, she did not acknowledge me; my presence seemed inconsequential to her. So I was surprised when she walked up to me, where I was seated by a family member, after the bathing scene was over. She offered, unsolicited, "Rebecca calmed down right away as soon as she got into the tub." Why did she bother to tell me this? If she had perceived me as lacking influence, why would it matter that I should know that? Although I perceived her to be at the top of the power hierarchy, perhaps she was not secure in her role. Certainly, there had been recent turnover in high-level administrative offices, and she may have misjudged me to be more powerful than I was. Or perhaps she was simply concerned with information management. Given the administration's difficulty in "selling" Snow 1 to families, joining me and a family member may have been calculated. She may have tried to soften the staff's actions by expressing Rebecca's own acceptance of them. She also may have tried to influence what I was to write in my report with information that I later learned was distorted. As Timothy Diamond observed, "Language enters into, shapes, and sustains power relations" (Diamond 1992: 239). The DON's words intended to preserve those relations.

After Rebecca was back in her room and calm was restored, I spoke with one of the NAs from the bathing incident about Rebecca's ease in calming down. She looked at me puzzled and explained that Rebecca had not calmed down a single bit, but continued pushing and hitting and re-sisting the bath to the bitter end. The head nurse confirmed this the next day, showing me her scars left from scratches on her hand and forearm.

Outcome

About an hour after the incident, I knocked on Rebecca's door, half expect-ing her to evict me for not having helped her; I was surprised when she did not. Perhaps my separation from those who participated in the forcible bathing enabled her to retain some trust in me. Perhaps she appreciated my refusal to observe her ordeal. Perhaps, too, her softened spirit indi-cated that her will was injured. Renée Shield notes how grouchiness and angry bickering are rare in sicker residents and may be linked to health and survival (1988: 170–171).

Sobered and still tearful over the day's events, Rebecca looked numb as she confessed her main reason for hating baths: she despised publicly exposing her body, which was disfigured by a double mastectomy. The rou-tine of being taken to the bathing room, being undressed, secured into a chair, and then raised and lowered into the tub prolonged her exposure, magnified the shame of her disfigurement, and felt degrading (Kayser-Jones 1981: 47–48). The humiliation of the day's incident, she confided, was too much for her to bear. It only worsened once her psychologist explained that today's ritual would recur until she fully accepted baths.

During the next couple of weeks, Rebecca frequently clutched her chest and gasped for air. The head nurse did not take her seriously, explaining her fondness for overly dramatizing a mild heart condition. Two days later, Rebecca had expired. The unit physician reflected, "Maybe she was sicker than we realized." Maybe she had also given up her desire to fight.

Discussion

Rebecca's violation of the behavioral expectations of the institution and "community" is more complex than it may appear (Macklin 1990: 62–66). When she refused to behave by the institution's expectations, the staff exer-cised their muscle and transferred her to a "lesser" unit, partly out of punish-ment, partly in response to complaints from her fellow residents. This would be understandable if the staff had exhausted other measures first and if they offered the resident a chance to suggest alternatives (Aroskar 1990: 183–87);

in fact, neither occurred. The staff from her old unit ignored recommendations from the psychiatric consultant and did not try to secure the pads she was willing to use. Later on Snow 1, her initial willingness to receive a sponge bath dissolved as she faced a staff hardened by her disruptions.

Under the direction of the DON on Snow 1, Rebecca's wheelchair-bound body was subjected to domination by NAs who were commanded to coercively bathe her without being given other options (Aroskar 1990: 187). Both Rebecca and the NAs were forced to submit to the hierarchical power structure of the nursing home.

From one perspective, it would appear that the institution imposed a negative, repressive, instrumentally driven brutish power (cf. Habermas 1984, 1987; Dreyfus and Rabinow 1983: 130) over a physically disabled, relatively helpless old woman; other nursing home ethnographies[18] have documented similar excesses. From another perspective, however, Rebecca was not entirely passive. Her ability to make rational decisions was not impaired; indeed, she *chose* to act as she did. As a rational being, she functioned as an *autonomous moral agent* capable of deciding how to behave. More importantly, she violated demands of any "community" of residents living in close proximity to each other (Macklin 1990: 65). According to some moral theorists, the nursing home administrator's application of power to reform Rebecca's undesirable behavior (Hindess 1996: 17) for the betterment of the larger community[19] was a justifiable act.

Despite her rational state when "choosing" not to conform to the staff's hygienic requests, it would be a farfetched distortion to regard Rebecca as entirely "free" in her dealings with the staff. At best, one might argue their strategies were repressive. Residents have the right to refuse baths in some homes (cf. Foner 1994: 44), and some ethicists have argued against *ever* forcing a resident to take a bath (Aroskar 1990). Since it involves touching another person, bathing—like caregiving more generally—they argue, requires consent. That lacking, Rebecca should have been given the opportunity to explain her concerns and to suggest alternatives, rather than be forced to conform (Aroskar 1990).

As extreme as they were, the strategies were not intended as a simple-minded domination of an old woman, but as a measured *encouragement* that she adjust her conduct. They were what Foucault calls normalizing

---

[18] See especially those by Kayser-Jones (1981), Foner (1994), Diamond (1992), Savishinsky (1991), and Shield (1988).

[19] Such liberal notions which assume that free rational individuals in a participatory democracy submit their will to that of the general public are problematic in the nursing home setting where power is not equitably distributed (Foldes 1990: 35).

techniques (Foucault 1977 [1975]), intended on promoting the welfare not only of Rebecca, but of the entire unit (cf. Dreyfus and Rabinow 1983: 195–96). Still, given the context of a physically limited elderly woman on a locked unit, the lack of symmetry between the power available to her and to the staff more accurately approximated a relation of domination that afforded only a minimal margin of freedom (cf. Hindess 1996: 102)—a situation that some ethicists insist can never be ethical (Aroskar 1990: 187). *As ethically problematic as this was with someone who was rational, it becomes even more so when such powers are imposed on a cognitively impaired person who cannot understand the purpose of such actions.*

According to bioethicist Arthur Caplan, nursing homes restrict autonomy by either coercively applying force or by not providing choices (1990: 48); Rebecca's autonomy was denied on both counts. Where reason is compromised (as with dementia), autonomy is further denied—a misfortune in light of evidence that residents who retain autonomy and choice are healthier and live longer than those who do not (p. 48).

For Rebecca, abrupt violence came at a price. Her newly mild manner signified a surrendering of spirit and autonomy (cf. Macklin 1990: 69) without which her will for life faltered. Given the drastically reduced range within which she could exercise agency, her remaining potential for resistance offered no guarantees (Hindess 1996: 141). Though her spirit momentarily dulled, her urge to resist persisted. Within the power structure and world of limited choices she now inhabited, the only acceptable path of resistance may have been to let go of life.

FURTHER READING

McLean, Athena. (1994). What kind of love is this? *The Sciences*, 34(5), 36–40.
McLean, Athena. (2001). Power in the nursing home: The case of a special care unit. *Medical Anthropology*, 19, 223–57.

CHAPTER 6

Historical and Cultural Context of Caregiving in Snow 2: Three Case Studies

THE CULTURE OF CAREGIVING AT SNOW 2

With as much turnover as Snow 1 had sustained over the years, Snow 2 was remarkable for its stability. Several residents, the charge nurse and three NAs had been with the unit since it opened 19 years earlier, and another NA arrived soon after. The other residents had lived there from two to four years. Family members were welcome there and generally felt confident about the care their relative was receiving. Administrative staff regarded Snow 2 as the "most stable" unit in the nursing home, and at the start of my study the DON called it her favorite.

On all the shifts, the NAs and nurses in Snow 2 were black except for the head nurse and a new young female NA on her shift. There were only two males, both NAs: a younger man who sometimes rotated through the unit on the day shift, and an older man on the evening shift who had been with the unit almost from its opening.

Jenny, the Head Nurse of Snow 2

Jenny, a Jewish woman in her mid-fifties, had headed Snow 2 for the last dozen years. The DON had gone to nursing school with her and regarded her as an extremely competent, intuitive clinician, and together with the ADONS, valued her judgment implicitly. Jenny's entire career was devoted to long-term care, and before coming to head Snow 2, she had worked for many years at another prominent Jewish nursing home in the area. Whenever Jenny felt a resident was too cognitively competent for her unit, she let the administration know this, and invariably the person would not be admitted. When I asked how she achieved this, she simply smiled and stated, "I have my ways."

Jenny had kept the unit stable by "fighting with anyone who tries to take my residents away!" This meant, for example, keeping a close watch over residents before moving to hospitalize them if they appeared ill. Her 30 years of long-term care experience convinced her that maintaining a stable location for those with dementia was in their best interest. She also prided herself in having improved the condition and quality of life of residents who arrived at her unit in much worse shape. Some residents who came to her unit incontinent were now continent. Others who came in wheelchairs could now walk. Although she insisted that these residents were just as impaired as persons admitted to Snow 1 when they arrived, she was convinced that her efforts, and those of her staff, transformed them. This may have explained why Snow 2 residents often appeared less impaired than those on Snow 1 and challenged the rumors that her refusal to accept more impaired resulted in their ending up on Snow 1.

Jenny's Philosophy of Care

In contrast to Hazel's rigid criteria for prioritizing care, Jenny promoted a standard of care for Snow 2 that valued flexibility and attention to individual needs, as brought to her attention by attentive family members or NAs. To fulfill these, she sometimes relaxed expectations (e.g., that everyone must receive a bath when scheduled), and sometimes she pressed her finest NAs to their very limits.

Jenny believed in the minimal use of physical and chemical restraints (psychotropic medications). If a resident presented behavioral problems, there had to be a good reason, and she tried to get to the core problem. That is how she managed to make such strides with very demented persons. She also believed in the importance of keeping residents ambulatory to enable them to take care of their own toileting needs and to remain continent. In her view, toileting programs—taking residents to the bathroom every two hours—had been developed more for NAs than for residents; people have urges that cannot be so predictably scheduled. When NAs are too busy to respond to toileting needs, elders may develop incontinence. This is why retaining their mobility is so vital.

Jenny tried to create a homelike environment for the residents by not caving in to multiple imposing institutional demands. Because administrative staff trusted her, she was able to stretch institutional rules without suffering consequences. For example, Jenny was more relaxed than CCs on other units about allowing some residents to sleep late and to get up when they felt like it rather than to hurriedly force them to receive morning care in preparation for breakfast; NAs could always reheat their meal later. This allowed for a happier resident who was less likely to fight her morning care because she did not feel like getting up. If a resident were having a rough day, Jenny would also postpone scheduled clinic appointments to avoid the additional stress of long waits in the waiting room. Jenny devised creative ways to get elders to eat, like mixing food groups like soup with pureed vegetable to increase their palatability. As seemingly minor as this gesture was, she received a citation for violating state regulations by not having included a formal order for this in the elder's care plan. Still, Jenny preferred to work informally. Her concern was for the needs of the resident, not for some generalized regulation.

Because she had seen that nursing home residents often function at a lower level than their potential, she trained her staff to watch for signs suggesting that a resident could function more autonomously than previously had been assumed. She had discovered that formerly independent elders can get very agitated if they are forced to become dependent on others; considerable improvements had occurred whenever she paid attention to their existing strengths. She was also willing to extend her staff and the staff members of other shifts to satisfy family members' requests to maximize the quality of life of their elders.

Jenny believed attention to an elder's personal needs was at least as important as completing and charting the ADLs (care tasks). Sometimes this meant that ADLs in fact were not charted—in violation the recently instituted OBRA regulations—and she had to guess, for example, whether a resident had already received an enema. Jenny treated each resident as a unique person, trusting her own nursing judgment, rather than any rigid ADL protocol as her care guide. This sometimes meant she had to defy standard practices and develop maverick solutions to very difficult cases. Because of the support she received from the administration, she often succeeded.

A "Well-managed Unit"

During my visits to Snow 2, Jenny indeed seemed to have everything under control. She conveyed a quiet assurance that instilled a strong sense of confidence in her as the unit head. She was on top of all her residents and immediately began telling me about them and their families. I had the sense I would learn much from her. Whenever an elder would come to the nurses' station to ask a question—no matter how many times—she would calmly answer the question or try to take care of the problem. If a family member called or made an appearance, she was pleasant and able to answer questions immediately. She even managed the environment with soothing music to calm the residents.

While the unit gave the appearance of being "well managed," it did not feel overly controlled. In fact, the unit had a relaxed quality that Jenny had deliberately cultivated with her staff. She explained how she trusted them to do their jobs without a lot of oversight because they were mature, had abundant experience, and had learned to cooperate well as a team. All but one of the NAs on her shift were in their late 50s or early 60s, and three of the five had worked together on the unit from its inception, with a fourth arriving soon afterwards. If an NA had a problem with a resident, she would discuss it with Jenny, develop a new strategy, and if it worked, share it with the others. Jenny also recognized the demanding lives the NAs led outside of the work place and tried to accommodate their needs (e.g., to phone home outside of break-times—something most head nurses would not allow). By lessening their personal burdens, she felt she would help free them to extend themselves more with the residents. Such autonomy was a rarity in the punitive system that most NAs faced. In turn, her staff loved working on Snow 2 and would complain about their treatment by other CCs whenever they worked overtime in other units.

As in Snow 1, NAs were assigned to rotating groups of about eight residents for two-week periods. However, at Snow 2, the groupings were not sequential, and NAs could make private exchanges of residents amongst themselves. This sometimes made it difficult to keep track of which NA was in charge of a given resident. It also allowed NAs to work with residents they preferred, while still offering some semblance of order by retaining groups to satisfy the administration. The old-timers on the unit really liked this system, but the newer staff preferred assignments that were more predictable.

Although the nursing home had a rule against assigning a specific NA to particular residents, the private exchanges were a vehicle around the rule. For example, Elaine, who had worked on the unit for three years, had a gift for working with difficult, combative residents, and so most of the NAs were willing to exchange difficult residents with her. Jenny deliberately would introduce these residents to Elaine, hoping she would develop a relationship with them and want to work with them. The system worked well for both residents and the staff, except that some of the senior NAs refused to participate as a matter of pride.

As well managed as the unit seemed, I was struck by the invisibility of the Snow 2 staff, even the care manager, during my first few visits to the unit. I assumed they were busy in residents' rooms conducting rounds or off at clinical visits elsewhere in the building. In contrast to my visits at Snow 1, where a number of staff members moved in and out of rooms while others walked me around the unit to help orient me to the residents, Jenny spoke to me alone behind the nurses' station the entire time (a good two hours). I only began to see NAs appear when it was time for them to leave their shift.

Shift Culture and Cooperation

Gradually I learned the reason for invisibility of the NAs and that Snow 2 was not only "well managed" by the head nurse; the three most senior NAs also found ways of managing the unit, and it was not always clear who was managing whom.

The Day Shift (7:00 a.m. to 3:00 p.m.)
Relative to Snow 1, Snow 2 was well staffed. In addition to Jenny, there were two LPNs—the care manager, who dispensed treatments and assisted Jenny with the NAs, and a nurse who dispensed medications. This freed Jenny to remain at the nurses' station most of the time fielding questions and problems, and completing forms and documentation. There

were five NAs daily on this shift, from a pool of seven regulars. The care manager plus four of the NAs had worked on the unit almost since it had first opened, another worked there three years, and the other two were recent hires.

On Snow 2, the senior NAs had developed ways to work together to avoid work. Having been there so long, and having "paid their dues," as one NA put it, they were ready to lighten their load. They also resented the punitive practices of the administration since they had worked with administrations in the past who had been more respectful. Newer staff without this history harbored less resentment toward the administration and were more responsive to their supervisors' requests. Jenny learned to depend on Elaine, an older and dedicated worker, or Karen, the newest NA on the unit, for special jobs like toileting a resident or taking someone to a clinic. One day when they were both busy, Jenny asked, "Where is everyone else?" A few minutes later when I went to the back room, I found the CM and NAs sitting down chatting. I learned that they would regularly "hide" (their own words) or sit down to watch television in a resident's room between their rounds and their regular break time.

Jenny was sympathetic to their position, since they had been hard workers, were aging themselves, and worked under a difficult administration. As long as she could rely on Elaine or Karen, she did not confront them. Karen seemed good-natured about helping but had an amused respect for the three senior women and hoped to be accepted by them. She gradually shifted her alliances away from Elaine, whose work ethic and high standard of interpersonal care threatened their own work practices.

Even though Elaine suffered from severe back pain, Karen was the only NA who would sometimes help her lift heavy residents; the others refused to help because they resented her for setting an "impossible" work standard. The senior women worked well together as a team, covering for each other both in their work and in their attempts to escape it. Two were steady workers, very attentive to basic physical care with residents in their group and skilled at alleviating residents' fears to make them more cooperative and easier to manage; the others were authoritative and less patient with residents.

The Evening Shift (3:00 p.m. to 11:00 p.m.)

The care manager on this shift felt more heavily burdened with responsibilities than did the staff on the day shift. She was required to deliver treatments and medication as well as to keep up with documentation while supervising a very difficult and often dependent staff. The NAs on this shift included a woman who had worked on the unit since its beginning and a man who had been at the home for over 30 years and worked on the unit for more than a dozen. Together he and another older woman were very reliable and cooperative with the CM and the other NAs. The remainder were new to the unit and often fought amongst themselves, making her job more difficult. The 3:00 p.m. to 11:00 p.m. CM complained that Jenny's laxity with her staff increased her own burden by increasing the workloads—and complaints—of the NAs on her shift.

The Night Shift (11:00 p.m. to 7:00 a.m.)

The night care manager was fortunate to be working with two diligent NAs. She was burdened, however, with great demands from the nursing administration to provide one-on-one attention to selected residents. With three other residents to look after, as well as paper work and supervisory responsibilities, she sometimes felt overwhelmed and was on the verge of quitting.

Relationship Among Shifts

On the day shift, NAs with seniority were known to not complete tasks from their last round—like diapering residents, changing dirty linens, or getting residents out of bed to change sheets, only adding to the work load of NAs on the later shift. The 3:00 p.m. to 11:00 p.m. CM appealed to the 7:00 a.m. to 3:00 p.m. CM, who referred her to Jenny; as a friend to the NAs, she preferred not to deal with them directly. Anytime the 3:00 p.m. to 11:00 p.m. CM tried to meet with Jenny and an ADON to discuss the problem, the meeting got cancelled. Things got better for a short while, only to deteriorate once again, leaving the CM frustrated and angry.

Jenny got along well, however, with the CM on her own shift because she appreciated her relaxed style. All the CMs would occasionally get annoyed with Jenny when she failed to communicate important information to them. This made them appear unprepared in her absence and brought undeserved criticism from ADONs.

Relations of Unit Staff with Other Staff Members

In contrast to Snow 1, the Snow 2 medical staff—the PA, unit physician, and psychiatrist—worked together well with the nursing staff and each other. Communication was excellent, and there was regular discussion about residents with Jenny and her entire staff. Dr. Bacon, the unit physician, visited the unit daily, not only to review charts but to mingle with residents and examine them; he didn't simply sign the PA's recommendations because he spent at least as much time on the unit as she did. He considered the geriatric post his primary commitment, so did not run off after a cursory review of residents' charts.

Dr. Mallory, the unit psychiatrist, was aware of the considerable variation that could occur in residents' conditions within a brief amount of time, so she welcomed and even elicited information about their behavior and its changes from both nurses and NAs before making medication recommendations.

Dr. Bacon was conservative in using psychotropic medications for agitation or behavioral disturbances because he feared their side effects could contribute to falls and hasten deterioration. He was willing to try a medication, however, if the psychiatrist encouraged it and the family was willing to try it. The medical staff and Jenny agreed that the family should be informed before prescribing psychotropic medications because the issue was so "loaded." Dr. Mallory pointed out that even if there were no *legal* considerations in not informing families—something OBRA was challenging—there were certainly *emotional* considerations that needed to be addressed.

Even though Dr. Bacon sometimes disagreed with Dr. Mallory—who was more prone to medicate elders for depression—they respected each other's professional opinions and, with Jenny's input, would negotiate—and often renegotiate—the use and withdrawal of medication with various elders. Dr. Bacon, however, could reject any suggestion from Dr. Mallory and often did.

As clinicians, they were highly sensitive to nonmedical concerns that should shape treatment decisions. Dr. Bacon determined whether an elder was agitated or depressed in relation to her previous behaviors and personality. Dr. Mallory was sensitive to the nonmedical conditions that could stimulate problematic behaviors. She was convinced that BDs are not random events related to disease process, but clear signs that something else—environmentally, emotionally, or physically—needs attention. She first explored whether something was wrong medically or whether the behavior had another reasonable source. *These medical practitioners were in some ways less biomedical in their views of BDs than were some of the nonmedically trained staff on both units.*

While the clinical team held regular meetings, the social worker was less involved since Jenny had largely taken over her role of communicating with families. The rest of the team—the nutritionist and activities specialist—worked quite well together. The music therapist for Snow 2, however, came only once a week and involved only the better functioning residents in activities.

Communication with Families

Jenny's mother had lived in another unit of the home for many years, so Jenny knew nurses throughout the building and was particularly sensitive to the feelings of families and residents. Unlike Hazel, who was reserved and uncomfortable with families, Jenny thrived on dealing with them, which is why she preferred to bypass the social worker and communicate with families directly. She appreciated families' rights to information, and either she or the unit physician would contact families about possible changes in a resident's medication, freely discussing options with them. In contrast to Hazel, she openly shared information from the elder's chart about her current status and treatment. She even welcomed family members to care conferences when their relative was being discussed, even though it sometimes slowed down business. Given her belief that family involvement was vital to providing quality care, she set a standard of expectation for families that the care managers could rarely meet, or even chose to. At the same time she insisted that she would never support preferential care just to satisfy a family member's wishes unless it was in the best interest of the residents.

Although Jenny deeply cared about the residents on Snow 2 and tried to accommodate their needs, her relaxed approach to organizing care was sometimes abused by senior NAs whose relations with the administration had suffered. Somehow—by gathering the energies, and even sacrifices, of other unit staff—she nevertheless was able to provide many of her residents with exceptional care. The following case studies are testimonies to this fact. In these studies, the residents will be identified by their surnames (amended for confidentiality), in keeping with the practices of Snow 2.

CASE STUDY 1: MRS. NOBLE: DIGNITY IN ADVANCED DEMENTIA

> Daughter: "I'm the only one who knows who she was long ago from a different time and world: the last great post-Victorian woman."

Daughter: "It is more peaceful now that the person isn't there."

"She maintained her grace, nobility and dignity unto the end."[1]

At 91, Mrs. Noble carried herself with the poise, grace, and an air of haughtiness that had always distinguished her. She scoped out the room carefully searching for Elaine and looked intently toward her until she caught her attention. As the NA approached from the opposite side of the room, Mrs. Noble kept keen watch, and when she walked up, Mrs. Noble broke into a smile. Elaine was her favorite person—a caregiver who always seemed to understand her, even though she no longer spoke English. As her dementia advanced, even her native German deteriorated to single words or phrases—or to a stream of garbled German. Still, sitting tall and upright in her chair, Mrs. Noble remained an elegant and imposing figure.

Mrs. Noble's History

Mrs. Noble grew up in Germany in an affluent family with servants, completed finishing school where she learned French, and before marrying, became a singer and entertainer. A stunning, talented beauty, she was indulged by both her father and husband. According to her daughter Renée, Mrs. Noble could also be temperamental, frequently breaking out in "fits of emotional outbursts and loss of control," something the family learned to "endure." Her privileged life had been shattered when the Nazis sent her husband to an internment camp for many months and burnt down her house. After much difficulty, the family succeeded in locating a spot on the very last legal boat out of Europe.

After sustaining these losses, Mrs. Noble's capacity to nurture seemed to disappear, and by her pre-teenage years, Renée was forced to become her mother's nurturer. While the family eventually regained a middle-class life in the United States, Mrs. Noble seemed more emotionally sensitive than in the past. While readily lashing out in anger at others, including Renée, she herself felt easily wronged and would not rest until receiving an apology. Everything in their relationship had to be accounted for;

---

[1]   Comment by the rabbi from the nursing home at her memorial service at the family synagogue.

her mother's love became conditional. She also needed "constant emotional massaging" and "indulging of her ego," something Renée refused to do; their relationship had become conflictual ever since this period. Still, Renée retained strong images of her tall, beautiful mother and, still later, of her mother dining with Renée's own young daughter, both donning fancy hats and white gloves. Renée relished an image of her mother as an elegant, stunning woman, as meticulous about her appearance as she was powerful and world wise; she tried to preserve this image in the family's memory.

Moving to the Nursing Home

After her husband died, Mrs. Noble spent several years in an independent living facility close to Renée's home. She had no cognitive impairments at the time but had severe ulceration in her legs and was able to get some limited help at the facility. Increasingly she depended on Renée, who was consumed by the need to attend to her daily in addition to her other work and family obligations, and their physician felt it was time to seek full-time nursing home care.

Mrs. Noble agreed to move to a unit appropriate for persons with physical problems only. During that time, Renée visited her mother several times a week, handled her laundry, and was actively involved in activities at the home. She even organized a fashion show in which Mrs. Noble modeled. Mrs. Noble remained mentally sharp during this time, and was able to take care of herself, maintaining an interest in looking attractive. She continued to visit with her grandchildren, but rarely related to the other residents because she felt superior to them.[2] When Renée found Mrs. Noble courting two men, so "out of character" for her, she suspected she was losing her "edge" a bit.

About that time, Mrs. Noble increasingly showed cognitive "slips" and personality changes, fancying herself at a high-society tea, and later becoming even more demanding than was typical for her. One day she insisted that Renée immediately see her. Renée rushed only to find her dissatisfied with how the housekeeper had arranged her bedspread. As

---

[2] There was a clear social hierarchy at the home between Jews from Germany, who were culturally and socially more privileged, and those from Russia and Eastern Europe, where they lacked those privileges. The common Jewish background did not overcome these perceptions of class difference.

her emotional outbursts and "irrational" demands increased, the staff reassessed the appropriateness of her remaining there. Her fits of temper and unreasonable demands, which had always been there, became still more severe. Mrs. Noble then suffered a major lapse of memory, abruptly losing recognition of her daughter and the fact that she had ever been married. A broken hip sealed her fate; after surgery she was transferred to Snow 2.

Mrs. Noble's Transfer to Snow 2

By the time she arrived at Snow 2—four years after moving to the home—Mrs. Noble had deteriorated dramatically. Hip replacement surgery had taken a cognitive toll; she lost her ability to speak English, and she showed evidence of paranoia. She avoided the other residents here as on the other unit. Within a year she could no longer walk, became incontinent, and showed extreme agitation during her morning and evening care. Her German deteriorated, and she could only speak a few words or phrases—a form of nonsensical "gibberish," according to Renée. Mrs. Noble also lost interest in keeping up her appearance. Her singing became limited to a high-pitched eerie croon she expressed whenever she was irritated. She would often sit alone giggling to herself, or playing with her juice box, utensils, or other objects. While she retained her poise as she sat upright studying her surroundings, Mrs. Noble could unexpectedly hit, bite, pinch, or pull hair, and out of fear, most of the NAs preferred not to work with her.

Communicating with Her NAs

In spite of these problems, two NAs, Veronica and Elaine, were fond of working with Mrs. Noble, and each would try to exchange another resident in their group for her. Veronica now worked on a different unit but would visit Mrs. Noble daily. She enjoyed Mrs. Noble's "spunkiness" and felt they communicated very well whenever "she is clearly here," even though there were many times when she was not. Veronica first met Mrs. Noble while working as a bathing assistant for the unit. Veronica became intrigued with the way "she carried on so crazy in the bath." She soon discovered that many of Mrs. Noble's actions were deliberate responses to things she disliked, such as getting water on her hair. Once she realized the sense in her responses, she took her gestures quite seriously and tried to "read" her wishes from her body language. Veronica also learned to "play" tag with her by gently tapping her shoulder, then teasingly pulling back while Mrs. Noble, full of smiles, repeated these gestures. Through such games, Veronica gained Mrs. Noble's cooperation so she could complete her care routines (washing her, diapering her, brushing her teeth, and grooming her), but she always made sure that Mrs. Noble made the last tag. *Caregiving thus became an intersubjective give-and-take.*

Unlike the rest of the staff, Veronica and Elaine felt Mrs. Noble's actions were very sensible. If either of them did something that offended Mrs. Noble—like diverting attention to another resident—Mrs. Noble would express hurt or anger; similarly, she would find ways to communicate pleasure. I saw several examples of this during Veronica's visits. Whenever Veronica turned to another resident, Mrs. Noble would frown and rapidly shake her hands, cry, or start to hum eerily in a distressed tone. As soon as Veronica returned, Mrs. Noble would take her hand and hit it in a choppy fashion or try to twist it. Veronica would apologize, and Mrs. Noble would immediately soften and smile. Sometimes she would teasingly threaten to leave, and Mrs. Noble would laugh, knowing she was just joking. There was continued eye contact between the two during such exchanges.

Veronica could tell how angry Mrs. Noble was by checking her hand; if it was rigid, then she was seriously annoyed. She could also detect that something was not right by her mood. For example, she was much less calm on days when Elaine was gone. Sometimes Veronica would decide to trim her nails, or gently shave a little hair from her face, promising not to hurt her. Mrs. Noble would calmly accept this—something she would never have tolerated from anyone else, other than Elaine. Veronica always ended her visits by assuring Mrs. Noble she would return and ask if that were okay; she would not leave until Mrs. Noble responded, "Ya." This reaffirmed their established trust.

Elaine's Approach to Caregiving

Elaine also had a knack for communicating with Mrs. Noble. Like Veronica, she believed that Mrs. Noble let her wishes be known through her actions, and always tried to "read" them. She read her gestures, the tone of her voice or song and her facial expressions. Elaine respected Mrs. Noble's right to know every step of the caregiving process, ensured that she understood, and secured her approval as they proceeded. If Mrs. Noble were having a difficult time, Elaine would never push her, but return later when she would generally be ready. If Mrs. Noble resisted, Elaine tried to determine and correct the problem. Elaine worked under the conviction that residents, no matter how demented, "do everything with a purpose," and she was invested in learning that purpose. Before eating any meal, Mrs. Noble would carefully mix all food groups together with her spoon until they were of a single smooth texture. Rather than rush her to finish her meal as other NAs were prone to do, Elaine saw that the gesture was calming, perhaps because it returned control to Mrs. Noble—an excellent cook in the past—by allowing her to "cook" her meal herself by stirring it before she would eat it. Elaine always respected her wish to complete this ritual before eating. Whenever Elaine tried to change Mrs. Noble's diaper, Mrs. Noble would assist her by moving her body toward her, rather than working against her as she did with so many of the other NAs. Elaine's approach to work *with* her by engaging her as a person—not *on* her as if she were an inert body—paid off for both of them.

Elaine felt that many of the other NAs misread Mrs. Noble's actions as combative or provoked her by being insensitive to, or unconcerned with, her wishes. For example, when she would take her to the bathroom, Mrs. Noble would hold Elaine's hands very tightly because she was afraid of falling. The others misinterpreted this as her attempt to fight them. In addition, if Mrs. Noble did not like a particular food, she would purse her lips as a sign of rejection. If another NA kept pressuring her to eat it, she would register annoyance by screaming or pushing them away. Moreover, if an NA hurried Mrs. Noble in order to complete her care tasks without taking account of her own wishes, she would understandably lash out. To Elaine there was no question whether Mrs. Noble's actions were meaningful; they simply needed to be understood.

The rest of the staff, she admitted, viewed her and Veronica as "crazy" for giving legitimacy to Mrs. Noble's actions. They attributed her and Veronica's successes to discovering "which of her buttons to push," not to the trust they had built by respecting and engaging with her as meaningful *agent*. In their stimulus/response behavioral model, Mrs. Noble became a programmable body manageable by manipulating buttons, not a person with whom intersubjective communication (and appeals) could occur.

Whenever Elaine took days off from work, she would usually stop by to visit Mrs. Noble or to brush her teeth—something the other NAs often neglected to do because they were afraid of her. Attending to Mrs. Noble went beyond her shift; it was not just a job, but also an act of caring and love.

Similarly, Mrs. Noble made it clear that she preferred Elaine and would find ways to express her discontent if another NA had been assigned to her or if an old-timer insisted on being her caregiver. One day she communicated how the NA who was caring for her had been negligent. As she sat between Elaine and the NA, she showed Elaine an untied restraint and tensed her eyebrows, as if to say, "Look what she did! She put me in danger!" She then turned to the NA who was supposed to be caring for her, showed her the untied restraint, and made a fist that conveyed, "Look what you did! You put me in danger!"

Mrs. Noble's Bath

Mrs. Noble had a reputation for being very difficult and combative during her baths. When Veronica was working as the bathing assistant, she and Elaine discovered that she remained cooperative until they brought out a hose to rinse out her hair. As soon as Mrs. Noble saw the hose, she would panic and begin to fight. They speculated that the hose resembled something frightening, even life threatening, perhaps because of her years in Nazi Germany. The NAs stopped using the hose and instead rinsed out her hair with cups of water. Mrs. Noble would then remain calm.

Changes in Mrs. Noble's Relationship with Her Daughter

Renée abruptly severed her relationship with Mrs. Noble after her move to Snow 2. She was stunned to learn her mother was transferred to that unit and found it extremely painful to visit her there. Renée felt her mother still recognized her as someone close but could no longer place her: "Even my touch or a soft, gentle word means nothing." Her own serious illness from months earlier had weakened her, and Renée decided to virtually stop visiting her mother. She also discouraged visits from her adult children because she wanted them to retain the image of their grandmother as fashionable and powerful.

Renée rested assured that she "did what had to be done" in cutting off the relationship. After years of therapy and emotional suffering in dealing with Mrs. Noble, Renée felt she could finally gain some comfort and be at "peace" because "the person was no longer there." Although seeing her mother decline had been extremely hard, now that there was "nothing left," she could allow herself to be removed; it "was almost a relief."

"Now," she explained, "my life is for the living." Yet she admitted that her mother had retained the ability to connect with others. She also retained some sense of her European background, sitting tall and gracefully as she dined, while keeping her knife in her left hand to help carve and slide her food onto her fork.

During the few times Renée did visit her mother, Mrs. Noble expressed rage toward her. On one occasion, she told Renée something sternly in German, pushed and hit Renée, and then pulled Renée's hair into her plate. Another time she screamed viciously at her daughter. Jenny and most of the staff assured Renée that her mother did not know what she was doing. Elaine and Veronica saw things differently. They were convinced that everything Mrs. Noble did was deliberate and purposeful. They had never seen her lash out at anyone unless she was frightened, threatened, pressured, or hurt. Nor had they ever seen her attack anyone or register anger or alarm without good reason. They were convinced that Mrs. Noble acted differently with Renée out of rage that she had been abandoned.

A Turn for the Worse

A few months after I stopped studying Mrs. Noble, I learned that she had been hospitalized because of dehydration and a urinary tract infection. The timing for this setback could not have been worse. When she returned, she discovered that one of the things in her life that gave her pleasure, her television (which she used to watch children's programs like *Sesame Street*), no longer functioned. Much worse, Elaine was no longer on the unit.

During Mrs. Noble's hospitalization, Elaine had received word that a transfer request for a full-time position as a bathing assistant had just come through. Because she was rearing her adolescent granddaughter, Elaine wanted to be home with her on weekends, so she needed a position that did not require weekend duty. One care manager surmised that she left because she felt overworked and inadequately appreciated. Both reasons were probably correct.

Elaine's Visit with Mrs. Noble

When I visited Elaine on her new unit, she expressed great concern about how Mrs. Noble, for whom she had cared almost exclusively the last three years, would fare in her absence. Elaine was missing her terribly, and when she heard that Mrs. Noble was not eating, she came to visit her. I too thought that Mrs. Noble was looking less vigorous than usual, uncharacteristically slouched down in her chair and not maintaining eye contact. Earlier in the day, I brought her a cookie to establish some rapport. Although she accepted and played with it, she did not eat it as she typically would.

At the end of her shift, Elaine came up to visit Mrs. Noble. Mrs. Noble did not display the usual anger she showed when Elaine was gone for a while. Rather, she just glowed in her presence, smiling continuously while Elaine was with her. Elaine walked up to the table where Mrs. Noble sat and pulled up a chair beside her. Mrs. Noble caught her eye and smiled, maintaining strong constant eye contact for the entire time Elaine was there, a good thirty minutes. Elaine offered her a cookie and some orange juice, and Mrs. Noble accepted both immediately. She started drinking and eating while "speaking" to Elaine excitedly in a garbled German for the entire visit. At one point, another resident spotted Elaine and quickly walked up to her to give her a hug. Elaine returned it with warmth. Mrs. Noble got jealous and deliberately spilled the juice Elaine had given her. Elaine explained that she had to greet her other friend too, but she still loves her; Mrs. Noble recovered quickly and began to smile again.

During this reunion, another resident, whom NAs described as self-centered and unpleasant, appeared to be taking great pleasure in watching their affectionate display. The pleasure of the moment was too much even for this woman to resist, and at several points, she laughed aloud, all the time looking in their direction.

A Premature Eulogy

Renée was troubled that her mother had been placed on an IV and antibiotic without her wishes. Having seen her father suffer a prolonged death, she would have preferred that her mother only receive hospice care with neither antibiotics nor IV. She had written an explicit DNR (Do Not Resuscitate) statement, however realizing this was a gray area. Dr. Bacon said that Renée had approved the hospitalization and he felt that the IV was noninvasive and temporary, since it was not the lifeline that a tube feeder would be. He and Renée had negotiated final measures many times, perhaps because of her ambivalence about her mother. He thought—apparently incorrectly—that her most recent position allowed for heroic measures.

Meanwhile, Renée began to write her mother's eulogy. She explained, "No one else could do it." No one else could possibly know who Mrs. Noble had been "in a different time and world." Although I felt that she had anticipated death prematurely, I surmised that she was waiting for Mrs. Noble to pass on as a relief to both of them. During a conversation with her, she began to reflect on qualities that she and her daughter had acquired from Mrs. Noble—propriety, appreciation of niceties, and graciousness. She went on to say that these proprieties were German, not Jewish, in origin and that she preferred the warmer—if less polished—style of Russian Jews like her husband.

Mrs. Noble held on for another 15 months and was quite stable during most of that time. About a year after her first hospitalization, she had another setback with pneumonia and was returned to the unit to die, but remarkably survived. With Elaine no longer there, she had eventually "mellowed out," according to Jenny. No one replaced Elaine; instead, the staff took the approach to "just leave her alone and not bother her." "Benign neglect seems to work," Jenny offered. "Sometimes you just have to let them alone to work it out."

Three months after her battle with pneumonia, Mrs. Noble suffered another one that took her life. Her daughter called me to invite me to her memorial service. In her eulogy, Renée spoke of her mother's heritage as a fine German Jew, of her beauty, graces, and talents. She remembered how, as a little girl, she would proudly walk down the streets of Berlin holding her hand. She spoke of Mrs. Noble's domestic world full of lilacs, fine linen, porcelain, and abundant beauty. She also spoke of how, in spite of these riches, Mrs. Noble had once called Renée her "greatest gift."

The rabbi ended by noting how gracefully Mrs. Noble had carried herself to the very end, in spite of her biological failings. Mrs. Noble, she said, was an example of "the ideal Jewish woman who carries herself with grace and gives of herself lovingly to her family."

Discussion

Although persons with dementia vary widely in the types of capacities they lose and retain, Mrs. Noble retained an especially odd mix. She was no longer continent, could not carry on a verbal conversation, and required total body care, but she retained an uncommon poise and sensitivity to her environment and those within it. She carried herself with the demeanor of someone who had once lived well, and characteristics of her former self—her fondness for attention, self-absorption, and moodiness—not only remained, but had intensified. Despite her compromised memory for persons and events, her semantic memory enabled her to still eat in the European fashion and to develop new relationships. She could not communicate verbally, but she managed to acquire new ways to let her wishes be known.[3] Thus she continued to operate successfully as a social agent. Under her new circumstances as a resident at the home, and with significant disabilities incurred over time, Mrs. Noble developed new selves out of her relations with others to help her survive in that world.

Her acceptance and ongoing acknowledgment from Veronica and Elaine sustained her long after relations with her family had decayed. To both Veronica and Elaine, Mrs. Noble retained her sense of agency as she communicated with them through smiles, crying, gestures, resistance, and if necessary, fighting. Mrs. Noble did not express her needs any differently to Veronica and Elaine than to the rest of the NAs; what was different was the acknowledgment they granted them. This led them to explore and correct whatever core problem might be upsetting her, thus retarding her frustration and escalation of behavior. The other NAs tried instead to find the "right buttons" that would control her behaviors; such instrumental approaches proved unsuccessful.

Veronica genuinely enjoyed Mrs. Noble because of her spunkiness and learned to "read" Mrs. Noble's wishes in order to eliminate problems that could upset her. Playing tag with Mrs. Noble helped Veronica complete her tasks, but it was pleasurable for both of them, not just an instrumental strategy.

Elaine had a more mature relationship with Mrs. Noble—and a different motivation. As a spiritual person, she believed that Mrs. Noble, as a creation of God, required loving attention. Out of love and concern for the residents, she gave much of herself. Even on her days off, she would come to the unit to make sure Mrs. Noble had received decent care. Caregiving for her was not simply a matter of completing tasks; it was a moral rendering and a way of being in the world. In working with Mrs. Noble,

---

3 Persons with advanced dementia, particularly Alzheimer's disease, are said to have lost their ability to learn new information. It is curious, then, that Mrs. Noble, like so many other elders I observed, seemed to have learned new ways of relating interpersonally to communicate her desires. Does not learning how to resourcefully use one's capacities for purposes of communication also constitute new learning? Relational skills, such as face recognition, remain even after one's ability to capture and retain new facts becomes less secure. I would argue that in society the relational skills are the more important.

and others like her, Elaine accepted her "moral obligation [to] prevent the loss of the person to the disease" (Gadow 1988; Downs 1997: 598) and to help preserve her person. However, in spite of her lasting concern for Mrs. Noble, she was forced to move on because of family obligations.

The strategy of "benign neglect" that the Snow 2 staff adopted after Elaine left allowed them to avoid burdensome tasks. Elaine regarded this as "neglectful," not "benign." Nonetheless, benign neglect allowed Mrs. Noble some freedom from their demands and minimized the agitation that occurred whenever they did push her.

Renée had great difficulty identifying that giggling old woman talking to herself in German "gibberish" as the strong woman who had so dramatically affected her life. At the same time, with her mother purportedly no longer able to recognize her as a daughter and her belief that "the person is no longer there," Renée felt more peaceful than she had for much of her adult life. While Lockean scholars would agree with Renée that the person was gone, those adopting a relational view might claim that the "person" of Mrs. Noble indeed could not survive without continued acknowledgment from her daughter or others.

When Renée spoke of the absence of her mother's "person," she was referring more precisely to the absence of a particular self or selves (of the self[2] variety)[4] that had been so prominent before Mrs. Noble was affected by dementia. On the other hand, Renée acknowledged that aspects of her mother's former self (or selves) were still apparent, such as her European style of eating and ability to relate to others. Neither did her emotional outbursts and excessive demands cease; in fact they became even more accentuated as her dementia worsened. Also, new "uncharacteristic" relationships with two male friends at her previous unit, suggested the emergence of yet newer selves.

Such retention of selfhood argues against the "loss" of the person, however compromised her memory or hidden some of her former selves were. To Renée, the person who epitomized "the strong, imposing, highly educated post-Victorian woman" that she hoped to preserve in family memory—a very particular self[2] that conveyed a very partial story about Mrs. Noble—was gone. What remained was all too familiar—the demands, complaints, expectations, and violent outbursts—the less tolerable and less pleasant aspects of her other selves. Up until she perceived

---

4   More precisely, the "person" who required social acknowledgment for survival is the social self or selves (s^2) formed through particular historical relationships (e.g., between Mrs. Noble and her daughter) and maintained through ongoing contact. I would refer the reader to chapter 2, p. 50–51, 54–56, for fuller discussion.

that "the person is not there," Renée remained attentive to her mother. With "the person" missing, however, she found no further reward in relating to a woman whose only surviving selves had caused her so much suffering. With the idealized self no longer in view, Renée could claim that the "person" is not there and break off relations. While doing so afforded her "peace," it led Mrs. Noble to lash out in rage at the rejection.

The eulogy enabled Renée to publicly celebrate and reaffirm the idealized self that Mrs. Noble would carry into posterity. While her premature preparation of the eulogy might have seemed macabre, it was quite consistent with her need to clutch onto the image of her mother that she most valued, but that was now missing in the living Mrs. Noble. Absent in her memorial were those unpleasant qualities Renée preferred to forget; only those warranting glorification figured into her carefully crafted eulogy. Renée declared the "death" of her mother when Mrs. Noble was still alive by announcing that "the person is not there." She was forced to wait until her mother's actual death before she could bestow "life" to her again.[5]

CASE STUDY 2: MRS. FINE: THE "WICKED WITCH OF THE WEST"

"I have nothing—just this, while they have a very big house." (8/11/93)

"My life is full of nothing, and it just gets worse." (9/28/93)

"That is their world, and this is mine; I like it here; there are two good doctors here." (12/28/93)[6]

The last six years were rough for 85-year-old Mrs. Fine. Before coming to Snow 2, she had endured the loss of her home and close male companion, six hospitalizations, and multiple nursing home admissions. About a year prior to her nursing home admissions, she became confused, suffered a stroke, and fell and broke her hip. The stroke left her with a severe speech impediment and her ability to walk suffered as well. Following hip replacement surgery, she experienced periods of depression and delirium, as well

---

5   I thank Sharon Kaufman for bringing to my attention the significance of this reversal of "life in death" and "death in life" as elaborated in her article (Kaufman 2000). See also Leibing (2006).

6   Actual comments of Mrs. Fine during the period of study.

as confusion and hallucinations. These led to brief psychiatric hospitalizations the year before her nursing home admission. She also showed signs of greater cognitive impairment. Although one of her daughters tried to keep her at her home, Mrs. Fine's tearfulness and complaints were more than she could handle, and she arranged for her mother's admission to the nursing home.

Her daughter pulled her out of the psychiatric hospital as soon as possible because she could not bear the effects of the antidepressant on her mother: "I couldn't stand that syrupy sweet woman. I wanted my critical mother back!" While this quality endeared her to her daughter, it gained her the reputation with some staff in the nursing home as the "wicked witch of the west."

Her son-in-law did not mince words about his mother-in-law: "She is domineering, interfered in her daughters' marriages, and even caused me to be separated once. Money is her God. Whenever she sees her family with something nice, she worries that they bought it with her money."

Indeed, the favorite daughter of her resourceful Russian Jewish father, Mrs. Fine learned to be very practical and frugal. From her German Jewish mother, she gained the motivation to complete high school with high honors—quite a feat for a woman of her generation—and also acquired her intellectual snobbery and a taste for the arts.

Admission to the Nursing Home

Mrs. Fine first arrived at the nursing home with a diagnosis of major depression, multi-infarct dementia associated with her stroke, and periodic delirium (which presented with symptoms of paranoia, delusions, and hallucinations). She also had arthritis and a history of falls. While continent at the time, she seemed hostile and too demented for cognitive testing. When tests were administered, she could not even identify her location, age, or married name. She also stated that her husband had died one year ago, when it was actually 20 years ago.

During her three years at the nursing home, Mrs. Fine presented a somewhat unusual medical history with variability in functioning, inconsistent diagnoses, and a history of frequent moves within the facility. Less uncommon, her dementia diagnosis shifted back and forth between Alzheimer's disease, multi-infarct dementia, and mixed dementia. But her clinical picture was irregular and did not follow the expected pattern of progressive decline. Despite her very poor performance on the Blessed cognitive test and a mini-mental status exam[7] (scoring 4 out of 30) soon after admission, she performed much better on both tests three years later (now scoring 21 out of 30).

Since her admission, Mrs. Fine lived on four different units, including Snow 2. At her first unit, she became agitated within a few months and started hitting other residents. The staff decided that she had declined and transferred her to a second unit. There, her behaviors only worsened, and they placed her on a tranquilizer. Her gait became unsteady, she fell, and later she was restrained in her wheelchair. Her care plan indicated that she had become incontinent and was in need of complete hygienic and grooming care (her ADLs). Mrs. Fine also began ritually stripping publicly in the middle of the night and continued to scream at the other residents. Since her behaviors did not resolve, the staff transferred Mrs. Fine to Snow 2.

Mrs. Fine's Transfer to Snow 2

Once Mrs. Fine came to Snow 2, Jenny reassessed her capabilities during a one-on-one interview. She also determined that Mrs. Fine's anger stemmed from her increasing loss of control and dependence on others. Her anger was most apparent during her ADLs; it appeared she wanted to be the one to decide when to do these.

To help promote Mrs. Fine's independence, Jenny explored the possibility of getting her into a physical rehabilitation program so she could start walking again. The physical therapist had previously deemed her a poor candidate for therapy due to her past uncooperative behavior, so denied her the opportunity to begin therapy in the past. Jenny secured Mrs. Fine's promise to cooperate in physical therapy, and Mrs. Fine, true to her word, became ambulatory once again with the help of a walker. Her restored independence helped to improve her mood considerably, her prescription for tranquilizers ended, and she stopped stripping in public.

---

[7] Although the two tests measured somewhat different cognitive elements, the Blessed, for example examining information, memory, and concentration, and the MMSE, memory orientation, concentration, language, and constructional ability (Sano and Weber 2003: 27–28), the difference in Mrs. Fine's performance went beyond differences in the tests. It reflected differences in disposition toward being tested as well as actual differences in her cognitive status during times of testing.

Later, a male NA found her removing her diaper in order to use the toilet. When he reported this to Jenny, she discharged the diaper order. Mrs. Fine was redefined as "continent," and the staff were told to respect this and to help her get to the toilet should she request help. Still later, an NA discovered that although she enjoyed getting baths and would accept assistance with her evening hygienic care, she resisted receiving such help early in the day. Jenny explained to Mrs. Fine that she would not be pushed to receive help except during those times, and she was rarely combative with her care after that. Jenny also informed her staff and the CMs and NAs on other shifts about this change. The night shift were asked not to use diapers, even if she wet the bed. The care plan encouraged her independence, help with requested toileting, and the termination of diaper use. Mrs. Fine improved so markedly that staff visiting from other units could not even recognize her.

Now that she was doing so well, her family encouraged the home to transfer her to a different unit, where residents were functioning at a higher level.

Mrs. Fine at a Different Unit

Mrs. Fine fared poorly on the new unit. She did not like her room, complained incessantly about her roommate, and became aggressive with the staff and other residents. She was placed on a tranquilizer, became more confused, started to strip again publicly, and frequently screamed in anger. The care plan indicated that she had declined cognitively, had become completely incontinent, and had greatly reduced her ability to communicate her needs. Now she required "complete assistance" with grooming, hygiene, bathing. She was back in her wheelchair and needed to be restrained. Her decline led to the very loss of independence that was a principal source of her angry mood. In addition, cognitive testing showed extreme impairment and suggested, "testing corroborates global cognitive dysfunction."

It was Jenny's guess that Mrs. Fine had gotten "lost" on this large unit, with its long narrow halls that made it difficult to keep track of her. Her decline, increasing irritability, stripping activity, and her fights with her roommates and others led to her transfer back to Snow 2. This time she was able to move into a highly coveted private room.

Back at Snow 2

For two weeks, Mrs. Fine continued her nighttime stripping. However, that seemed to stop as soon as Jenny took steps to restore some of her autonomy again. She was removed from restraints and her wheelchair, encouraged to use her walker, and assisted with bathing and hygiene only at times that were agreeable to her. Once she was able to walk on her own, she regained her continence as well. Mrs. Fine's speech *aphasia* (difficulty in finding words)—brought on by her stroke a few years back—had become more severe, making it even more difficult for her to find words and express her thoughts. This difficulty frequently left her tearful and frustrated and only intensified her agitation. Jenny encouraged her staff to be patient with Mrs. Fine to allow her adequate time to gather and articulate her thoughts. These steps helped to improve her verbal communication and to reduce her irritability. Once again, her care plan encouraged supporting her independence and ability to communicate.

A Brief Hospitalization

About eight months after moving back to Snow 2, Mrs. Fine experienced left-side weakness and an inability to speak. She was sent to a hospital for a brief period. Tests indicated that she had not suffered another stroke but, more likely, a TIA (transient ischemic attack), or partial block of oxygen to her brain. Additional neurological assessments showed that she had mild cortical atrophy, no new visible areas of damaged tissue beyond the infarct that physicians detected in the past. The neurological exam showed signs of dementing disease as well, this time assessed as Alzheimer's.

After she returned from the hospital, Mrs. Fine's speech aphasia became somewhat more marked. She continued to be aggressive with other residents, to whom she felt superior, and could not tolerate their visibly disturbed behaviors. During mealtimes she would compare her food with that of other residents and complain. She would frequently hit or yell at other residents or throw food or beverages at them. Although this resembled her previous behavior at the home, a new set of behaviors focused on her family—an obsessiveness about photographs of various family members (repeatedly removing, replacing, or misplacing photographs from her bulletin board), her tearfulness over a daughter who died in early adulthood, and fears that her son-in-law had murdered her daughter. If she had not heard from her daughter every few days, she worried that she had died. She also devised a story explaining how her son-in-law managed to secure her entire estate, forcing her to live here, penniless (McLean, 2006).

Nurses found their own ways of dealing with her. When she complained about food, Jenny would ask the NAs to find uneaten foods from other residents' trays that might please her (e.g., unopened juice or pudding). A couple of NAs would directly confront her about her "unacceptable" behavior. When she would demand something immediately, Jenny would try to comply and then explain that she needed to be more polite next time. The 3:00 p.m. to 11:00 p.m. CM repeated that she would come to her only after she was free. If Mrs. Fine insisted, she warned that she would not come at all if she continued being demanding. All of these seemed to be effective, at least for a while.

If Mrs. Fine were fighting with other residents, the staff would separate her from the others and suggest she return to her room. There, they would find her very tearful, looking at photographs of family members she dearly missed, or perseverating (that is, repetitiously ruminating) about their fates. She began to comment that her life was over and no longer worth living. Sometimes she would scream that someone had been going through her belongings and that something valuable was missing. At other times, she would insist that a man had entered her room. She would occasionally be up at night, yelling on and off throughout the shift. On occasion, she even reverted to disrobing at night.

"Treating" Mrs. Fine

While the staff dealt with specific complaints or incidents, Dr. Mallory, the psychiatrist, felt she needed to do something more general to ease Mrs. Fine's emotional discomfort. Because Mrs. Fine evidenced paranoid thinking, Dr. Mallory considered placing her on Haldol®, a fast-acting antipsychotic medication, until she discovered her poor reaction to it in the past. She asked Jenny's opinion, but Jenny remained noncommittal. She generally preferred to avoid antipsychotic medications because of their dangerous side effects. Although she felt that Mrs. Fine needed something, she was not sure what. Dr. Mallory was looking for clear changes in behavior to justify starting her on medication; she thought perhaps her altercations with other residents were new, but Jenny disagreed.

At the time of this research, the only antidementia medication available was tacrine, but it was used only for people with early dementia. Dr.

Bacon, the physician for the unit, felt there was no actual "treatment" for patients like Mrs. Fine. He had known her since she first arrived at the home and was certain that her behavior now was not really different than it had been in the past. He was not in favor of starting her on any psychiatric medication. "What we are seeing," he insisted, "is just Mrs. Fine." Her behaviors continued to reflect her own personality, albeit they were somewhat more exaggerated. In his view, Snow 2 was equipped to deal with them. He was pleased with the improvement in her functioning and did not want to risk this by introducing psychotropic medications.

Dr. Mallory was not sanguine about using antipsychotic medications with elderly patients, especially when dementia was involved. She realized that certain tranquilizers, especially benzodiazepines, not only made people dizzy, placing them at risk for falls, but could have disinhibiting effects, which could compound agitation. Mrs. Fine's exhibitionistic disrobing may have been simply a side effect of her medication. Even antidepressants can increase agitation in some persons, as happened a few months back when she placed Mrs. Fine on one. On yet another antidepressant, her confusion worsened within a short time. Still, Dr. Mallory did not like to see Mrs. Fine needlessly suffer, and she believed she could help her with the right mix of medications; she simply could not understand Dr. Bacon's position. She also advised moving Mrs. Fine to a higher functioning unit, unaware of her history in the home and better success in Snow 2.

The two physicians differed in their view of the benefits versus risks involved but were able to discuss their views and negotiate on a plan. Dr. Bacon reluctantly agreed to have Mrs. Fine start on another antidepressant, and for a while, her mood improved. She even came back from an evening at her daughter's home, feeling that her son-in-law had actually welcomed her. She fully accepted the need to return to the nursing home, noting, "That is their world, and this is mine." This woman, who had repeatedly shared how much she detested the unit, added, "I like it here; I have two good doctors here."

Dr. Mallory considered the antidepressant instrumental in improving Mrs. Fine's mood. She no longer spoke of dying, and her paranoia reduced dramatically. Her performance on the mini-mental status exam showed higher cognitive functioning than at any time since her admission several years earlier. However, her speech became markedly worse at an unfortunate time because she was about to participate in a discussion group with Dr. Mallory to mingle with higher-functioning residents. Still, she and Dr. Mallory, who clearly enjoyed her company, had developed a strong relationship.

About a month later, the staff reported an abrupt increase in her level of irritability, particularly with the staff. She refused medications, threw food she disliked at other residents, and seemed hostile even to her favorite nurses. Dr. Bacon discovered a severe urinary tract infection (UTI) and sent her to the hospital for treatment. UTIs often exacerbate irritability and can even be accompanied by psychotic symptoms.

Once back from the hospital, Mrs. Fine's annoyance with other residents escalated once again, despite her medication. As Dr. Bacon confidently stated, "This is just Mrs. Fine." The antidepressant was withdrawn again, and her mood remained unchanged.

When I visited her a few weeks later, she looked quite satisfied. She was glad to be back from the hospital, but disappointed that her daughter had not visited. Instead of worrying that her daughter was dead, as she was wont to do, she casually commented, "Well, it doesn't matter as long as she's okay."

Later she told me that she tore off a sign that was on her door. The sign, which read, "Nurse in Charge," had been placed on her door because of a suspected infectious virus she might be carrying. "I just tore the 'Nurse in Charge' sign off my door," she proudly stated. "*I'm* in charge."

"You are protesting?" I asked.

"Yes," she firmly stated.

It appeared she was back to her old spunky self.

Discussion

Dr. Bacon had followed Mrs. Fine since her admission. He was convinced that her variability "is exactly what we would expect from a resident with her history"—referring to the multi-infarct diagnosis. He was hesitant to medicate her, fearing that medication side effects might make matters worse for both Mrs. Fine and the staff. She had achieved a good level of functioning and independence, notwithstanding her depressive mood and complaints and intolerance of others, which were characteristic of her personal baseline. "Why then medicate her?"

From her perspective, Dr. Mallory saw an older woman who was suffering from fear, hallucinations, uncontrolled mood, and death wishes. She wanted to ease Mrs. Fine's suffering so she could enjoy a more comfortable existence. Dr. Bacon did agree to try Dr. Mallory's suggestions, but in the end determined that she was better off without the medications. Although during my last couple of months on the unit Mrs. Fine was functioning much better than she had been earlier and her cognitive assessment showed gains, her mood remained mercurial. Most of the time, she would complain about her environment and worry about her family and money. There were occasions when she seemed accepting of her living situation and did not feel encumbered by constant ruminations about her deceased daughter, and these occasions seemed to be increasing in frequency. Still they were no guarantee that she was becoming fully stable in her moods.

Dr. Bacon saw no problem with this variability; it was "to be expected." Having learned about her personality from her family, and observed her himself since her admission, he was not ready to quiet this woman, even though her behaviors were extreme. Certainly, the Snow 2 staff proved able to handle them in most cases, and they did not pressure him to medicate her.

While Dr. Mallory had hoped to improve her emotional comfort, Dr. Bacon was more concerned about upsetting the delicate balance that allowed Mrs. Fine to function independently at her current level. Even if her complaints and talks about death marked some suffering, they were also a mode of expressivity she had used her entire life, free of medications. And after tasting the "syrupy sweet" woman that antidepressants brought out, even her daughter wanted back the "critical mother" she had known all her life.

Dr. Bacon appreciated this expressive quality of Mrs. Fine as part of her personal history and targeted his interventions at maintaining it, rather than some other idealized standard emotional baseline. Although they differed in approach, both physicians were intent in supporting the *person* of Mrs. Fine, whether that meant accepting her behaviors or softening them. As her condition changed, they continued to revisit the pros and cons of medicating her, developing an ever-changing treatment plan that might optimize the quality of her remaining years.

Similarly, Jenny was able to look beyond the dementia to Mrs. Fine's circumstances and her confinement to the unit. In light of these, she viewed her anger as understandable. Even though Mrs. Fine's speech aphasia made conversing with her slow and difficult, Jenny took time to talk with her to see if she could improve her functioning and then took steps to do so. Locating Mrs. Fine's anger in her forced dependence on others, Jenny developed a plan to restore much of her independence—in striking contrast to the units where her desperate acts of protest were taken as evidence of symptoms needing containment.

Mrs. Fine's dementia exacerbated her condition by allowing a freer expression of attitudes and behaviors that had always been part of her personality. The point of treatment and care, as seen by the Snow 2 team, was not to suppress these expressions—as they often signaled a genuine problem; it was to get at the core of what stimulated them to minimize the impacts and improve her functioning. This approach served to preserve—not pathologize and suppress—the obdurate, cantankerous person, however difficult, who had always been that way. While Jenny achieved this by facilitating Mrs. Fine's independence, the tougher NAs further dignified her person with their greater expectations and demands. Through their combined interpretations, care strategies, and interventions, the Snow 2 staff validated Mrs. Fine as a person, well beyond her dementia, enabling her to function at a level unimaginable in the other units. In acknowledging her need for independence, they nurtured a fundamental human agency that the other units denied.

CASE STUDY 3: MRS. GOLD: A CASE OF "SPECIAL" CARE

> Daughter: "I concentrate on my mother's successes and focus on what is left—what she can still do. My sister writes her off: 'Oh, mom's just demented.'"

> "I am young and should be dancing...."[8]

Mrs. Gold was the 78-year-old mother of Ella, the best friend of the DON, who had known her since grade school. Ella's parents were frail and for the last year had been living together in an apartment at the nursing home complex where the special care units were located. Ella's sister had advocated moving their parents to a long-term care facility in the suburbs, closer to her own home. The family could have afforded a more luxurious facility, but Ella encouraged them to move to this nursing home complex, because it was close to her job and she could easily drop by daily to visit them. A nurse would check in on them daily, and she felt secure knowing that she could depend on the DON to exercise her clout should that be necessary. The decision proved to be a wise one.

---

[8] Another spontaneous comment by Tula, the unit poet.

Deterioration in Mrs. Gold's Condition

Ella's father was suffering from Parkinson's disease, and her mother had been showing signs of cognitive impairment for many years. As her father became weaker and her mother more impaired, it became clear both to Ella and to her father that her mother needed round-the-clock care. Mrs. Gold was diagnosed with a probable mixed dementia and an aphasic speech impairment that distorted her words, reducing her communicative efforts to speech fragments. She also suffered severe pain from peptic ulcers. Her husband told me that her memory began to decline six or seven years earlier with insidious onset; her speech problems developed about four years later. Her ability to understand him and to take care of herself had increasingly deteriorated during these years; she even ceased to recognize what to do with toilet paper. Her confusion had worsened to the point where, along with her extreme speech aphasia and inability to communicate more than single words or fragments, clinicians believed she was beyond cognitive testing.

Mrs. Gold was no longer able to dress herself or sufficiently organized to select her own clothes, and she would become frustrated and angry if her husband called upon her to do so, screaming or hitting him. Mrs. Gold had also become self-abusive, sometimes hitting her head in frustration or repeatedly throwing her body on the floor until she was exhausted. During these times, Mr. Gold couldn't find anything that helped, not even hugging or kissing her. His own condition was also worsening, and dealing with his wife was very difficult. After realizing he could do nothing more to help her, he resigned himself to moving her to the nursing home.

Differing Perceptions About Mrs. Gold's Condition

Ella reported a more positive clinical picture of her mother, which her father considered falsely optimistic: "You can't imagine what she can't do." While detecting occasional signs of cognitive difficulty going as far back as 12 years, Ella detected actual memory problems only a few months earlier. Mrs. Gold's inconsistent pattern of cognitive decline and improvement had also led clinicians to shift their diagnoses multiple times.

While acknowledging her mother's bouts of uncontrollable anger, Ella felt she could appeal to her whenever she lost control by explaining how much she was upsetting those around her. For example, during a recent visit to Ella's home, Mrs. Gold fell to the ground and started banging her head. Ella told her mother how she was scaring her grandchild, and she immediately stopped, saying, "Poor boy." Events like this led Ella to think that her mother understood more than others had realized.

Ella also offered more reasonable explanations for her mother's behavior. For example, she explained how her mother would wake up early and be eager to go out. Her father would want her to get dressed first, but she was unable to dress herself or select an outfit. Despite this inability, however, her mother retained an excellent sense of style, which her father lacked, and would get displeased with his selection; that would further intensify her frustration. This would then escalate into overt anger and, possibly, self-abuse. Ella also attributed some of her mother's bizarre behavior to pain from a peptic ulcer.

Ella's Relation with Her Mother

Mr. and Mrs. Gold were well-educated, financially secure people. They led a socially and politically engaged life and regularly entertained guests at formal dinner parties. Mr. Gold was a "brilliant" businessman, according to Ella, and Mrs. Gold had advanced degrees in the fine arts and was an educator. Both had high expectations for their two daughters, but Mr. Gold had been supportive while Mrs. Gold had been exacting and demanding. Her relationship with her daughters was very tumultuous during their teens and through their mid-twenties. While her sister remained distant from her mother, Ella had since made amends with her, despite vestiges of anger that would regularly surface. At this point she was closer to her mother than either her father or sister and was more inclined than they to try to "read" and understand her. By thus trying, she felt successful in getting her mother to communicate her thoughts using words or groups of fragments that made sense.

Ella understood that her father was himself ill and tired of dealing with these difficulties day in and out. She felt, however, that her sister had "written Mother off" without any effort to try to understand her. "She's just demented!" she would comment bluntly. Ella took a different view: "What matters is what she can still do." She got her mother involved in dancing several years earlier, which Mrs. Gold continued to enjoy. Ella encouraged these areas of her mother's life, sometimes to the point of both their frustration, as when Mrs. Gold failed to meet Ella's expectations.

Although she attributed a rational basis to many of her mother's behaviors, Ella did not discount the possibility that some of her behaviors might stem from hallucinations. She was also not averse to her mother's taking antipsychotic medications if they could be helpful.

Selecting a Unit for Mrs. Gold

Mr. Gold resigned himself to the reality that his wife needed nursing home care. Ella discussed various possibilities with the DON, who invited her to visit different units. Although Ella preferred sending her mother to a unit with better-functioning residents, more natural light, and a prettier color scheme, the DON suggested Snow 2 because of Jenny's willingness to accommodate the family's desire for individualized care. Jenny offered to assign Elaine to provide consistent care for Mrs. Gold during the day shift, despite "official policy" against permanent assignments. The 11:00 p.m. to 7:00 a.m. CM also agreed to assume responsibility for Mrs. Gold while conducting her other duties. The 3:00 p.m. to 11:00 p.m. CM refused to commit a special NA to Mrs. Gold but seemed willing to give her considerable attention.

Despite this support, Ella had concerns about the lack of stimulation at Snow 2 and the difficulty of finding volunteers to spend time with her mother there. Mr. Gold also questioned sending his wife there because, as a former volunteer to the unit, he realized "what a sorry lot they were." At the same time, he thought that the staff might give his wife "special attention" because her warmth, affection, and engaging personality would be a welcome contrast to the other residents. Ella's sister continued to bristle at the idea that her mother would be in a unit with so many impaired residents. In the end, the sisters agreed to give Snow 2 a try, and Mrs. Gold was admitted there.

The staff on Snow 2 tried to be sensitive to Mrs. Gold and respectful of her background. After hearing her tell Ella that the staff "treat us like children," Jenny no longer included her in activities such as ball tossing. Instead, she would give her some papers to sort—something more familiar to her as a former teacher. One time when this backfired, and Mrs. Gold started pulling charts from the nurses' station, the PA came up to her and said, "Thank you. I need to take these back now. Doctor's orders!" Mrs. Gold willingly handed them over with a smile.

From the very beginning, Mr. Gold came to see his wife daily for brief visits. Sometimes she welcomed him with pleasure; at other times, she would act as if he were not there. She always responded to Ella, but not always favorably. With the move to Snow 2, Mrs. Gold's emotional outbursts subsided, and she never expressed anger or self-destructive behavior to the staff. In fact, her warm hugs and kisses earned her the reputation of being exceptionally sweet. Mrs. Gold would still get angry with Ella, though, particularly if she pushed her to do more than she could. One day, Ella took her mother to a piano performance at a different unit. Afterwards, Mrs. Gold merrily danced to some music with her daughter. When Ella pushed her mother to play the piano, however, she refused and got angry. At other times when they were at odds, recognizing a favorite nurse would improve Mrs. Gold's mood, much to Ella's chagrin. Despite the tension that regularly surfaced in their relationship, however, Mrs. Gold looked forward to Ella's daily visits every morning on her way to work and often again in the evening.

Mrs. Gold's Deterioration in Snow 2

Mrs. Gold appeared quite vigorous when she first entered the unit. Within one week however, she began to deteriorate. She started to lean heavily to one side whenever she would try to walk—a new development. To prevent her from falling, the staff placed her in a seat-belted wheelchair during the day. At night, they placed her in a posey restraint (straps attached to the bed rails) in her bed and lifted the side bedrails. Mrs. Gold hated the restraints and fussed to get out of them. At one point, she banged her wheelchair so hard that it fell over, fortunately not injuring herself. She was then given Serax®, an antianxiety medicine, to help calm her. The combination of Serax® with the medications she had been on for several months—a painkiller for her ulcers and Navane®, an antipsychotic medication—appeared to exacerbate her unsteadiness and agitation.

Seeing her mother like this, Ella decided that she needed one-on-one care. However, the monthly nursing home bills were diminishing her parents' resources, and the family was in no position to pay for a private companion. Ella could not find a volunteer willing to come to this unit, so considered moving her mother to a unit with volunteer help. Jenny, who did not like to lose residents, convinced her to keep her mother on Snow 2, promising she would do everything she could to accommodate Mrs. Gold's needs.

Dr. Bacon, the unit physician, decided to withdraw Mrs. Gold gradually from all medications and she began to restore her balance. However, Ella feared her mother would be in pain without her ulcer medication so she asked Dr. Bacon to place her on it again. Dr. Bacon complied, but she became very confused and more agitated and unsteady on her feet and developed a dramatic reversal in her sleep pattern, where she remained awake all night long. Mrs. Gold also began repeatedly stripping off her clothes and shoes, especially at night. The sleep impairment was new for her, and Dr. Mallory appealed to Ella to let her give her mother a sleeping pill at night to try to correct the pattern. Ella refused.

Dr. Bacon reluctantly placed Mrs. Gold again back on her medications, and she began to improve. He then gradually withdrew the psychotropic medications (the Navane® and the Serax®), but Mrs. Gold once again had a setback. Again, he restored the medications. Then Ella noticed that her mother was overly sedated and asked him once again to withdraw them. He did so, very gradually, this time with eventual success. It took about two months before Mrs. Gold was back to her pre-admission status, despite an infection that led to a brief setback.

The nursing staff felt that Ella's initial interference with the ulcer medication had triggered her mother's problems. They also felt she was unrealistic and overly demanding of the staff during the two-month recovery period. Furthermore, she was successful in gaining the backing of the administration to secure unreasonable expectations from the staff. Even Dr. Bacon, who was incredibly patient with Ella and accommodating to her requests, found her forceful approach offensive. In the end Mrs. Gold improved, but at quite a cost to the staff.

Restraints as "False" Protection

During this period, Mrs. Gold would stay up all night and be drowsy throughout the day. Since she was very unsteady on her feet, the staff would sometimes place her in a belted wheelchair or bed restraint. She hated the restraints, and the staff attempted to limit their use as much as possible. Jenny used the belted wheelchair only when Mrs. Gold was so unsteady she was at risk of falling. Mrs. Gold could unlock the seat belt without getting agitated. Whenever Ella found her mother in the wheelchair, she would take her for a walk. Ella told the staff she wanted her mother walking as much as possible. Because her mother's gait varied considerably, even within a single shift, the staff also varied the degree of freedom they would allow her.

The DON let it be known that Mrs. Gold was to be carefully watched. Jenny afforded Mrs. Gold more freedom than did the charge nurses (the CMs) on later shifts. They realized that if anything should happen to her, they would be in trouble, so preferred keeping her in a belted wheelchair until someone was free to be with her. However, they did not use a geri-chair and no longer raised the bars on her bed at night because these only agitated her more. Although Mrs. Gold did fall a few times without restraints, her greatest injuries occurred when she tried to get out of them. For this reason, Jenny and the regular charge nurses avoided restraints as much as possible. Ella requested that they be discontinued entirely but refused to sign a statement releasing the home from responsibility should her mother fall and injure herself without them.

It is not uncommon for injuries to occur during weekends when an irregular staff, who do not understand the nuances of care demanded by a resident, are working. The weekend CM, for example, placed Mrs. Gold in a geri-chair for protection. She objected by violently rocking and toppling it over, fortunately sustaining only minor bruises. That night, to further protect her, the CM put up side bars in her bed, even though there was no order for doing that. Mrs. Gold climbed over them and fell, receiving a haematoma on her head.[9] Restraints also led Mrs. Gold to rely on diapers, which Ella opposed.

The Administrative Mandate for One-on-one Care

It was at this point that the DON told the staff they must give Mrs. Gold one-on-one attention and stop using restraints, except for an occasional seat belt. Dr. Bacon ordered a special floor-level bed to prevent injuries from bed falls. A key goal was to return her to a normal sleep pattern, by tiring her out at night. A nurse supervisor came in at every shift to see if the staff were walking her enough to tire her out.

The nurses felt their nursing supervisors fostered preferential treatment and were insufficiently staffed to expect one-on-one care. At the same time, they recognized that Mrs. Gold did improve cognitively with this kind of care and thrived personally on it. What bothered them were the continual stream of demands by Ella and the administration when they were already so overextended. The administrators also insisted that Mrs. Gold be awakened, cleaned, and dressed for breakfast before the other residents so she would be ready for her daughter's morning visit.

---

[9] Growing recognition of such dangers have led many homes to discontinue the practice of restraining residents in their beds and to new regulations against them.

And despite their efforts, Ella did not hesitate to show dissatisfaction if she found her mother without a shoe or still in pajamas.

Mrs. Gold also seemed to act differently with her daughter than with the staff. She enjoyed attention, but used different strategies to get it with each. With her daughter, she would act helpless or faint, needlessly worrying her—behavior Jenny would not tolerate. At the same time, she rarely revealed the kinds of disturbances that made the lives of the nurses so difficult—like banging her wheelchair against tables and repeatedly removing her clothing or shoes after repeated dressings. Because she did not see these behaviors, Ella thought that the staff had exaggerated them.

Extraordinary Demands on the Staff

During the two months it took for Mrs. Gold to return to her pre-admission state, the staff offered creative solutions and exerted extraordinary energy to return her to that baseline. When the bed Dr. Bacon ordered didn't work out, he ordered two others until an acceptable solution was found. The staff from all shifts paid close attention to her, keeping someone with her at all times and walking her regularly to tire her out. Elaine was exceptionally attentive, and the CMs from later shifts made sure someone would be watching her, or kept her with them as they conducted their rounds. But even these actions did not satisfy the supervisors.

CMs from the later shifts resented the extreme oversight and intense degree of attention that nurse supervisors mandated without providing additional help. If a supervisor found Mrs. Gold sitting alone in a wheelchair, she wanted to know why she was not being walked. If she found her walking on her own, she demanded to know why she was not being assisted. If some of her clothes or shoes were off, the supervisor insisted that she immediately be dressed, no matter how often Mrs. Gold would remove them. During the night shift, the charge nurse, who had only one or two assistants to care for 40 residents, was becoming overwhelmed with her responsibility to look after Mrs. Gold. This was a particularly strenuous time of the day because of Mrs. Gold's pattern of sleep reversal. When Mrs. Gold was willing, she placed her in a geri-chair between walks, so she could keep an eye on her while doing her paper work or conducting rounds. At other times, she was forced to keep her tagging along with her as she cared for the other residents. If Mrs. Gold started removing her clothes, she had to replace them. This could continue repeatedly throughout the night and would severely distract her from other business. The administration never followed through on their discussion to hire an additional NA to help her.

An Illustrative Vignette

It was not only the requests that disturbed the CMs, it was the demanding tone with which the supervisors made them. Upon finding Mrs. Gold still seated after dinner, one supervisor commanded, "I don't want her sitting in that chair all night; I want someone to be walking her." Such demands were all too common.

The injustice of this supervisor's demands struck an ironic chord one evening as she spoke with me about Mrs. Gold's problems. She explained that walking was necessary to tire out Mrs. Gold and that the demands on the staff would only last a little while longer until her sleep pattern would return to normal. As we spoke, Mrs. Gold walked up to her and gestured her to come with her. The supervisor laughed awkwardly and said, "Oh no, I don't have time." When Mrs. Gold walked up to her again later, she repeated, giggling, "Oh no, I have my rounds to do!"

The supervisor then softened her tone a bit as she faced the CM and said, "I know it's hard, but if you tire her out, it will be better." The CM looked at her in disbelief. Later she asked, "How can she expect so much from us when she runs away herself?"

Providing such a high level of care did not occur without consequence. The charge nurses from the later shifts were so overworked that they were on the verge of quitting, and one did transfer out. By then Mrs. Gold was back to her own sleep routine and steady on her feet again.

Discussion

This case study illustrates both the delicacy of the elder with dementia as well as the value of minutely attentive caregiving for optimizing her condition. It shows the immense vulnerability of some elders to medication changes, while illustrating the extraordinary energy that went into restoring unnecessary disabilities that can result from such adjustments. This case study also represents an all too uncommon example of a positive outcome that resulted from family will, administrative pressure, and staff diligence. Ella's positive expectations led to persistent demands for medication adjustments and highly attentive caregiving. Despite her excessive optimism about her mother's condition, the requests it produced led to major improvements in her mother.

At the same time, the demands placed upon the nursing staff were excessive and demoralizing in the absence of adequate resources and administrative support. Equally problematic, and ethically troubling, was the administration's consumption of limited staff time and resources to a single resident, away from others with similar needs. As much as Mrs. Gold thrived under this attention, many other residents' needs were undoubtedly sacrificed as a result. Certainly Mrs. Gold was not the only elder who disliked restraints, or the only one who might have benefited from a special bed. Nor was she the only resident who might have benefited from discontinuing sleeping pills or retained some degree of independence and continence by being walked. Even on a more accommodating unit like Snow 2, such measures are too often neglected.

Ella, out of her good fortune in knowing the DON, was able to secure one-on-one care for her mother, but she was not alone in considering her mother to be entitled to such care given the high cost of the special care unit. However, she was spared the disappointment so many other family members face when they discover that the individualized care is not to be had.

Optimizing the condition of elders like Mrs. Gold is an ongoing, consuming process that varies with changes in the elder's condition. The Snow 2 staff succeeded in minimizing Mrs. Gold's agitation, steadying her gait, and returning her to a normal sleep pattern by adjusting and readjusting her medications, purchasing special beds, and giving her one-on-one attention. The supervisors correctly predicted that special attention would be needed only for a temporary transitional period until she was stabilized. Indeed, she became stabilized after a couple of difficult months, after which the demands on the nursing staff lightened. Still, their patience and diligence were heroic.

From my observations, whenever a single setback occurs after medications are withdrawn, the nursing staff typically note this on the chart in order to prevent staff from withdrawing the medication in the future. Dr. Bacon's repeated additions and withdrawals of the same medications were extremely rare, and in the end this proved effective. Dr. Bacon was receptive to doing so because he worried about the risks associated with psychotropic medications with cognitively impaired elders, and he was willing to find a way to eliminate them.

The medical and nursing staff designed treatment directed at preserving Mrs. Gold's existing strengths, restoring potential functioning, and preventing further decline through experimentation, innovation, and devoted personal attention. Her "special" care was person-oriented, tailored to her unique needs, and directed at eliminating medical problems or drug effects that impeded optimal functioning.

In a system driven by cost efficiency, the care model used with Mrs. Gold may appear unrealistic. Snow 2, which has its own restricted care economy, made an exception for Mrs. Gold because of her daughter's relationship to the DON. However, even when cost efficiency is taken into account, models of care that lead to positive outcomes like Mrs. Gold's cannot be ignored. The challenge is to develop person-centered care that may be high-intensity at times, but sufficiently productive that both the resident and staff are rewarded. Such care will require a supportive and adequate staff and supervisors whose vision includes preferential treatment not only for select residents, but for all of them.

Postscript

Soon after Mrs. Gold recovered her balance and prior sleep pattern, Ella considered moving her mother once again to a unit with higher-functioning residents and more musical activities. Given Mrs. Gold's fragility and the support she had received from the Snow 2 staff, I questioned the wisdom of such a move.

Several months later, after I had left the unit, I called Ella to ask her how her mother was doing. She said that she had been doing even better than when I last saw her, but that she was no longer residing on the unit. I was shocked. Ella's sister, who hated coming to Snow 2, decided their mother would be better off at a new facility closer to her own home. Although Ella initially objected, she liked the stronger activities program she found there and finally submitted to her sister's pressure. Ella felt the new facility was beautiful and had a more extensive activities program, but she claimed that the staff refused to make the kinds of accommodations to which Ella and Mrs. Gold had grown accustomed. The change proved disastrous for Mrs. Gold, according to her daughter. Mrs. Gold became more confused and agitated once again, was placed on antipsychotic medication, and declined further. According to Ella, the staff at the new facility attributed the decline to the *inevitability* of the disease process—the *natural* expectation for a woman with her condition. As such, minimal effort was expended to restore her to her prior state, as they judged her as having progressed beyond recovery. Thus, the medical staff there felt reluctant to expend effort to titrate medications in hopes of restoring her functioning. The facility was also out of easy reach for Ella, and without her daily visits and the lack of attentive treatment, Mrs. Gold further declined. Ella felt impotent to do any more for her mother because she feared that returning Mrs. Gold to Snow 2 would at this point only exacerbate her confusion.

CHAPTER 7

Comparing Caregiving of Snow 1 with Snow 2

The case studies from the previous two chapters provide examples of two contrasting approaches to dementia "care" giving, with extremely different outcomes for the recipients. These *internal unit-level differences* in caregiving were not part of a deliberate research design, but developed naturally over time under the direction of the head nurse on each unit, and provide important clues about nonmedical factors that can profoundly affect outcome.

The Snow units differed in the ways that their staff interpreted BDs and the strategies they adopted for dealing with them. They also had different care priorities for caregiving, ways of organizing their staff to meet perceived care needs, and collaborative relations with other professionals and families to help minimize BDs and maximize the functioning and quality of life of residents. The resulting differences in outcome for the residents in the case studies were dramatic. While elders in the Snow 1 continued to decline, those in Snow 2 maintained or even improved their functioning, despite the similar diagnoses of elders in the two groups. One can only imagine how different the fates of all residents might have been had they resided on the other unit.

It would be a mistake, however, to present Snow 2 as an ideal unit. Although it clearly outweighed Snow 1 in its success with the behaviorally disturbed elders in the case studies, it did so by placing excessive pressure on particular staff members. In addition, despite its successes in these cases, Snow 2 fell short of extending adequate quality care to many of the other residents of the unit. Similarly, while Snow 1 had clear shortcomings, it also had strengths, such as the greater personal interest its young NAs took in the biographies of their residents. Still, there were vast overall differences in the outcomes of behaviorally disturbed residents of the two units. This chapter will draw on material from the case studies in chapters 5 and 6, together with additional findings from my research, to examine characteristics that profoundly differentiated the two units and enabled Snow 2 residents to fare better. Additional conditions affecting caregiving on the units will then be addressed.

CHARACTERISTICS DIFFERENTIATING SNOW 2 FROM SNOW 1

The head nurses of the Snow units exerted considerable influence in shaping caregiving because they held particular assumptions about persons with dementia and their care needs, were in a position to promote certain caregiving approaches and priorities based on those assumptions, and could organize their staff to implement these. However, their ability to effect the kind of care that matched their expectations was limited by the support of their nursing and professional staff. The characteristics that differentiated the two Snows, then, reflected in great part, but not entirely, the head nurse's vision about quality care.

Four characteristics differentiated and shaped the quality of care and outcomes of residents on Snow 2 from those on Snow 1:

- the staff's ability to look beyond the disease to the *person* with dementia and pay attention to his or her wishes, feelings, and behaviors
- their relative preference for a person-centered intersubjective approach to dementia care over a standardized task-centered instrumental approach

- the level of flexibility and willingness of the head nurse to organize her staff to satisfy nonstandard personalized care priorities within the given care economy
- the degree to which open communication among the head nurse and professional and nursing staff and with families enabled a sharing of knowledge that could promote optimal caregiving

1. Looking Beyond the Disease to the Person

Looking beyond the disease to the person with dementia requires *taking the resident seriously as a human being.* Thus it credits elders with dementia as having *agency,* or intentionality and purpose behind their words and actions that it sees as more than empty gestures, expressions, or behaviors produced by the dementia. The Snow 2 staff was more receptive to this perspective, which was described in chapter 2 as the *communications perspective* on behavioral disturbances.

In her work as an NA of Snow 2, Elaine attributed a *purpose* or *intentional communication* behind *everything* a resident said or did, including BDs. As a caregiver, she felt an essential part of her job was to understand an elder's communication and any problems or concerns signaled by it. Jenny, the head nurse of Snow 2, also took residents seriously, even though she was somewhat less convinced than Elaine was that *all* BDs were meaningful. As a nurse whose entire career had been devoted to long-term chronic care, Jenny was attentive to finding ways to improve the functioning and life quality of residents in spite of their impairments. With the residents on her unit, she was thus tuned in to disabilities that could be corrected and to the potential for improving such functions as mobility and continence. Although she was realistic about the inability to treat the dementia itself, she tried to minimize disabilities that contributed to the elder's overall impairment.

For example, despite Mrs. Fine's long history of confinement to a wheelchair, Jenny was willing to take steps that had never been tried before to allow her to function more independently. By observing and listening to Mrs. Fine, Jenny concluded that Mrs. Fine's agitation resulted from her reluctant dependence on others, so she helped Mrs. Fine begin physical therapy to regain her ability to walk. After spending three years restrained in a wheelchair and being viewed as incontinent, Mrs. Fine learned to walk with the technical aid of a walker and eventually regained her continence. She thus became more self-reliant, more content, and able to function at a much higher level in spite of her dementia. As Mrs. Fine's autonomy increased, the severity of her dementia seemed to decline. Remarkable improvements such as these, which are not expected in dementia, have been labeled *rementia*, or a reversal of the dementia (Kitwood 1989: 5). What is more likely is that her previously untreated disabilities, excessive medications, incontinence, BDs, and confinement in restraints—together with the unhappiness these produced—made her behave and present as more impaired than her capabilities allowed. The improvements were achieved because Jenny was willing to take Mrs. Fine's words and actions seriously.

Similarly, when Mrs. Gold complained about being restrained in her bed or the geri-chair, the Snow 2 staff responded to her requests while still ensuring her safety. They ordered a very low bed that allowed her to be unrestrained. One nurse would ask her to stay in the geri-chair just a bit longer until she could take her for a walk. Another would let her tag along during rounds. Eventually, when she was more steady on her feet, Mrs. Gold was seated in a wheelchair with a belt she could unbuckle; once she became safe on her feet, she was free to walk on her own again.

In contrast to the Snow 2 staff, Hazel, who headed Snow 1, seemed unable to differentiate the person with dementia from the disease itself. Thus, the diagnosis of dementia served to stigmatize residents of Snow 1. Because of their cognitive impairments, Hazel distrusted and disregarded *anything* they said or did. To Hazel, BDs provided evidence of the organic irreversibility of their disease—something she could not change—rather than communicative information about their condition or inward state— which she could address. Given her training in acute care, she was accustomed to treating persons whose symptoms stemmed from a specific, usually treatable, cause. Since dementia itself could not be treated, she lost sight of the possibility of *any* kind of recovery and concluded that all she could do was to provide maintenance and custodial care. She thus placed a low priority on correcting "excessive" disabilities (OTA 1992), such as hearing losses, and disregarded suggestions from families about how to minimize them. For Hazel, the problems of the residents of Snow 1 were too great to be corrected by means of the localized solutions families frequently suggested.

The Pathologization of Agency in Snow 1

Hazel's acute care training predisposed her to a strongly biomedicalized view of residents with dementia. As a result, she tended to regard their words and actions as the *disease artifacts* of the dementia itself and ignored the messages and meanings they may have contained. By attributing their behaviors entirely to disease process and ignoring the intentionality behind them, Hazel pathologized the agency of these elders, declaring their actions meaningless and rendering the elders powerless to communicate feelings, needs, or wishes. By disregarding the communicative content of their BDs as expressions of genuine need, she also thwarted her staff from adequately addressing their problems, often exacerbating them. Such exacerbation was not more evidence of pathology, but an understandable response to the violence of being denied their agency (Sabat and Harré 1992: 453).

When Margaret's screams increased in intensity and frequency, Hazel concluded her disease precipitated the decline. She never considered that the disease, *which could not be corrected*, made Margaret less tolerant of adverse environmental conditions—like noise or getting water in her ears—*that could be corrected*. Hazel didn't believe that Margaret's agitation—which only escalated when left unresolved—could have been prevented by using the rubber bonnet that prevented her ears from getting wet. Hazel's refusal to use the bonnet stood in sharp relief to the way in which Elaine and Denise of Snow 2 immediately stopped rinsing Mrs. Noble's hair with a hose as soon as they realized it upset her. Their intervention prevented the kind of escalation or agitation that continued unceasingly in Margaret.

The Snow 1 staff also pathologized Carl and Vicki's romance as the product of diseased brains, not evidence of possible new selves[1] emergent from their relationship. Carl's desire was redefined as pathology and "treated" with psychotropic medications. The staff tried to protect Vicki from his advances despite her own desire for them; lacking reason, the desires of both of them were entirely disregarded. When Carl's "treatment" failed, the couple were permanently separated, and each severely declined. Interventions such as these "circumscribe human possibilities and therefore cut short human development" even at the latest stages of life (Moody 1988: 35). Despite severe impairment in memory and other cognitive functions, the pair retained the will, but were not permitted to pursue a meaningful relationship.

The continued capacity of the couple to relate by presenting their social identities (i^2) (See chapter 2, pp. 50–51, 54–56) to the other helped to sustain each of them as they faced the unraveling of their former selves; their own

---

[1] The "selves" referred to here are the variety of selves (s^2) produced intersubjectively through a particular relationship with another person any time during the course of development during that person's life. (Please see chapter 2, pp. 50–51, for further discussion.)

abilities were cut short, however, by the staff's inabilities to see beyond pathology. Other clinicians have described how similar events have led elders to stop eating and eventually die from a "failure to thrive" (Robertson and Montagnini 2004). Such occurrences are the all too common outcomes of policies that reduce relational capacities of sentient human beings, however demented, to the products of disease.

In another case at Snow 1, Hazel and the PA assessed a woman's complaints of intense stomach pain as "standard," given her history of chronic constipation, and possibly evidence that her dementia was worsening. After two weeks of her needless suffering and considerable pressure from her family, the nurse ordered an X-ray, which revealed a serious blockage. If the staff had taken her complaints seriously and acted sooner, the woman could have received medication and been spared suffering.

When another resident's earnest pleas for release from his geri-chair went unheard, he managed to tip it over and damage it. After being seated in an ordinary chair with a posey (a strap-like restraint), he seemed actually quite content. However, as soon as the geri-chair returned from the shop, Hazel insisted that he use it, despite his desperate pleas. A federal government listing registered geri-chairs as less severe restraints than poseys, and since the nursing home was trying to reduce the severity of restraints to fulfill a federal mandate, Hazel wanted to use the geri-chair. What were ignored were the man's own preference and *experience* of what was restraining. *Rather than using the federal listing as a guideline to better serve the man, the man became an instrument to better serve the mandate!* The status of the institution's restraint use mattered more than the persons for whom the mandate had been developed in the first place. *Used in this way the mandate ironically served to induce, rather than relieve, misery.* How different he would have fared on Snow 2!

2. Person-centered Intersubjective versus Task-centered Instrumental Approaches to Caregiving

A caregiver's perspective about caregiving derives from the way in which she regards the person with dementia and her needs. Because of the vulnerability of the elder who is placing trust in the caregiver, there is also a *moral dimension* to the caregiving relationship. The caregiver who tries to understand an elder's communications as she proceeds with care is likely to view caregiving as a *person-focused, intersubjective* endeavor that must be respectful and supportive of the elder. Intersubjective care is above all person sustaining, reinforcing the subjectivity of the elder by engaging with her interpersonally throughout the caregiving process. Because the emphasis is on preserving the person, such care approaches respect the elder's wishes and personal preferences and are sensitive to the elder's identity and history.

In contrast, a caregiver who does not take into account an elder's personal feelings and wishes during the process of "care" giving is likely to view it as an *instrumental task-focused* enterprise. Instrumental acts are done to objects, in this case, bodies, in contrast to intersubjective caregiving, which is done *with* persons. With instrumental caregiving, completing the task, not rendering care, becomes the goal; thus the person becomes the means for accomplishing the task, rather than the reason for doing it. This may be why the elder who receives instrumental "care" may be seen as actually "getting in the way" of the task. Instrumental caregiving regards medications and other technologies mainly as tools to *manage* the elder so that the caregiver can complete the tasks, rather than as aids to helping the elder herself. In such cases, the caregiver exercises control over those who are unable to resist—a practice some bioethicists consider to be potentially immoral (Gadow 1988; Martin and Post 1992: 57).

Snow 2

For Jenny and Elaine, caregiving was an intersubjective endeavor involving the elder every step of the way. While mindful of the need to complete her care tasks, Elaine was equally mindful of the need to preserve the dignity of the person for whom she assumed responsibility. This required sensitivity to the elder's feelings, mood, and comfort and to some extent attention to her history. For example, Elaine observed how Mrs. Noble insisted on mixing all her food together before eating it. Although it delayed her from moving on to other care tasks and residents, Elaine was patient and allowed her to perform this ritual because doing this relaxed her and helped her remember how she had prepared her own meals in the past. The act of stirring and mixing her food returned a measure of control over her highly managed life, and contributed to her desire to eat. Through her patience and efforts to "draw out" Mrs. Noble (cf. Lyman 1993: 31), Elaine did what she could to support her person. She worked skillfully, not only in maintaining aspects of her older pre-morbid self (cf. Martin and Post 1992: 57), but also in advancing Mrs. Noble's current self in the institutionalized setting.

Elaine could have made her own life easier by adopting the "benign neglect" attitude of other NAs that justified ignoring care needs. Recognizing the importance of hygiene for health, she refused to do so. Instead, she would find ways to work with the elders by talking, laughing, touching, and if necessary, using diversion. If these failed, she would try to determine and correct the source of the problem (e.g., a pain or itch) or leave and return when the resident felt ready. She would *never* use force or impose her will over the elder; doing so was entirely unacceptable.

Knowing she could not effect cure, Elaine tried to preserve the identities[2] and personhood (See chapter 2, pp. 39–47, 50–51), of elders through caregiving that diminished their dependency and vulnerability (Gadow 1988: 7). By engaging subjectively with the elders and preserving their vitality, Elaine accepted the "moral obligation [of] preventing the loss of the person to the disease" (Martin and Post 1992: 57). She adopted an ethics of *intimacy* (Martin and Post 1992: 57) as she involved herself with them strictly as a *way of being*. For Elaine as a spiritual person and masterful caregiver, such caring embodied an *ethic of love* and was a *moral act*, meaningful in and of itself, independent of outcome (Gadow 1988: 7). As elders like Mrs. Noble experience the unraveling of their selves, caregivers like Elaine sustain their personhood[3] through intersubjective engagement that reinforces their unique identities, affirms their personal worth, and respects their dignity. This is the core of person-preserving dementia care that graced those under her care.

Snow 1: The Limitations and Risks of Instrumental Dementia "Care" Giving

From Hazel's perspective, however, caring as an end in itself seemed wasteful given the other compelling needs her limited staff needed to address. Through her acute care training, she came to regard *cure* or recovery as the goal. With neither in sight, she gravitated toward a *nihilistic* view of dementia care that regarded anything more than bodily maintenance and custodial care as "unrealistic" and wasteful in a tight care economy. By favoring standardized "maintenance care" over residents' own feelings,

---

[2] Identity here can refer to any single or combination of types of identities (i^1, i^2, i^3) discussed in chapter 2, pp. 50–51. Preserving identity[1] (i^1) would refer to preserving the will of the elder. To preserve identity[2] (i^2) would mean protecting the ability of the elder to project one or more selves, new or old. A third level, that is also appropriate in Elaine's case, would be identity[3] (i^3), which refers to yet a higher level of cultural understanding about the preservation of the person in caregiving beyond any reliance on a former self.

[3] I am speaking here of relational personhood, based on sustained acknowledgment from others, rather than attributional personhood, which depends on personal attributions such as cognition or reason. See chapter 2, pp. 44–49, for further discussion.

wishes, and expressions of need, she promoted a program of *instrumental* "care" delivery that directed her staff, above all, to complete and chart their ADLs. The focus here was the *body* and the *task*, not the person or her dignity. Indeed when a family member asked the staff to do something (like replace a diaper with a panty) for reasons of personal dignity, she would privately comment, "Whose dignity, hers or the resident's?"[4]

Hazel's instrumental approach too often ignored needs that were pressing, feelings that were legitimate, and conditions that warranted attention, such as the bowel blockage of the woman mentioned above. Addressing these needs would have improved the quality of residents' lives, prevented the exacerbation of their symptomatology, and possibly resolved their BDs before they could escalate to the point of intractability, as occurred with Margaret.

Hazel felt that NAs who took considerable amounts of time to relate with those under their care were trying to avoid "real" work. This is why she preferred Rose, the fast, efficient NA whom families and residents dreaded, over the slower, attentive NA they adored. Hazel's only complaint with Rose was that by working *against* residents, she tended to get injured and miss workdays! As she plowed through her work, Rose *managed* the residents who "got in the way" of completing her "care" tasks by yelling, pushing, or holding down their hands so tightly that they became bruised. Such exercises of power over defenseless, failing elders damage both bodies and spirits and raise the specter of immorality to which bioethicists have alerted us.

Rose did not see it that way. As a recent Asian migrant to the United States, she saw no reason to respect elders whose own children had abandoned them to a nursing home—something she couldn't imagine doing to her own mother (cf. Shield 2003: 208).[5] To her these elders had already lost their dignity, so did not deserve her respect. They had ceased to be

---

4 Hazel actually raises and problematizes an important point. The uses and misuses of the term "dignity" deserve exploration. Although a valid concern, questions must be asked about how dignity is used, by whom, and for what purposes. One example is illustrated by the state official who claimed that Jenny had violated the rule that food groups must not be mixed because of "reasons of human dignity." There is danger in applying such an objective and standardized view of dignity, however. What if the elder prefers to have her food groups mixed, or won't eat it otherwise? Must her dignity be maintained by violating her own wishes. Clearly such objectified notions of dignity are misguided.

5 Renée Rose Shield (2003) found similar attitudes from foreign-born NAs at the home she studied. However, while they also believed that families should provide direct care to their aging parents, they did not show this kind of negative attitude to the elders themselves.

soulful persons, so she "processed" them like objects on an assembly line. To Kitwood, such "care" giving involves "treachery" and "intimidation" that is itself destructive of persons (1990: 181–82). Indeed, as seen in the Snow 1 examples, *such approaches preserve neither persons nor bodies.* Nonetheless, this ethic of cold, detached labor suited the instrumental tasks Hazel had defined.

Any program of dementia care built on instrumental goals risks fostering a mentality and practices that are dehumanizing and immoral and that may attract dominating persons who disrespect those under their care. Such programs may even congratulate these practices! Because of these risks, gerontologist Harry Moody objects to instrumental gerontology (Moody 1988: 33). Even caregivers who are not predisposed to such practices may become instruments of control in caregiving settings that are directed by instrumental goals. This is what occurred with the nurses on Snow 1 who were directed by their Director of Nursing to apprehend and forcibly bathe Rebecca—an event that took its toll both on her body and person, even in the absence of dementia.

3. Flexibility in Arranging for Non-standard Care

Dementia, as we have seen, is never standard in its manifestations and course. While standard care (e.g., grooming, toileting, bathing) is required for all residents, how it is performed varies with each resident, caregiver, and the relationship they have (or have not) achieved. In addition, residents vary widely in their additional care needs, such as for prosthetic devices like walkers, dentures, glasses, and hearing aids. This is why individualized care plans and care priorities cannot be standard. Still, planning, organization, and ingenuity are often required to accomplish the standard, let alone nonstandard, care routines within a care economy of limited NAs and shift hours. Given their conceptual differences about persons with dementia and their care needs, it is not surprising that Jenny and Hazel set radically different care priorities and arrangements for nonstandard care.

Snow 2
Jenny promoted a standard of care for Snow 2 that valued flexibility and attention to individual needs, as determined by her own assessments, as well as those of families and her staff. In satisfying individual needs, she worked within the limitations of her care economy to utilize the strengths of her existing staff while also deciding what elements of standard care, such as

the resident's dental appointment or bathing another resident, could be postponed so she could attend to nonstandard needs she wanted to address. Often, she had to "stretch" her finest NAs and nurses to achieve this.

Jenny did not feel the necessity of equally rationing care to all residents at all times because "it all works out in the end." Too often, however, care did not become more equitably distributed over time. Behaviorally disturbed elders took far more staff attention and energy than withdrawn residents; even when such residents' families advocated for them, equitable distribution was rarely achieved. Relatives of very proactive or well-connected family members, like Mrs. Gold's daughter, however did benefit from Jenny's flexible system. Sometimes the bathing assistant would need to spend additional time with an agitated resident who had not received a bath in a couple of weeks, limiting her time with other residents. At other times, Jenny would cancel a clinic appointment if a resident seemed too impatient to be able to sit in the waiting room that day; this freed an NA to do other things. For the most resistant residents, resorting to a benign neglect philosophy (although not without its problems) could free an NA to walk another resident to the bathroom, look for a lost pair of glasses, or change an outfit.

Jenny's responsiveness to family requests led her to arrange the schedules of her staff to provide more attentive and personally reinforcing care to certain residents, arguably at a cost to others. Although institutional policy did not allow her to assign a particular NA permanently to a resident (except in Mrs. Gold's case, where they demanded it), Jenny found a way around this that would satisfy families' requests and help her to handle difficult residents. She would encourage Elaine, her most skilled NA, to develop a relationship with the elder and later informally adopt him into her assigned group through exchange of another resident. This was intended to please both caregiver and receiver. The only glitch was any refusal of NAs to make the exchange.

Jenny believed in the importance of preserving as many functions of her residents as possible. Her experience convinced her that the best way to help an elder retain continence was to empower her to walk independently. Jenny thus responded to families' requests for walking their relative to keep them ambulatory. To do this, however, she was often forced to rely either on Elaine or on a new NA, since senior staff made themselves unavailable. Senior staff would only walk those residents with a special doctor's order to walk as part of their *standard* care plan.

Snow 1

In contrast, Hazel had established a rigid hierarchy of caregiving priorities that elevated physical care over care of the person. Her top priority was maintenance and custodial care (e.g., regular hygienic care), protective care (e.g., using restraints), and medical attention (e.g., injuries due to falls); residents' own complaints of discomfort in the absence of a visible sign received somewhat lower priority. The next priority was applying, repairing, or ordering prosthetic devices such as hearing aids. At the very bottom came personalized requests (e.g., to locate a pair of glasses or lost article of clothing) from a resident or family member.

Unlike Jenny, who appreciated how far prosthetic devices could go toward eliminating an elder's "excess disabilities," Hazel felt that such devices were overrated for this population since they could do little to overcome their larger incurable cognitive impairment. Thus, she gave low priority to families' requests to get dentures made, find glasses, or replace batteries in hearing aids. She disliked using her staff to locate glasses or hearing aids because she expected that they would only get misplaced again. Residents who were fearful or uncooperative with dentists might require two or three visits to get the dentures made, only to refuse to wear them. She did not think it was worth her staff's time to deal with devices that had such short-lived benefits.

Hazel also maintained a strong ethic about equally rationing out care among her residents, so she objected to families' nonstandard requests to treat their own relative in "special," apart from standard, practices. When one woman asked that her diabetic husband be toileted more frequently than provided by his two-hour toileting program, she refused, even though his condition demanded an increased intake of fluids. Similarly, she disallowed the use of the rubber bonnet for Margaret because looking for it and using it would have cut into the bathing assistant's time with other residents, even though it reduced Margaret's screaming. Her overriding concern with fairness through equal rationing of *standard* care left serious *nonstandard* care needs or preventative measures unaddressed.

4. Communication Among Nurses, Professional Staff, and Families

Elders with dementia are extremely sensitive to minor adjustments in their treatment, medication, or environment (e.g., increases in noise or a move to a new room). As we saw in Margaret's case, slight changes in medication instigated significant increases in her verbal expressions of distress and set in place a precipitous decline.

Collaboration among those most familiar with the elder helps to minimize declines and improve functioning. Family members who are attuned to changes in the elder can offer observations and suggestions about what had worked in the past. A physician, psychiatrist, or social worker who has known the elder over her history in the nursing home can also recognize changes others may not notice. Finally, nurses, especially NAs who have the greatest amount of hands-on contact, may be the most familiar, and best equipped, to describe the subtle changes in an elder's day-to-day behaviors or mood. Open communication of clinical information among these parties helps promote informed treatment decisions.

Communication Between the Head Nurse and Families

Jenny fostered open communication with family members from Snow 2, sharing information about their elder's condition and welcoming their input about improving care. Families were given access to their relative's chart, invited to ask questions, and encouraged to offer their own observations and suggestions. If a family showed concern about excessive sedation, Jenny looked into the matter and immediately brought in a medical specialist to talk with them. She included family members at any team meeting where staff discussed their relative, not only at the initial admissions meeting which families typically attended. Older spouses were especially comforted to hear feedback from different staff and to provide their own input. Jenny had observed how AD and other dementias affect not only behavioral and cognitive changes in the individual, but also impact family and other relationships. As a clinician, she saw the suffering of families and tried to reduce it. She even was sympathetic with Ella, who placed incessant demands on her Snow 2 staff, because she appreciated how hard it was for Ella to see her mother deteriorate.

Hazel was professional but somewhat aloof in her dealings with Snow 1 families. While she would answer their general questions about their relative's overall condition or the unit's policies, her primary loyalties were with her institution, of which she was very protective. She was thus hesitant to give families information and trained her staff to direct all inquiries to her. She followed a former supervisor's advice to never show families their relative's chart without a physician or PA present to answer questions. She did respect medical training though and would show the elder's chart to physicians who had received administrative approval. Having attributed decline in dementia to the inevitable course of an intransigent disease, she was unmoved by families' concerns about rapid deterioration. When a woman who was alarmed at her husband's decline noted how he had been driving just six months earlier, Hazel dryly responded, "They all were."

Although pleasant during casual conversation with families, Hazel would withdraw if challenged or pressed for more information. Even when she did follow families' requests to schedule tests, she rarely shared their urgency in getting back the results. To her, such concerns paled in light of the overall severity of the disease. Many families felt uncomfortable approaching the nurses' station with questions or requests, only adding to the ordeal of visiting their declining relative. Hazel categorized families into "realistic" and "unrealistic" groups. The former resigned themselves to accepting what Gubrium (1975) called "bed and body" work; the latter expected the staff to do whatever possible to minimize impairment. To Hazel these could not alter the inevitable.

While Jenny's ethnicity may have enabled her to be more comfortable with the families, it does not fully explain her different attitude toward them. Other Jewish nurses with parents at the home did not deal with families the same way she did. Thus the differences between Jenny's and Hazel's attitudes toward families went beyond any ethnic identification with them. It also had little to do with their personality styles. While Jenny was more willing to work cooperatively with families, she was neither warmer nor more outgoing with them than was Hazel; Hazel, in fact, could be quite warm until she felt a family member unreasonably pressed her or made unrealistic demands from her. Thus the differences in their ways of relating to family members were not a result of differences in their personalities either but in *their genuine beliefs about what they could or could not do to help the elder with dementia* within the resources of their care economy. These beliefs in turn shaped their relative optimism or pessimism about the benefits of correcting excessive disabilities and their responses to families about attending to these matters.

Communication of Medical Staff with Families and Nurses

There were also differences in the quality of communication that occurred on the two Snow units by physicians with both families and nurses. Dr. Johnson, the physician for Snow 1, played into a potentially adversarial relationship between families and staff by giving into families' requests to alter their relatives' prescriptions without first consulting the nursing staff. One resident injured a nurse after Dr. Johnson responded to the wife's requests to reduce his medications, only to later denounce the wife as demanding. Dr. Moore, the psychiatrist assigned to the unit also blamed the woman for being "narcissistic" and "entitled" even to make such demands. He accused a highly attentive daughter of "struggling with guilt issues." Such offensive pathologizing served only to close off further communication with families.

In contrast, Dr. Bacon showed considerable empathy with families from Snow 2. He regularly communicated with Ella and the nursing staff about ways to restore her mother's sleep pattern and balance while ensuring her protection without restraints. He responded to Ella's requests to adjust medications because of pain or over-sedation, and when this resulted in setbacks, he continued to make adjustments until Mrs. Gold reached her former baseline.

Dr. Bacon was also very involved in Mrs. Fine's case. Having followed her since her admission, he opposed Dr. Mallory's (Snow 2's psychiatrist) recommendations to medicate her grouchy personality: "This is just Mrs. Fine." He did not want to upset the delicate balance achieved in her stability and functioning by introducing another medication. Like her daughter, he preferred Mrs. Fine as her usual grouchy self. His medical experience in chronic care taught him to treat her in the context of her history, rather than by a standardized dementia protocol. Although Dr. Mallory had a different assessment of Mrs. Fine's condition, she was equally invested in helping Mrs. Fine. She studied the medical charts and talked with Jenny, the NAs, and Mrs. Fine herself. While she was unsuccessful in convincing Dr. Bacon to try an antidepressant, their open discussion about the pros and cons of medicating her were beneficial for Mrs. Fine.

In contrast, the medical staff for Snow 1 preferred to work in isolation from other professionals. When Dr. Moore, the psychiatrist, was asked to complete a routine evaluation on Margaret, he changed the medication on which she had been stable for many years without discussing the matter with nurses, the PA, or physician, or the family. He based his decision strictly on chart information and observations during his limited visits to the unit. His personal views about the potential lethal effects of antipsychotic medication on the "demented brain" and the OBRA mandate to use milder medications and/or smaller doses also affected his decision. While these were worthy additional considerations, in the absence of information about Margaret from her family and staff, they proved inadequate. Even as Margaret's condition deteriorated on the new medication, he continued to make adjustments without taking into account vital information from the family or staff about the delicacy of her condition.

Neither the PA nor Dr. Johnson, the unit physician, questioned the wisdom of Dr. Moore's recommendation. Dr. Johnson's professional interests lay elsewhere, so he would quickly review the charts, sign off on scripts, and move on without spending time directly examining residents himself.[6] He was instrumental in his approach; like some of the NAs, he simply "processed" them.

ADDITIONAL FACTORS AFFECTING CARE ON THE UNITS

Clearly, the head nurse's philosophical perspective, her ability to creatively utilize her staff in a restricted care economy, and the sharing of knowledge among family and staff affect the caregiving program she develops. However, additional factors can work to restrict the care-giving possibilities afforded by her approach. Thus, despite Snow 2's success in providing person sustaining dementia care, factors internal to the unit and institution limited it from bringing such care to more of its residents. Similarly, while the therapeutic nihilism and instrumental orientation on Snow 1 discouraged person-preserving care, other factors also limited Hazel's ability to advance her instrumental care program.

The nurse's ability to realize her program is facilitated or limited by her relation with both the administration and the unit staff. Support from the nursing administration can free her to take risks in trying different approaches to caregiving and staff organization. However, as direct providers of care, the NAs are key to the program's success. Their actions in turn have been shaped by their relationship with their head nurse, their history and experience with the unit and nursing administration, personal attitudes toward and perspectives on residents, and their appraisal of the head nurse's caregiving approach to care.

The Head Nurse's Relation with the Nursing Administration and Her Own Staff

Given the hierarchical structure of nursing, the head nurse plays a major role in organizing care, but her influence is tempered by the way she is regarded by the administration and her staff. Since Hazel was *acting* as the head nurse, she constantly felt that she was under a supervisor's eye and probably less secure in deviating from a rigid interpretation of administrative policies than if she had been in a permanent position. Further, her

---

[6] Toward the end of my research at the unit, a later institutional policy mandated monthly examinations with each resident.

predecessor had trained her to run a tight ship. These led her to be tough with her staff but insufficiently confident in her own position to go out of her way to support them as fully as her predecessor did.

In contrast, the nursing administration regarded Jenny as an outstanding clinician and implicitly trusted her judgment, perhaps to a fault. As the result, they gave her free rein to run her unit without interference. As a compassionate person, Jenny, at the same time, was troubled by the punitive practices of the nursing hierarchy and felt very protective of her staff, whom she regarded as skilled and mature. Their appreciation of her support, however, was overshadowed by the adverse effects of the punitive nursing administration on the NAs' morale and work ethic.

Consequences of the Relations Between NAs and the Nursing Administration

On both units, many of the NAs were not motivated to help out with residents beyond those in the group assigned to them on a two-week rotational basis. They would either argue that the other residents were not their responsibility—even though they officially were—or they would find ways to escape the job entirely. Although the motivations of NAs were different on each unit, their actions equally sabotaged their head nurse's program.

On Snow 1, Hazel's staff felt she was too tough on them while at the same time not adequately protecting them from the punitive administration. (See chapter 5.) Because she was so hard on them, they were also reluctant to go out of their way to help NAs who did not "pull their own weight" in their work, especially with their groups. Out of resentment, they didn't readily respond to her requests for extra help and worked less quickly and efficiently than she preferred. Their refusal to "put out" also reflected the "equal distribution" ideology of the unit, which affected not only the amount of care rendered *to* each resident, but the amount of care rendered *by* each NA.

On Snow 2 despite their appreciation of Jenny's support, the NAs with long tenure (20 years or more) resented how aloof, demanding, and unnecessarily punitive the nursing administration had become. As the institution grew and changed, this administration, which in the early days had been very accessible and involved in the life of the units, underwent considerable turnover. Many long-serving nurses and NAs were unhappy with how they were currently treated as expendable. They knew supervisors who seemed mean spirited and even abusive, disengaged, and unconcerned about their welfare or morale. Old-timers from Snow 2 challenged these perceived abuses by finding ways to avoid work and putting forth a minimal work effort—which is why they resented Elaine for working so hard. Some even became lax in completing minimal demands of their own shift, by leaving soiled diapers and linens for the next shift to change. This severely limited the reach of Jenny's person-centered program.

NAs' Approaches to Residents, Teamwork, and the Unit's Philosophy of Care

Without Elaine's genuine caring, dedication, and skill with residents on Snow 2, it would have been difficult for Jenny to have advanced the intersubjective caregiving that sustained residents like Mrs. Noble. Still, demands by the nursing hierarchy to provide such care for Mrs. Gold involved an engaged relational caregiving by many nurses and NAs beyond Elaine, albeit without Elaine's seemingly endless patience. Still, it demonstrated the possibility that good nurses without Elaine's extraordinary dedication, when pressed, could indeed advance such care. Rose, of Snow 1, displayed the epitome of instrumental efficiency. While Rose and Elaine were on opposite ends of a caregiving spectrum, each left a mark on her unit by most fully realizing the head nurse's care philosophy.

Like Elaine, the NAs with long tenure on Snow 2 were also skilled, but their relations to their work and residents had soured, together with their relations with the administration. While glad to be working on their unit, they did not seem excited by the rewards of relational caregiving. Years of experience made them suspect that some elders "know more than they let on," but they often responded to them by exerting their power to chastise them, rather than supporting their agency. When one resident banged on the table, for example, asking for help, a senior NA pulled her wheelchair away from the table so she could no longer pound it, saying, "If they act like babies, you treat them like babies." While the NA's strategy effectively stopped the pounding, it also denied the possibility of discovering the actual reason for the elder's behavior.

The senior Snow 2 staff had become astute as to how they could "work the system." They developed strong teamwork but used it also to cover for each other as they escaped into an empty room to chat or watch television between breaks and after completing their rounds. This made them unavailable to help Jenny address residents' care needs. Thus, while cooperation among the Snow 2 staff was considerably better than on Snow 1, it worked to empower the NAs to find ways to cover for each other by escaping from their work rather than strictly helping each other care for their residents.

The NAs on Snow 1 also found excuses to avoid helping residents outside of their assigned group. The senior NA on that unit was a very hard worker, and she resented the higher expectations and apparent lack of appreciation from Hazel. In response, she encouraged her friends not to help the NAs she viewed as lazy. Cooperation and teamwork on Snow 1 thus became limited to a few friends. Despite these issues, the Snow 1 NAs did not share and were not affected by the intense resentment toward the nursing administration of the senior NAs of Snow 2. In addition, perhaps because they were overall younger, they seemed more intrigued by the elders under their care. They tried to learn about their histories and often interpreted their impaired behaviors in meaningful terms. Hazel's instrumental program, however, did not offer the personal rewards of a person-oriented approach, and they lacked enthusiasm for advancing her program.

Consequences of Poor or Misdirected Team Work for Residents
Residents on both units suffered because of the lack of cooperation among the Snow 1 NAs and the misdirected cooperation among the Snow 2 NAs. As a result NAs from both units repeatedly ignored calls from residents begging to be toileted. As one NA noted about another, "She hears but she does not respond." Hazel did not encourage them to respond to such requests unless a toileting program was an official part of the elder's care plan. While Jenny did appreciate the validity of many of the residents' requests, she also did not pressure her NAs to satisfy them. It was unclear whether she was trying not to be seen as the extended arm of the despised nursing administration or had herself become a victim of her laxity with her staff.

Inequitable Care
Perhaps the most unfortunate victims were residents who had lost the verbal capacity to advocate for themselves. The needs of those who did not demonstrate BDs or whose families did not intervene on their behalf did not receive the same level of attention as the more demanding residents and families. Such was the plight of the quiet or nontroublesome victim. One elderly man complained that the nonverbal communicative gestures of his minimally responsive wife were completely ignored by the Snow 2 staff,

who regarded her as "vegetative" and therefore ignored her (cf. Kayser-Jones 2003: 59). He observed, for example, how one NA had continued to stuff food into her mouth while conversing with another NA, inattentive to the fact that she was spitting it out.[7] After seeing that, he tried to be around during mealtimes because he did not trust that his wife was safe with the staff and wanted to oversee her feeding. Thus even Snow 2, which provided examples of stellar care for persons with BDs, did not adequately use its staff to extend quality care for everyone.

The Responsibility of the Head Nurse in Promoting Her Program of Care

It was unclear whether Jenny was oblivious, in denial, or simply not bothered by the way her staff could be inattentive, unavailable to work, or negligent in leaving tasks undone for the following shift. Given their own lack of youth and long tenure on the unit, she may have been unwilling to chastise them. The care manager also did not want to push them, especially since she was a friend of theirs and had been there from the unit's opening. It was easier for both nurses to rely on Elaine than to confront the old guard, even though doing so pushed this already overworked woman to her limits and would leave Jenny without a substitute after she eventually left the unit. As Elaine observed, it would have been easier to advance a strong person-centered program if the senior NAs had all quit so they could begin with a fresh staff.

For her part Hazel did what she felt was necessary to serve her residents adequately and was tough on her staff to accomplish this. Her demands in the absence of support, however, backfired because they made her staff more reluctant to work even harder, especially in a task-centered program that lacked the personal rewards of a person-centered one.

Summary

Caregiving on each unit was shaped by its head nurse's philosophical perspective about dementia care, which derived from her assumptions about the resident with dementia, his care needs, and what could be done to help him. It was further affected by the willingness of all the staff to communicate with each other and with families in order to optimize care. The opposing perspectives of the head nurses of Snow 1 and Snow 2 resulted in

---

7   Unfortunately, I observed gross inattentive feeding like this on both units 1 and 2.

caregiving with contrasting emphases on the person versus the disease, person-centered versus task-centered approaches, flexibility versus rigidity in organizing the staff, and shared versus withheld communication among staff and family. These different emphases in care led each head nurse to advance radically different caregiving approaches—the nihilistic instrumental approach of Snow 1 and the more optimistic intersubjective person-centered approach of Snow 2. Each determined how care needs should be prioritized and how the staff should be organized to meet them. In addition, the willingness of the Snow 2 medical staff to communicate and cooperate with each other, the nursing staff and families allowed for indefatigable efforts and produced ultimate success in improving the functioning and overall well-being of many Snow 2 residents. This stood in sharp contrast to the patterns of staff communication in Snow 1.

The success of any program of dementia caregiving in fulfilling its goals—whether it is oriented toward the person, like the examples from Snow 2, or toward the task, like those of Snow 1—is the combined result of a strong head nurse, a supportive administration, and a willing caregiving and professional staff. With any of these missing, the program will suffer. In comparison to the instrumental orientation of Snow 1, Snow 2's person-oriented dementia care approach was unquestionably superior in its philosophical approach and outcomes for its residents. However, like the program of Snow 1, it suffered for reasons that were unrelated to the philosophy of the program itself. The next chapter will discuss these issues further and consider the conclusions and implications we can draw from this comparative study.

CHAPTER 8

Conclusions and Recommendations for Future Dementia Caregiving

DISCUSSION AND REVIEW OF FINDINGS

On the Nature of "Care" Giving

Giving care to another person is fundamentally different from giving or delivering an object to someone. This is because caregiving involves a *relational transaction* between the caregiver and the care receiver that inevitably affects the *nature* of the care or service being rendered. When this relational dimension is missing, there can be no genuine *care transaction*, only action directed at accomplishing some *instrumental goal*. In such cases, the very absence of a relational dimension affects both the "care" giving and care receiving experience. This is particularly true with dementia, where the elder requires ongoing acknowledgment and support from the caregiver in order to counteract the subjective unraveling of self or selves resulting from the disease. Here there is *no possibility of curing, only of validating and healing the person.*

Dementia "care" giving is directed at giving "care" to those who need it. As simple as this may sound, how this occurs depends on what is meant by "care," how care "needs" are defined, and who is defining them. Unlike objects, care is not a thing that can be readily given to another person. Nor is care something that is done *to* a person, like a procedure to an object; *such would be an instrumental procedure, but it is not care.* Rather, care is intersubjective; it is a mutual relationship and ongoing negotiation that involves both caregiver and receiver.

Richard Martin and Stephen Post call *caring* one of the highest human values because it involves the sustenance of one human being by another—a practice fundamental to the continuation of all societies (1992: 56–59). In dementia care, sustenance concerns not simply bodies, but also persons. Caring for the person is necessary to offset the fragmentation of his or her identity (Kitwood and Bredin 1992: 277; Lyman 1993: 30). Unlike bodies, which are attached to individuals, persons are produced out of human relationship, and in dementia especially, they must be replenished continually (Kitwood and Bredin 1992: 285). *Dignity* is the defining characteristic of personhood, according to Kitwood, because it is rooted in human relationship and the social acknowledgment and respect of one person by the other.

How care needs are defined also affects the quality of caregiving. If one considers care needs to include correctable organic conditions or physical abnormalities or injuries, then service providers can use treatment procedures, medications, and rehabilitative therapy to *cure* the patient or help recover lost functioning. Such procedures or techniques, however, are also likely to include a subjective dimension when the service provider extends interpersonal support, encouragement, and/or hope to the patient; this is the relational provenance of care and healing. It can be part of any care transaction, whether it involves cure or not.

In dementia, although cure is not possible, care and healing can be realized. Dementia care can include medical treatments and rehabilitation for other disabilities, as well as preservative services, such as hygienic maintenance and custodial protective care. The "care" giver can perform individual care tasks (such as ADLs) strictly as *instrumental procedures* for the institutional employer in exchange for a salary. In such cases, the recipient of these procedures can be seen as marginal to the process since his body becomes a vehicle for purposes outside of relational care. Alternatively, the caregiver can treat these procedures as intersubjective rituals of care in

which the elder actively participates and through which he receives recognition and dignity. In these cases the *care procedures* can be *preservative of
the person* with dementia and can *heal* the elder who is undergoing personal
fragmentation due to the dementia. Such an exercise produces mutual
gains for both care receiver and caregiver that extend well beyond the institutionally prescribed task or the paycheck.

Who defines care needs also affects caregiving because it raises issues
concerning the exercise of power. This is of particular concern when the
care receiver is vulnerable due to advanced age or his condition. When
these external *institutionally* defined care needs are imposed on the elder
without equally considering his *personally* defined needs, the care receiver
may be more resistant to receiving such "care," and may display more BDs
as a way of communicating his own needs. Thus, no matter how caregiving
is defined and who is defining it, it must be regarded as a *moral enterprise*
since it addresses and entails fundamental human vulnerabilities, both of
ailing care receivers and their more powerful caregivers.

Caregiving in this Study

This study compared two divergent approaches to giving care to institutionalized elders who presented both dementia and disturbed behaviors (BDs).
These divergent approaches occurred within the same facility in identically designed special care units. However, they were based on strikingly
dissimilar assumptions about dementia, the affected person, the nature of
behavioral disturbances, and what could be done for the elder. Dramatic
differences in outcomes in the six case studies provided affirmative evidence
of the superiority of intersubjective person-oriented care over instrumental
task-oriented care.

Chapter 6 illustrated the positive outcomes associated with dementia
caregiving in which the care receiver is personally engaged in the caregiving process. In these case studies, every elder, no matter how impaired, was
regarded as integral to the caregiving process. The Snow 2 staff involved
in their care was also committed to trying to understand and satisfy the
elder's own perceived needs and the meaning of their BDs as caregiving
proceeded. In contrast, elders from Snow 1 were viewed as if they were irrelevant to their care and as if their own perception of their needs did not
matter. The exceptionally positive outcomes for the residents from the Snow
2 case studies demonstrated the value of engaging the person in the caregiving transaction. In contrast, the negative outcomes for residents from

Snow 1 offered evidence not only of the limitations, but also of the *injury* that can result from instrumental caregiving that ignores the person.

Despite the differences in their caregiving approaches and the outcomes, the head nurses of both units were undoubtedly responsible, hardworking individuals who wanted the best for the elders under their care. Their backgrounds, however, led them to accept very different assumptions about dementia, the persons it affected, and the kind of care they should provide. These assumptions shaped their philosophy and approach to dementia caregiving and the priorities they set for their staff.

Hazel was exceptionally gentle and respectful of her residents during one-to-one caregiving transactions, and the Snow 1 families and residents appreciated her clinical skills and bedside manner. At the same time, her acute care background, directed at cure, led her to adopt a highly pathologized view of dementia that predisposed her to an instrumental approach to caregiving directed at efficiently completing standardized care tasks. Although she found this approach personally unsatisfying—and even dreaded the day she might need such care—her assumptions and training had led her to believe it was all she could do for her residents. In contrast, Jenny, with her strong background in chronic care, appreciated the importance of minimizing correctable disabilities while attending to individualized needs of her residents. She worked with the Snow 2 nursing and professional staff to develop relationships with elders that promoted their dignity and addressed these concerns.

Snow 1: Pathologizing Agency and Ignoring the Person in Instrumental "Care" Giving

A behavioral disturbance (BD) provides clues that the disturbed elder has some need or wish, is emotionally upset, or is physically ailing. Caregivers can explore BDs for their meaning content, or disregard or attempt to control them. As illustrated by the case studies from Snow 1, disregarding BDs, or trying to manage or control them without attempting to understand their source, often exacerbates the behaviors and can precipitate the decline of the elder. In addition, regarding BDs as disease artifacts lends itself to pathologizing and invalidating as "diseased" *any* action by the elder—no matter how reasonable—through which he attempts to communicate needs or discomfort. This is what occurred when a Snow 1 resident complained of abdominal pain, but none of the staff took her complaint seriously. Pathologizing the elder's agency and ignoring BDs cuts off the communication about the problem and serves as the basis for denying legitimacy to the person; both are damaging to the elder with dementia.

Refusing to accept communication from these elders is equivalent to denying their humanity. As Jules Henry observed about nursing home life over 40 years ago, "If in every human contact something is communicated, something learned, and something felt, it follows that where nothing is communicated, learned, or felt, there is nothing human either" (Henry 1963: 404).

The head nurse of Snow 1 viewed dementia as a hopeless, totalizing disease that devastates bodies and minds. Since reason is compromised in damaged minds, Hazel no longer trusted that the affected elders could accurately communicate their needs or wishes. Thus, she disregarded the possible meaning content of their words and actions, including the BDs, which she viewed as artifacts of the disease. The intentionality or purposefulness behind their words and actions got lost in the process. Once she identified the elder with the disease, the person with dementia and his agency ceased to exist. That is because personhood was treated in Snow 1 as an attributional status that depended on an individual's retention of reason. Only those retaining reason would retain the status of "person," since the validity of their intentionality or action (i.e., their agency) and rights associated with being a person depended on that. (See chapter 2 for more elaborate discussion.)

Seeing dementia as an incurable disease led Hazel to the nihilistic view of caregiving that nothing could be done for the elder beyond basic physical maintenance and custodial needs. She thus promoted an instrumental task-oriented program of care that focused on completing such tasks. But as nurse philosopher Sally Gadow so eloquently describes, "Giving up on cure ... need not mean letting go of that relationship" (1988: 14). In fact, she recognized that a commitment to cure can work to "compromise if not sacrifice" the relationship with the care receiver. For Gadow, the "central moral choice [is] whether to hold onto or let go of the special covenantal relationship of caregiving" (p. 14). Clearly, resorting to instrumental care asserts a letting go of that relationship, and with it, the empathy that it demands.

In choosing instrumental caregiving, Hazel concerned herself with completing the institutionally prescribed task whether the elder wanted it or not; what she forgot was the sentient human subject. Here there was no relational transaction, only unidirectional action by the "care" giver to the receiver. As they went about their tasks, instrumental caregivers were *disengaged* as they "processed" the elder's body and checked off each task on the ADL list. Completing the list became the goal, and the elder, the "instrumental means" by which to accomplish it. At times, the elder even was seen as interfering with the "care" giving, rather than being remembered as the reason for it. This justified using measures to *manage* or *control* him through medication or even by force. Under this model, the caregiver is far removed from the elder in terms of vulnerability, power, and freedom to exercise control. At its worst, it can lead to morally questionable exercises of power by administrators, as occurred with Rebecca (case study 3, chapter 5) or caregivers such as Rose (chapter 7). In bypassing the person, instrumental caregiving lends itself to both dehumanizing and potentially immoral practices.

Hazel's heavy focus on pathology depended on *her particular reading* of a disease (or biomedical) model of dementia. It is important to point out, however, that the particular model that she adopted, together with the nihilism it implied, did not derive from a clear understanding of the pathology underlying dementia. As shown in chapter 1, that understanding remains ambiguous. Nor did she rely on a model that serves as a standard guide for biomedical practitioners. Certainly the physicians of Snow 2 did not adopt it as they sought measures that could improve their residents' conditions. Nor, of course, did Jenny as she sought ways to reduce correctable disabilities to improve functioning.

The particular biomedical model on which Hazel depended was not a widely accepted professional model at all, but a *pessimistic folk model* to which staff who were untrained in medicine, resorted when they decided they were unable to help persons with dementia. While adopting assumptions of continuous organic decay that were consistent with a biomedical perspective, her model provided a folk view about dementia, not one grounded in a refined scientific understanding of underlying organic processes.

Snow 2: Preserving the Person and Her Agency Through Intersubjective Caring

In contrast, Jenny, with her extensive training in chronic care, tried to improve the functioning, optimize the independence, and preserve the personhood of elders residing in Snow 2. In contrast to the other unit, personhood here is a *relational* status. Elders retained their status as "persons" because of the efforts of others to preserve their dignity and to "to keep their stories going" as biographical beings. Personhood here also includes respect for the person's continued exercise of intentionality and will, even when cognition is compromised. (See chapter 2 for further discussion.)

Toward that end, Jenny directed her staff to identify correctable disabilities, such as hearing losses, attention to which could improve overall functioning and independence and elevate the elder's sense of dignity. Identifying disabilities required attentiveness to the elder's statements and actions, including any BD that might be signaling need, desire, or distress. Even when Jenny and her staff could not identify a correctible disability, they kept the elder as the focus of care and validated him through ongoing acknowledgment and respect.

Jenny directed attention to the *person* who remained, rather than the losses that resulted from the disease. That person was a *relational* being who was not defined by attributions like reason, but by ongoing support and recognition from others. Toward that end, she encouraged her staff to develop relationships with elders that would facilitate caregiving and validate their worthiness. She viewed caregiving as an intersubjective process that could *only* occur through the active engagement of the elder. The intensity of the caregiver's empathetic regard for the elder was often a humble admission of her own vulnerability in the universe. This admission reduced the distance between the caregiver and receiver (Gadow 1988: 13), allowing for a trustful relationship. As caregiving proceeded, the caregiver would listen, observe, and try to interpret and respond to the elder's wishes. Her goal was to preserve the dignity of the person with dementia while negotiating with him to complete prescribed care tasks. This was arduous, endless work, especially in a care economy with very limited staffing. To a caregiver like Elaine who accepted this charge, the alternative was unacceptable and the rewards were uniquely gratifying.

Communication Among Staff and Families

The situations at Snow 1 and Snow 2 were further affected by the extent to which information was openly shared and discussed. Communication between nursing staff and families was poor on Snow 1 because Hazel restricted its flow. The medical staff also worked alone and did not take a personal interest in the residents. This limited the availability of information from knowledgeable parties that could have better informed treatment decisions.

In contrast, Jenny readily shared information about Snow 2 residents with whoever might be able to inform their condition and its treatment. This fostered open communication with family members that provided valuable input. The medical staff were equally open with the families, staff, and each other and very devoted to residents on the unit. The physician took a holistic approach to dementia care, taking into account BDs in light of their histories and personalities, rather than by objective indicators of pathology. Treatment decisions for Snow 2 elders were thus informed by the uniqueness of each resident's past rather than by a standard pathologization of their condition.

The Outcomes

These divergent approaches to dementia caregiving had dramatically different consequences for the elders in the units. Those from Snow 2 fared markedly better than those of Snow 1. The latter's caregivers were trained to disregard residents' requests or comments and to ignore BDs or control them through medication or pressure. Suppressing the BD rather than attempting to correct the underlying problem often led to further escalation of the problematic behaviors, even to the point of crisis. As seen from the Snow 1 cases studies, these elders declined, sometimes precipitously. Even in one case when dementia was not involved, using force to overcome a BD was followed by the elder's failure to thrive and an unanticipated precipitous death.

In Snow 2, Jenny trained caregivers to try to understand the communicative intent of the BDs, in order to correct the problem at its source. This validated the agency and dignity even of highly impaired elders. Even when the staff failed to interpret the source of a BD—if, for example, it represented a less accessible internal state—their effort to acknowledge the elder and to address the BD as more than a disease artifact imparted respect that often served to prevent the behavior from escalating. In each of the Snow 2 case studies, the elder retained dignity and a strong sense of self and in two cases showed dramatic functional improvements as well.

As relational beings, persons develop through significant involvement with other persons. They continue to retain a sense of social identity through their ongoing recognition by other human beings over the course of their development. Just as people become persons through significant engagement with others, so can their personhood be dissolved if social acknowledgment and relational contact are withdrawn. In dementia, the elder needs constant reinforcement and engagement as the memory of his various past selves fades. A caregiver who connects with fragments of formerly produced selves or helps to support newly emergent ones eases the terror from losses that result when memories fade. This is the kind of person-preserving care that Jenny had envisioned for Snow 2, and that was realized for many, but not all of her residents.

Institutional Obstacles to Actualizing Promising Caregiving Programs

Even when a program of caregiving is successfully designed to preserve persons, extend functioning, and promote relationships, there is no guarantee that it can accomplish these goals without the support and cooperation of both clinical and administrative staff. The high demands and minimal satisfactions of Hazel's instrumental approach thwarted many of her staff who would probably have thrived under the person-centered program of Snow 2. However, even though Jenny's staff claimed to appreciate this approach, not all of them always worked to promote it. Their bitterness toward the administration carried over to their work with their elders. This led some of them to resort to instrumental means of control or even to abscond from their responsibilities altogether. This was a tragic loss to the elders, the program, and the NAs themselves.

CONCLUSIONS AND RECOMMENDATIONS FOR FUTURE DEMENTIA CAREGIVING

The following conclusions and related recommendations derive from my findings from over 18 months of intensive observational study of the two special care units and reflect the consistency and intensity of differences I found. There are 10 principal conclusions and recommendations plus numerous subsidiary conclusions, identified by numbers (e.g., C 1.1, C 1.2) with related subsidiary recommendations (e.g., R 1.1, R 1.2). There is also a final overall conclusion and recommendation with many related final recommendations (FR 1, FR 1.1, FR 2, FR 2.1, etc.)

Conclusion 1: Person-centered caregiving is superior to task-centered caregiving. Intersubjective, person-centered caregiving is unquestionably superior to instrumental task-centered approaches for supporting persons with dementia who have BDs. This approach facilitates completing care tasks, minimizes BDs by responding to the triggering problem, and improves the elder's overall well-being. Far from being generic (cf. Capstick 2004: 131) or offering some market model of consumer choice (Stone 2004), "person-centered" caregiving attempts to preserve the person with dementia simply because she is one. It values the person both for her history and continuing expression of will and desire to relate to, and to be taken seriously by, another person.

Conversely, instrumental task-centered care, while admirably fitted to preserving bodies, is poorly suited to supporting persons and can even harm and precipitate serious decline. This approach pathologizes both the dementia and the person, ignores remaining capacities, and treats *all* efforts to communicate—whether BDs or ordinary expressions—as *disease artifacts* to be ignored. This approach denies potentially valid claims of the elder, erases or ignores his/her history, and handles the person as an empty shell.

Recommendation 1:

- The caregiver must adopt an attitude of respect, attentiveness to communications from the elder, and an approach to care as a negotiated intersubjective process, rather than one he/she directs.
- The caregiver should try to engage the elder's remaining capacities and competences and address her wishes (Post 2000b: 13, 50). Personal attention, validation, and subjective relational reinforcement with caregivers are vital in this approach.
- Even in very advanced cases of dementia, such relational caregiving is necessary to impart dignity to the elder as a valuable self.
- Caregivers must not ignore or pathologize the actions of elders with dementia, but try to interpret and respond to them. This should not only minimize BDs, but also improve the state of being of the elder.
- Nursing homes should make a deliberate effort to shift from instrumental, task-centered *management* of persons to their person-centered *preservation*.

C 1.1: Pathologizing and invalidating as "diseased" *any* action by which the elder attempts to communicate needs, discomfort, or other concerns cuts off communication about many valid problems. It also rejects the elder at the very time when she needs bolstering from internal fragmentation due to confusion and memory loss about the past. Rejection contributes to the expression of BDs and promotes shame, distrust, and withdrawal. Confusion and memory loss are independent of will, desire, feelings, and recollections and human expression of needs that are valid and must be satisfied. Invalidating the expression or recognition of the needs leads to a tragic denial that minimizes the elder's dignity as a person.

R 1.1:

- Caregiving programs must work to *counteract* the fragmentation of self that occurs with dementia and the loss of confidence and security this produces in the elder.
- Programs must work to reinforce dignity and help heal the person who is suffering from fragmentation.
- Programs must instill in their staff the importance of supporting remaining capacities in elders and of recognizing the legitimacy of many of their concerns and wishes and reasonably satisfying them.

C 1.2: Person-preserving caregiving is facilitated when the person responsible for organizing care is flexible in creatively arranging the staff to address personalized care needs.

R 1.2:

- Those responsible for organizing care must keep in mind the needs of the elder, rather than being completely bound by institutional directives.
- Institutions also need to provide more room for creative arrangements that facilitate person supportive care.

Conclusion 2: Person-centered care combined with disability reduction is optimal. Person-centered care combined with efforts to reduce correctable disabilities (e.g., hearing, vision, or ambulation), result in fewer BDs, even in elders who appear too uncooperative to participate in therapeutic activities. Dramatic improvement in functioning and mood may appear as *rementia* (or reversal of the dementia).[1] Such improvements facilitate caregivers' efficiency in working with residents.

Recommendation 2:

- Full assessments, accompanied by regular periodic re-assessments, to identify and reduce excessive disabilities should become a standard feature of dementia care, even when the resident may appear to be too advanced to gain benefits from such efforts, or they failed in the past.

Conclusion 3: Instrumental caregiving is dangerous. The dangers of providing solely instrumental caregiving must not be underestimated. Any program of dementia care built on instrumental goals risks fostering a mentality of *sanctioned abuse* through dehumanizing and immoral practices. Programs that encourage *management and control* of vulnerable elders and their behaviors are at particular risk for promoting instrumental approaches. What's more, such programs may attract dominating, nonempathetic persons who abuse their power in trying to manage and control elders in order to complete their work.

---

[1] Rather than an actual rementia, it is more likely that the previously untreated disabilities and/or side effects from excessive medications led to conditions (e.g., incontinence, severe BDs, and confinement in restraints) and associated despondent states that gave the impression that the elder was more impaired than she actually was.

Recommendation 3:

- Given this serious concern, dementia programs should thoroughly examine their existing practices and priorities to evaluate where their priorities can lead in order to avoid potential abuses.
- Gerontologists should re-evaluate the very goal of seeking better technical means for controlling the behaviors of elders (cf. Moody 1988: 33).
- Instrumentally oriented NAs should be reassigned to units with less vulnerable residents.

C 3.1: NAs involved in proving relational person-preserving dementia care require a high level of personal commitment, the ability to engage with others, and qualities (such as self-sacrifice, patience, and kindness) that are quite different from those desirable in acute care (e.g., detachment, speed, and efficiency). As Kane states, "A nurse is not a nurse" (2004: 253).

R 3.1:

- Deliberate hiring practices for dementia caregivers should encourage selecting persons with these qualities who are also responsible and competent to carry out the physical and emotional demands of the job.

C 3.2: Disengaged instrumental caregiving can be devastating to quiet "unproblematic" elders whose dementia has carried them beyond the point of overt verbal communication or manifestation of BDs. These elders lack any means, except subtle nonverbal communication, to make their wishes or complaints known. Even though they may be easy to "manage," they are frail and vulnerable to injury or harm if not attended to carefully. They can also be better sustained through person-preserving care attuned to their signals. The sanctioned abuse they experience through disengaged caregiving is also less visible, but not less immoral, than that which affects more vocal, aggressive, or purportedly troublesome residents.

R 3.2:

- Quiet, nonproblematic elders must be tended even more carefully, and their nonverbal bodily signals should be carefully observed, particularly during feeding to avoid choking.

Conclusion 4: Rigid Interpretations of Regulations can Counteract their Actual Intentions. Rigid interpretation of nursing home and government regulations, if applied without considering residents' preferences, can counteract the intent of the regulations.

Recommendation 4: It is essential that staff take into account a resident's own perspective in interpreting regulations intended to protect their rights.

C 4.1: Elders with dementia are fragile and vulnerable to decline when their treatment (such as the medication on which they have been stable for some time) is abruptly or drastically changed. Even changes in medications in response to federal regulations that require reducing doses or shifting to milder medications can destabilize an elder's condition.

R 4.1:

- Physicians and psychiatrists should take into account not only the elder's current condition, but the history of her personality, behavior, and past stability on medications before implementing changes.
- They should also consult with knowledgeable family members and staff.
- The physician should exercise judgment based on the elder's history in trying to remain in compliance with regulations to reduce, change, or eliminate medications incrementally.

Conclusion 5: Pessimistic views that shape dementia care are often based on folk beliefs, not biomedical science. Highly pathologized views of dementia as a hopeless condition for which little can be done are based on *pessimistic folk beliefs*, not on scientific evidence that definitively links dementia to specific pathology. Thus, while the biomedical model may predispose a caregiver toward instrumental care, it is not a necessary outcome of the model, but stems from a naïve employment of it.

Recommendation 5: The training of persons involved in dementia care should strongly emphasize the positive things caregivers can do to improve the functioning and well-being of residents, rather than encourage misguided views of unspecified disease processes they cannot change.

C 5.1: A nihilistic instrumental approach to dementia caregiving, grounded in an exaggerated emphasis on the pathology, *is less common among those trained in chronic care settings, whether physicians or nurses.* In fact, physicians trained in chronic care, in spite of their biomedical training, were often more concerned with "care" that would promote functioning and well-being than were nurses or NAs socialized to value "cure."

R 5.1:

- Dementia care programs should be staffed by clinicians—nurses, physicians, and NAs—and administrators who are trained in, and/or committed to, the value of a chronic care that reinforces the person and optimizes her well-being.
- Programs must encourage caregiver involvement and *ongoing* support (in addition to more intense involvement to help stabilize patients during difficult times) as well as the routine processing of emergent problems.

Conclusion 6: Person-preserving caregiving requires committed staff. A program to promote person-preserving caregiving can be successful only if the right persons are hired for the job and the entire caregiving staff is committed to this approach. A few committed NAs can actualize such care for some residents, but all the nursing staff is needed to extend such care to all residents. Relying on a few dedicated NAs to carry the program is impossible and leads to burnout and demoralization.

Recommendation 6:

- Careful hiring and training must occur to select responsible caregivers willing to engage themselves personally with residents.
- Ideally, the person who heads the program (in this study, the head nurse) should be centrally involved in hiring NAs and nurses to staff it to ensure finding people whose characteristics and values will advance its goals.
- Caregivers should possess qualities like compassion, patience, an ability to be flexible, and a willingness to simply "be" with the resident, rather than be oriented to outcomes.[2]

C 6.1: Learning to develop teamwork is crucial for successfully addressing the needs (such as help with toileting) of all residents that is vital for preserving their functioning. Shifting the focus from quantity of tasks to quality of interactions should minimize conflict among NAs who feel they have done more work than others have.

---

[2] These are the qualities that clinicians involved in training NAs with strong person-centered orientations look for, according to Mark Royer, Director of Training and Behavioral Health, Ingham County Medical Facility, Okemos, MI, who has over 30 years experience in the field.

R 6.1:

- Training should encourage teamwork that redefines staff priorities from tasks to people.
- Staff must recognize the legitimacy, and develop sensitivity, to responding to *all* residents' needs by working together.

C 6.2: Staff members who gain power due to seniority or other reasons may use it to avoid caregiving responsibilities and influence new staff to follow suit, much to the disadvantage of residents.

R 6.2:

- It may be necessary to recreate a program with a new team rather than continue working within troubled structures. This may involve shifting some or all NAs to different units. Examples include (1) situations where NAs use their seniority and power to avoid caregiving responsibilities, and (2) where staff relations and teamwork have broken down to the detriment of caregiving of residents.

Conclusion 7: Person-preserving care begins with a respectful caregiving relationship. An NA who learns an elder's habits and preferences and is sensitive to an elder's communicative gestures can offer more satisfying responses than an NA who is not so attuned. Similarly, elders will show less agitation and distress with such caregivers than with those who have not acquired such sensitivity or whose interactive style and touch is unfamiliar to the elder.

Recommendation 7:

- Once a strong caregiver/receiver relationship is established, the NA should be permanently assigned to that resident to promote that relationship.
- If a strong caregiver/receiver relationship changes later or the NA leaves, a new assignment should be carefully made to help build on the strengths of the previous relationship.
- Assignments should never be made for the convenience of the staff or institution or simply to rotate "difficult" and "easy" residents among the NAs.
- Other ways to achieve equity and fairness include a permanent case mix of easier and harder residents within specific groups or even allowing different numbers of residents per group in order to equalize the demands on staff time and energy.

Conclusion 8: Dementia caregiving is a demanding practice of consuming person-work in which both care receiver and caregiver need careful tending. We need to support the caregivers in whom we entrust the care of our elders. Caregivers are too often emotionally and physically drained in carrying out their work, while also being paid poorly and inadequately appreciated.

Recommendation 8:

- The enormous social value contributed by dementia caregivers must be recognized.
- Supervisors and the facility's administration should support caregivers in every way possible.
- Adequate staff should be hired to enable NAs to provide the kind of personal attention advocated here.[3]
- The nurse should request additional help when needed to prevent burnout, even if only for a short time. Hiring a part-time floater to help with needs, like toileting during meals and other times, would improve elders' quality of life while not overburdening NAs.
- NAs must be given abundant time away from work so they can refresh themselves. Working consistently in a rewarding program that builds in adequate time away should minimize burnout, turnover, and concerns about abuse of entitlements.

C 8.1: The conventional nursing home hierarchical structure promotes a unidirectional application of power by administrative staff who are disengaged from the everyday workings of the unit. This often leads NAs to feel disenfranchised from their commitment to elders and alienated from their work, thus inhibiting them from giving fully of themselves as caregivers.

R 8.1:

- The facility should strive to breakdown hierarchical barriers that divide administrative from caregiving staff by promoting mutual interdependence among all groups.
- Nursing homes should gradually move from a one-way accountability (NAs to administrators) to *mutual accountability* among all staff.

---

[3] See chapter 9 for further discussion of the need to improve standards for the number of direct caregivers needed per resident.

Conclusion 9: A strong caregiving program begins with a healthy administration. When upper level administrative staff are unhappy with their own working conditions, they will be less inclined to be sympathetic to other staff.

Recommendation 9:

- Conflict among administrative staff must be resolved so it does not affect the rest of the facility. This may require negotiation with the board and higher level executives of the home or corporation.

C 9.1: A rigid, suspicious, punitive administration can create irreparable damage to the functioning of the entire nursing home.

R 9.1:

- Supervisory unit staff and the administrative staff must be adequately involved with the life of the unit to appreciate the demands of the job and to respond to NAs concerns. They should offer respect, privileges, flexibility in work schedules and eliminate punitive policies.
- Morale must be bolstered, if not through significant increases in pay, then through paid and, if necessary, unpaid respites from the job and other perks.
- Administrative staff must provide more flexibility in scheduling of caregiver staff.

Conclusion 10: Direct caregivers (NAs) and families offer valuable input to dementia care plans because of their intimate knowledge of the elders.

Recommendation 10:

- Treatment and care planning, including questions about using medications, should include NAs and family members because their prolonged contact with elders provides valuable information about their current and past behaviors.
- Similarly, families should be informed about the possibility of changing treatments or medications ahead of time and be invited to participate in the deliberation process.

Final Conclusion: Dementia caregiving is a moral enterprise because of the high stakes for elders. The survival and quality of life of vulnerable, fragile elders at the end stage of their lives depend on decent dementia care. When this care is poor, they suffer immeasurably. Thus dementia caregiving *cannot be treated as merely another commodity* of products and services. High-quality person-preserving care that sustains those with dementia demands a special commitment and responsible action from everyone associated with it.

Final Overall Recommendation:

- All stakeholders[4] in the enterprise of dementia caregiving, at every level of production and consumption, must be *mutually accountable*[5] and *entrusted to act morally responsibly* to ensure the provision of quality dementia care of elders under their charge.

Because this overall recommendation involves so many stakeholders, I offer these additional related final recommendations (*FRs*) with direct relevance to each stakeholder.

FR 1:

- A larger vision of dementia caregiving should dictate the structure of institutional care, not the other way around. However, the vision is one that must penetrate, invigorate, and empower the entire staff and enable interdependence and *mutual accountability*, not just accountability of the lower-end staff to the top administrators.

FR 2:

- NAs, who are the backbone of dementia care, should be fully invested in accepting the demands of relationally sustaining those under their care. If they are not able or willing to provide respectful, person-oriented caregiving to elders under their care, they should request reassignment to a different unit where residents do not critically depend on intensive relational support.
- Caregivers who retain ongoing animosity to the work place, co-workers, the administration, residents or their families would also be advised to leave the unit if these feelings prevent them from engaging positively with those under their care.

---

4 Stakeholders include all of the following: NAs; nurses; supervisors; professional staff; and administrators who work in a nursing home; families who arrange for care; the board of directors who make decisions about running the facility, for-profit homes, and their stockholders; and policy-makers who make funding and regulatory decisions that directly impact the operations of nursing homes and the lives of their residents and all citizens.

5 I owe this concept to Trudy Bayer, a professor of Communications, at the University of Pittsburgh.

FR 3:

- Supervisory nurses must not only facilitate the work of NAs; they must also identify situations where staff members are unwilling to provide, or interfere with, the provision of person-preserving caregiving and attempt to correct the situation. Ignoring the situation constitutes a disservice to the elders.

FR 4:

- Since knowledge about a resident's typical behavior and personality are vital in making judgments about changes and the need for interventions, medical and professional staff should be invested in developing an ongoing relationship with those under their care, beyond their intermittent involvement with procedures or consultations. Over time they would become familiar with, and take into account, this information in making informed treatment recommendations.

FR 5:

- Communication among the administration, nurses and NAs must move toward a mutual accountability that depends on respectful dialogue to resolve concerns and facilitate provision of optimal care for the residents.

FR 6:

- Family members are equally accountable for remaining involved in their relative's caregiving after they enter a nursing home. They should be encouraged and supported by the nursing home staff to remain involved and contribute useful information to help the staff optimize their relative's care.

FR 6.1:

- Nursing homes should encourage visitation by friends and family to provide meaningful contact with residents unless there is clear evidence that they are upsetting or abusing the elder.

FR 6.2:

> • Families must also be respectful in their relations with the staff.

While families and caregivers are directly involved in the day-to-day care of the elders, they, like their elders, are too often at the mercy of stakeholders who are very removed from their experiences and yet have power to make decisions that shape it. The very distance of these stakeholders from those most affected by their decisions makes them immune from the consequences of their actions. It enables them to make decisions based on *macro*-economic considerations rather than considerations of the more profound, often tragic, *micro*-personal impacts of their decisions. The final recommendations concern these powerful stakeholders.

FR 7:

> • Since the operational and financial priorities set by the boards of directors of nonprofit and for-profit nursing homes can severely impact the life of their residents, they must establish priorities that best serve and sustain the elders being served by the facility, rather than focusing on presenting a particular image to "sell" the home to the public. A facility with better functioning, more content residents will eventually sell itself to the public.

FR 8:

> • Similarly, those responsible for decision making in larger for-profit nursing home franchises must realize what is at stake for elders when they cut back staff and services to maximize profits. Person-preserving care requires an even greater investment in staff time than instrumental care. When decisions are made to maximize profits in favor of adequate or decently paid staff this inevitably translates into losses for elders (Winzelberg 2003: 2555). The unfortunate deaths that occurred in some nursing homes because of decisions favoring stockholders (Bates 1999) provide a stark reminder of the price of placing profits over care.

FR 9:

> • Funding and regulatory policies should be examined and amended to provide adequate funding for caregiving that is person-centered and relational, rather than task-centered and instrumental.

- Policy-makers at all levels must also seriously consider the impacts of withdrawing funding to support quality long-term care, in and out of institutional settings, and must seriously re-evaluate the fiscal requirements for best serving this population.
- Policy-makers must re-examine OBRA regulations to consider where they have reinforced relational person care and whether they have impeded it and make the necessary changes.
- Above all, policy-makers must act in ways that are accountable to the best interests of the elders under their charge.

FR 10:

- Since all citizens will be facing old age directly, or through elders in their families, it is in their best interest to become educated on options and become strong advocates for funding and provisions that will ensure the availability of quality and desirable care for everyone.

As we look ahead to the future of dementia care, we also must keep in mind external barriers to providing the kind of relational care that is vital to promoting well-being of those with dementia. The next chapter will examine some of these barriers.

FURTHER READING

Basler, Barbara. (2004). Battle of the banned: Couple fights court order limiting visits to nursing home. *AARP Bulletin* 45 (10), 28–29.

Bates, Eric. (1999). The shame of our nursing homes: Privatization has produced millions for investors and misery for the elderly. *The Nation, 269*(12), 11–19.

Gadow, Sally. (1988). Covenant without cure: Letting go and holding on in chronic illness. In J. Watson and M. Ray (Eds.), *The Ethics of Care and the Ethics of Cure: Synthesis in Chronicity* (pp. 5–14). New York: National League of Nursing.

Martin, Richard, and Post, Stephen. (1992). Human dignity, dementia and the moral basis of caregiving. In Robert Binstock, Stephen Post, and Peter Whitehouse (Eds.), *Dementia and Aging: Ethics, Values, and Policy Choices* (pp. 55–68). Baltimore: Johns Hopkins University Press.

Moody, Harry. (1988). Toward a critical gerontology: The contribution of the humanities to theories of aging. In James Birren and Vern Bengston (Eds.), *Emergent Theories of Aging* (pp. 19–39). New York: Springfield.

PART THREE

looking ahead in dementia care

CHAPTER 9

External Barriers to Quality Dementia Care

Chapters 5 through 8 examined *internal* caregiving practices of two special care units as they affected the lives of persons with dementia. The evidence from the cases studies clearly pointed to the superiority of relational person-preserving care over disengaged task-centered approaches for sustaining persons with dementia.

Person-preserving dementia care, however, is both *labor* intensive and *subject* intensive. Elaine, a master of such care, showed that it is necessarily more *time* intensive than instrumental care. Person-preserving care involves much more than caring for bodies; it requires caring for what bioethicist Paul Ramsey called "embodied souls." Not only do person-preserving caregivers address the basic day-to-day physical maintenance care needs described in chapter 4; they also try to read and address the needs and desires of the person struggling with the fragmentation of identity and the effort to maintain a place in the world. The caregiver must tend to the elder respectfully and with patience, flexibility, and the stress of submitting to institutional constraints while trying to deliver much more. This form of caregiving is deeply emotionally demanding of the caregiver, who must surrender herself to the world of the elder in order to secure a trusting relationship. Because of the elder's ongoing cognitive vulnerabilities, it demands both an "empathetic regard" and corresponding sensitivity to "physical ministration" akin to that needed by someone enduring physical pain (Gadow 1988: 12). Thus, quality dementia care—like that Elaine rendered—is fundamentally different than basic maintenance care. Such caregiving is certainly not efficient and may not seem practical given other societal needs, but we have seen the unacceptable alternative. And, as Elaine showed, such care is not beyond reach.

Within particular nursing home units, intensive person-preserving care can only be achieved through considerable in-house support. However, there are many *external* historical, political, economic, and cultural impediments to its wider adoption in spite of the strong evidence in its favor. These include the historical legacies of former legislation, the larger regulatory and *political economic* context of struggle between competing stakeholders (e.g., the for-profit nursing home industry and advocates for promoting a high quality of nursing home care) that ultimately shape care, and specific cultural ideologies and conditions. This chapter will visit some of these barriers.

HISTORICAL LEGACY OF THE HILL-BURTON ACT: HOSPITALS AS A MODEL FOR NURSING HOMES

The institutional character of nursing homes can be traced to the Hill-Burton Act of the 1950s that developed standards of nursing home construction fashioned after hospitals and extended federal subsidies for that construction (Winzelberg 2003). This structural mandate imparted an enduring institutional imprint on nursing homes. The typically sterile large-scale medicalized setting, with its intercom system and constant stream of medical specialists and maintenance staff, proved a far cry from the semblance of home. The quality of its environmental stimulation also potentially aggravated BDs.

The bureaucratic structure of the institutional setting imposed regimentation, an artificial tempo over the lives of residents, and compliance with institutional rules, while the economy of scale demanded speed and efficiency from its workers. Regular times were imposed for satisfying all of life's needs, reframed as "services," but under the institution's time clock, not that of the resident, eliminating the possibility for the spontaneity of a casual homelike setting. This structure led to the unhappiness of countless residents, and for those with dementia, the pressures and multiple losses of control they experienced no doubt exacerbated BDs. Even where efforts were made to decorate rooms to *appear* more homelike, the size, structure, and regimentation of "services" impeded such achievements. Despite ongoing innovations in designs and outward appearances, many nursing homes retain an institutionalized character and mode of care delivery. By fostering a hospital model (fashioned to respond to acute care needs) rather than a social residential model (designed for everyday living), institutional care is unable to foster intimate caregiving relationships so vital to quality dementia care.

The Instrumental Bias of Institutional Care Economies

The hospital model, with its regimented structure, has favored an instrumental delivery of body care over the intersubjective rendering of person care. This approach divides caregiving into standardized units of staff time. All caregivers are seen as interchangeable as long as they follow identical procedures and protocols. The *person* of the caregiver does not figure in as relevant because he or she is valued as an efficient processing machine rather than relational being. The work itself is divided into manageable *body tasks* to be completed within specific units of time. Time is translated into dollars, and those unable to accomplish tasks in a given time frame can be exchanged for those who can. In order for homes to make profits or for nonprofit facilities to stay in the black, they must keep costs down, and this translates into maintaining the lowest acceptable level of staffing as defined both by federal regulations and the home's (or corporation's) own values. This in itself defines the extent to which individualized care is possible.

Tight economies of care promote a culture of care delivery that fosters depersonalized instrumental caregiving. The worker, as efficient processing machine, has little time or energy for the person. Nursing assistants in such systems are socialized to address rotational maintenance care tasks (the ADLs) rather than ongoing daily nurturance. A fluid interpersonal *rendering* of care becomes reduced to the fragmented devitalized delivering of care. Completing the ADL checklist is rewarded, not the manner in which care is done. The emphasis on tasks threatens the trust needed for developing the caregiving relationship (Ware et al. 2003), so vital in dementia care.

This instrumental bias was further advanced with the enactment of the Omnibus Budget Reconciliation Act (OBRA) of 1987 and the nursing home regulations it mandated.

THE OMNIBUS BUDGET RECONCILIATION ACT

In 1987, Congress enacted the Nursing Home Reform Act (NHRA) as part of the Omnibus Reconciliation Act to improve the standards of nursing home care through government regulations. More elaborate regulatory measures were implemented in 1990 and 1995. This legislation came in response to reports of grossly negligent conditions in many nursing homes and generally inadequate oversight of the nursing home industry. This Act significantly tightened regulations and made nursing homes responsible for reporting questionable incidents. At the same time, it placed enormous demands on the staff to document care, established rigid guidelines, and imposed economic, state licensure, and federal certification sanctions for deviating from its standards. These regulations helped to eliminate neglect and abuse in the worst settings. However, they encouraged an instrumental orientation to care even in the best of settings.

Despite some evidence that OBRA has led to improved care, profound deficiencies in care remain (Winzelberg 2003; Walshe and Harrington 2002: 477). Inadequate attention has been given, for example, to addressing correctable disabilities, such as hearing and vision impairments, exacerbated by Medicare not paying for these alleged "convenience items" or "cosmetic" requirements. In addition, under OBRA, bowel incontinence has actually increased (Walshe 2001: 131). Researchers have found that over half of all nursing homes fail to meet minimal standards researchers have established for nurse staffing requirements (Zhang and Grabowski 2004: 13–14). These kinds of deficiencies are particularly problematic for those with dementia who would benefit from improvements in their functional abilities and in increased contacts with staff. In addition, most quality indicators have identified only facilities that have *not* met minimal standards, but do not address severe limitations among those that have met the lowest acceptable standards (Mukamel and Spector 2003). Some serious irregularities also exist among states—and even among inspection teams within states[1]—in

---

[1] According to Kathy Hackney, of the Isabella County Medical Care Facility, November 17, 2004.

their oversight of homes and in the penalties imposed for violating regulations (Walshe and Harrington 2002). As a result, it is unclear whether possible improvements in the quality of nursing home care are genuine or are the artifacts of differences in the implementation of nursing home surveys (Walshe 2001: 121). In addition, state surveyors of nursing homes often miss serious "quality of care problems" (Walshe and Harrington 2002: 477).

A team of inspectors visits each facility annually, or more often if problems are detected, and exhaustively reviews medical and institutional records, interviews staff, and closely observes care practices on selected units, looking for possible violations. The style of regulation in the United States is one of deterrence and antagonism with the nursing home administrators and staff (Walshe 2001: 134). This feeling can permeate the entire facility and produce a perpetual state of strained relations, as I observed in my study. Regulation compliance has favored the survival of for-profit conglomerates—despite their greater deficiencies—over smaller single operations (Winzelberg 2003: 2555) because conglomerates can spread the cost of regulation across their business and develop expertise in compliance (Walshe 2001: 132). Such policies have encouraged standard "cookie-cutter" impersonalized instrumental caregiving.

OBRA's focus on specific outcomes has also promoted instrumental care, directed its staff's energies from residents to paper work and regulation compliance, and fostered rigidity and reduced innovation, while not adequately establishing standards for staffing dementia caregivers.

OBRA's Promoting of Instrumental Care, not Quality of Life

OBRA has mandated nursing homes to complete a resident assessment instrument—the Minimum Data Set (MDS)—for all residents in order to be able to identify and address changes in functional and health status. The extensive documentation of a resident's condition into numerous sections on the MDS was consistent with a care economy that divided caregiving into specific activities and units of time. The MDS emphasized medical and physical care *outcomes* at the expense of quality of life *processes* (Winzelberg 2003: 2554; Walshe and Harrington 2002: 476). In addition, the MDS has not been able to distinguish expected differences in quality among homes that have very different levels of staffing (Kane 2004: 253). It has thus been insensitive to those indicators of person-supporting caregiving that are relevant in dementia care.

Shifting Attention from Patients to Paper

The MDS has encouraged a focus on paper work, which does not necessarily reflect quality caregiving. Rather, paper compliance has substituted "caring to the regulatory standards" in place of "caring to the preferences of the resident." Neither does documentation offer guarantees that the staff has completed care routines. As suggested by one nurse's comment, "If it's not documented, it didn't happen"; the documentation is what counted.

Regulations have unintentionally diverted attention from residents to regulators and to the paper work by which they judge an institution's compliance with OBRA. This has shifted much of the nursing staff's time away from direct patient contact to filling out paper work, ironically reducing the contact hours that enable good care. The heavy demands of documenting changes in residents' conditions and potentially harmful incidents occupy much of a nurse's day. However, even when an institution attempts to correct this deficit by hiring outside staff to complete the MDS, the documentation is less likely to have an impact on care (Winzelberg 2003).

Thus as the home places importance in documentation for its own protection, regulatory pressures have inadvertently worked to favor documentation over actual contact with residents.

OBRA's Fostering of Rigidity and Discouraging Innovation

OBRA's regulations have been overly prescriptive in legislating standards that too often lead to rigidity in care options. The well-intended mandates for staff to minimize medications, substitute more mild alternatives, and provide periodic treatment holidays were worthy efforts to curb overuse or abuse of psychotropic medication as chemical restraints. At the same time, for elders who have been stabilized for some time on particular medications, adjustments can be disastrous, even when gradual changes in protocol are followed. Homes where staff make informed decisions not to alter a medication regimen on which an elder has long achieved stability—particularly when such attempts have proven counterproductive—can be cited for noncompliance and threatened with withdrawal of Medicaid payments for *all* residents; only withdrawal of the medication can restore funds.[2] Such rigid standards are universally imposed even

---

[2] According to Kathy Hackney.

though they are very uneven in their impacts, helping some, but serving to destabilize the condition of many others with dementia.

Other stringent rules, such as a prescribed maximum number of hours between meals, may benefit residents in negligent settings, but hurt those who prefer to follow a more relaxed pattern of waking up and eating, similar to one they followed at their home. The rush to artificially awaken, clean, and groom residents in preparation for breakfast so that the home will be in compliance with regulations defeats the very purpose of the regulations to protect recipients from damaging conditions. Too often, as I observed, elders who are forced to wake up as early as 6 a.m. become disoriented and startled, defensive, and agitated and are then declared "combative" and given anti-psychotic medication in order to complete their morning care. Such mandates, through the instrumental practices they promote, can thus result in the need for medications that the regulations ironically intend to reduce.

Under regulations directed at protecting residents, nursing homes must document and report any suspected cases of abuse between staff and resident or resident with resident. Fears of severe consequences for failing to file incident reports may also lead to unnecessarily cautionary reporting and a paternalistic bias to withdraw the few freedoms still available to elders on a locked unit.

Inspectors also can promote an unnecessarily concrete reading of the rules. The staff must treat pureed foods as separate food categories that must not be mixed when feeding the resident, even if the resident prefers them to be mixed. Only by documenting prior authorization to mix food groups as part of the care plan, can the rule be overturned. The rigidity of such regulations and the need to take special steps to circumvent them discourages efforts to provide personalized care. Nursing homes, fearful of penalties, sometimes are excessively rigid when interpreting and complying with the defined standards. In trying to develop more creative approaches for persons with dementia, many providers have turned to assisted living or special care facilities that are not as stringently regulated. These alternatives, however, are typically limited to the upper-income individuals who can afford to pay privately for such care (Wiener and Stevenson 1998: 92).

Inadequate Minimal Staffing Standards for Dementia Care

The NHRA (Nursing Home Reform Act) originally set minimal staffing requirements for RNs and LPNs, but not for NAs. Yet, recent studies have found that an increase of one NA hour per resident day significantly

improves quality of care (Zhang and Grabowski 2004), unlike comparable increases in RN or LPN staffing. In fact, higher numbers of NA
hours have consistently accounted for the most dramatic differences
in estimated quality among nursing homes (Schnelle et al. 2004: 246)
since contact hours facilitate resident functioning and responsiveness
to personal needs.

Too often physical restraints become labor- (and cost-) saving management substitutes for NAs, at the human costs of heightened depression,
physical and mental deterioration, and even mortality of the elders (Zhang
and Grabrowski 2004). Prior studies have established clear relationships
between quality care and increased NA contact hours with residents in
terms of reduced restraint use, reduced incontinence, increased activity
(Zhang and Grabowski 2004), and increased toileting assistance (Schnelle
et al. 2004: 226). These findings have led to calls for more stringent minimal staffing requirements (Zhang and Gabrowski 2004). Similar recommendations for minimal staffing requirements were produced by recent
studies conducted for the Centers for Medicare and Medicaid Services
(CMS) (Kramer and Fish 2001; Schnelle, Simmons, and Cretin 2001), the
Institute of Medicine (Wunderlich and Kohler 2001), and an independent
expert panel (Harrington et al. 2000; Harrington, Zimmerman, Karon,
Robinson and Beutel 2000). If these standards (2.8 to 3.2 hours per resident
per day, depending on resident need) were adopted by CMS, a full 92 per
cent of nursing homes in the United States could not meet them, and over
50 per cent of the homes would have to more than double their staffing (and
labor costs) to meet the minimum recommended standards (Schnelle et al.
2004: 227)!

Schnelle and his group of researchers found that a two-tier nursing
home system exists in the United States—an upper group staffed at, or
even above, the recommended levels and two lower groups that fall in a
tier that is far below minimal recommended staffing (Scnelle et al. 2004:
238). The homes in the upper group differed significantly from the other
homes in the engagement of NAs with residents, the amount of toileting
assistance they offered, and the amount of physical movement and repo-
sitioning of residents. The study concluded that NA staffing levels might
provide the best indicator of quality nursing home care far beyond any
differences detectable from MDS quality indicators (p. 247). But as Robert
Kane suggests, staffing levels may only be part of the story, since other
significant factors may include individual qualities of NAs, training, and
perspectives on (and the organization of) care (Kane 2004: 253)—*the very
issues addressed by this study.*

Even if homes attempt to increase their NAs and nurses, the tight nursing market that exists today would make that difficult. An estimated annual turnover of 100 per cent or more (Winzelberg 2003) is not surprising given the poor pay, few fringe benefits, punitive hierarchical working culture, and minimal opportunity of NAs for professional advancement (Holahan et al. 2002: 207). Quality care has been linked to higher wages and benefits and to lower staff turnover (Schnelle et al. 2004: 247). Where relationships are fostered between NAs and residents—as occurred on Snow 2—and when NAs participate in care planning activities, turnover is less of a problem (Winzelberg 2003: 2555).

In order to achieve the levels of NA staffing encouraged by the recent reports, significant increases in nursing home expenditures would be necessary. Already, labor accounts for two thirds of all nursing home costs (Gabrowski et al. 2004: 370). If nursing homes met adequate staffing requirements, labor costs would soar and could account for over 80 per cent of operating costs, or up to an additional $15 billion annually (Walshe 2001: 138). Severe shortages in the nursing and NA work force (Zhang and Grabowski 2004) would make recruitment efforts tough and costs even greater (Grabowski et al. 2004: 371). Given these expenses, the difficulty of finding and keeping staff and the unfavorable alternatives, it may be, as Robert Kane has observed, *that the time has arrived when we must seriously re-evaluate the role of nursing homes in long-term care* (Kane 2004: 253).

ECONOMIC BARRIERS

The High Cost of Long-term Care in the United States

In 2002, nursing homes in the United States cost around $5,000 per month, or $60,000 annually (Caro and Morris 2002: 13); current estimates approach $6000. Of the 1.6 million elders who reside there, only 30 per cent of the beds are reserved for private payers since most private payers cannot afford such expensive care for very long. Long-term care is not an entitlement in the United States, but it is available in the form of Medicaid for the indigent and as a safety net for those who have exhausted their private resources in paying for care. And even though dementia in the elderly is often treated as if it were a medical condition, the support and custodial care that this condition necessitates are not eligible for medical coverage through Medicare (Montgomery, Karner, and Kosloski 2002: 121), which will pay for up to 100 days of post-hospital skilled care, but not personal care. Until private resources have been exhausted, no funding is available for long-term care in the home or community even when disturbed behaviors—viewed medically as symptoms—are present (Montgomery, Karner, and Kosloski 2002: 121).

Devolution of Federal Funding for Medicaid and Medicare

Medicaid, through combined financing between the federal government and the states, is the largest funder of long-term care in the United States, accounting for 47.5 per cent, or about $47 billion in nursing home spending alone. Private payers (about 30 per cent), Medicare (12 per cent) and private insurance (8 per cent) have paid for the rest of nursing home care, with only 2 per cent from other public sources (Wachino, Schneider, and Rousseau 2004: 13; Miller 2002: 17). In 2002, the federal government, financed about 50 per cent of Medicaid long-term care services (Caro and Morris 2002: 7). Over the last 25 years, however, the federal government, as it has continued to cut increases in spending, has steadily passed on its responsibility for Medicaid spending to the states, under the assumption that local governments are better able to determine service needs. Medicare, which the federal government entirely finances, also has undergone severe budget cuts (e.g., 14 per cent during 2002 alone) (AHCA 2003) while restricting services (Feder, Komisar, and Niefeld 2000: 148). Because of fiscal tightening, at least 20 per cent of elders who have needed long-term care in the past have not received it (Feder, Komisar, and Niefeld 2000).

Gradually Medicaid spending has become one of the largest items in state budgets, averaging about 14.4 per cent in 2000 (Miller 2002: 20). Through the Boren amendment, federal law had required Medicaid nursing home reimbursements to be "reasonable and adequate" to operate while meeting minimal standards (Grabowski et al. 2004: 364), and nursing homes could sue the states if their rates were inadequate. As part of the Balanced Budget Act of 1997, the Boren amendment was repealed to give states more freedom in setting pay rates to nursing homes.

Despite the appeal of the amendment, between 1999 and 2002, payment rates grew generously (Grabowski et al. 2004: 367–68), in part because of the good fiscal shape of the states during the late 1990s. Since the economic downturn in 2001, however, and unexpected state budget shortfalls, virtually every state plans to either cut spending or reduce the rate of growth in Medicaid spending (Grabowski et al. 2004: 371) in the future. Considerable variation exists in the Medicaid rate each state sets for nursing home care, depending on its own economic health and the number of persons needing Medicaid grants. Although about 50 per cent of the revenues of nursing homes and 70 per cent of nursing home beds are for Medicaid recipients, the Medicaid rates may be set too low to cover costs. In the past, homes have tried to cover expenses by charging private payers more. As Medicaid reimbursement rates falter, however, the quality of care is expected to suffer. Low Medicaid payment rates are associated with poor quality because they limit the numbers of adequately trained staff and other inputs believed to affect quality (Mukamel and Spector 2003). This bodes particularly poorly for persons with dementia who need substantial contact with staff.

The federal CMS, which acts both as a major funder of nursing home services and as a regulator, may be in a conflict of interest (Walshe 2001: 138). On one hand, it has spent $400 million annually to regulate the nursing home industry and recently called for studies to determine staffing standards needed to improve quality. On the other hand, the scope of the staffing problem is so considerable (with over 90 per cent of homes not meeting standards recommended by recent studies), that if the federal government were to adopt these standards, costs would soar, and the federal government would be pressured into footing at least some of the bill. Thus, it has settled for learning what the minimal standards should be, but not adopting them.

CMS has been also slow to embrace nonmedicalized community-based services, despite their cost-saving potential and preference by the public (Lynch and Estes 2001). As states have acquired increasing fiscal responsibility for long-term care, however, they have increasingly opted for community alternatives through waivers and other mechanisms. States vary greatly in offering these options, from only 1.1 per cent of long-term care spending in Hawaii to 50 per cent in Alaska (Miller 2002: 20); on average they still consume a small but growing share of states' Medicaid long-term care pie (27 per cent by 2000) (Grabowski et al. 2004: 368). Programs like the Program of All Inclusive Care for the Elderly (PACE), which provide a full spectrum of home and community care, are gaining states' attention since federal legislation has recognized them as eligible for Medicaid and Medicare reimbursement. The move toward community care has been slowed, however, by nursing home lobbies, bureaucratic inertia, and state fears about costs (Holahan, Weil, and Wiener 2003: 325).

Even states that have embraced community options have had to cut back on innovative programs that allow elders to employ friends or families as their Medicaid-paid caregivers. Medicaid home care grants have been grossly under-funded, and local agencies for the aged have had to make up for inadequate costs, often from charity funds.[3] Assisted living facilities, which are invading the nursing home market, do not receive Medicaid support in some states. Even in the 41 states that do pay for assisted living facilities, only 9.1 per cent have received Medicaid funding, which still limits coverage for this service (National Center for Assisted Living 2001a). In fact, over 75 per cent of funding for assisted living facilities comes from personal or family funds, compared to only 29 per cent of nursing home funds.

To lower expenses, Medicare has tightened the kinds of services it will cover and set more rigid eligibility criteria for services, shutting out those with dementia. For example, Medicare had automatically denied claims for physical therapy of persons diagnosed with dementia (O'Boyle 2002). After pressure from constituents, the policy was reworked to consider therapy claims on a case-by-case basis. Still, a person with dementia can be denied access if the therapist feels the elder will not be able to follow a sequence of instructions. In addition, if progress cannot be demonstrated within a fixed period, Medicare will stop paying for services.[4] Those with dementia may take longer to progress successfully, yet not be permitted to try because of those restrictions, drastically limiting their functional potential, independence, and quality of life.

The nursing home industry is in a "crisis" because of continued cuts in Medicaid and Medicare payments, poor quality of care, nursing shortages, and reduced occupancy (Holahan, Wiener, and Lutzky 2002: 208) as community care options become available (Holahan, Weil, and Wiener 2003: 325). Sharp increases in liability insurance, following egregious cases of neglect and legal battles during the 1990s, added to the industry's woes. One of every ten nursing homes recently filed for bankruptcy (Winzelberg 2003: 2555), and some homes have even closed. The financial instability of the industry makes it even less likely that federal regulations will impose the tighter staffing standards that are desperately needed if person-preserving care is to become a reality.

---

[3] Personal communication, Barbara Frankenfeld, Commission on Aging, Isabella County, MI, November 17, 2004.

[4] Despite's Medicare's strict rubric, innovative physical therapy programs exist that have enabled highly cognitively impaired elders to regain mobility by reducing expectations for "progress" and changing the definition of requirements for expected weight-bearing. By prescribing regular daily walks with staff just to the point of pain, not only have demented patients succeeded in physical therapy, but their recovery time has competed with that of nondemented patients in traditional therapy. Personal Communication, Mark Royer, Ingham County Medical Care Facility, November 5, 2004.

The For-profit Nursing Home Industry

Over 93 per cent of homes in the United States are privately owned. Two thirds of all homes are for-profit and 56 per cent are owned by multi-site corporations (Walshe and Harrington 2002: 475). Many of these operate subsidiary firms, like physical or occupational therapy, for which they bill Medicare at the retail rate even though they incur far lower costs (Bates 1999: 16). Although some homes have pulled out of the industry because of tight operating conditions, others have fed off the public system for years, in some cases by robbing elders of decent care (Bates 1999: 12). The public financing over the past 40 years of a mainly for-profit industry, beholden to its stockholders, has further compromised quality care (Winzelberg 2003: 2555).

When Medicaid reimbursement rates fall, the for-profits reduce spending to maintain profits (Walshe 2001: 140). However, increases in Medicaid spending do not translate into increases in staff and quality in noncompetitive markets (Mukamel and Spector 2003). Competition for Medicaid nursing home recipients will result in higher quality only in more competitive markets. The nursing home market is generally not competitive because the federal government passed Certificate of Need (CON) legislation to limit Medicaid expenditures. It also set moratoria on new construction, effectively eliminating competition.

When there is no competition, for-profits have no incentive to improve the quality of their care, given the lack of economic rewards. In noncompetitive markets, for-profit nursing homes are thus likely to provide lower-quality care (Mukamel and Spector 2003). Given competing obligations to stockholders and the elders they serve, the stockholders win out. It is not surprising that for-profit chains have both lower staffing levels and more average deficiencies in care (Walshe and Harrington 2002: 478, 484). The domination of the nursing home industry by for-profit corporations has severely compromised the quality of dementia care.

The new case-mix adjusted Medicaid payment system pays higher rates for more disabled residents. Since sicker patients bring in greater reimbursements both from government funding and private payers, some researchers have even grimly suggested that this payment system may provide the for-profits with economic disincentives to improving functioning.

Finally, many nursing homes are part of a larger corporate entity that includes subsidiaries that produce diapers, walkers, and medical equipment regularly used in nursing homes. In strictly economic terms, the more e supplies are used, the greater the corporate profit—both in additional monthly charges from the nursing home and in the additional profits to such subsidiaries. Promoting continence maintenance may thus be economically disadvantageous to the corporation. This may help explain why bowel continence has actually worsened despite OBRA (Walshe 2001: 131).

Unless there is a commitment of the federal government to increase Medicare and Medicaid payments for long-term care or somehow tie performance to reimbursement, and a willingness of large chains of for-profit homes to sacrifice some profits for quality, dementia care in nursing homes may only worsen.

CULTURAL BARRIERS

Public Imaginary Regarding Dementia:
The Potency of a Disease Model

Through deliberate efforts, described in chapter 1, dementia has shifted in the public imagination from an innocuous vision of senility in the community to a terrifying specter of decay in the nursing home. A broad folk adoption of a biomedical model of dementia has produced an image of a disease for which nothing can be done short of a techno-medical cure.

In a disease model of progressive, irreversible, and inevitable decline, disturbed behaviors are seen as symptoms of this decline. Cognitive impairments become signs of a person lost to the disease and fully defined by it. What is left is a body that continues to need custodial and maintenance instrumental care. Such a conceptualization urges for continued body care, while minimizing the importance of the interpersonal nature of that care.

As caregivers defined persons by their dementia, as they lumped together similarly diagnosed persons, they forgot their unique identities. Dementia was assumed to follow a common course of decline requiring a *leveling* standard program of symptom control—through physical or chemical restraint—and task-oriented care. A delivery system that imposes severe limitations on care may reinforce this nihilistic attitude among caregivers who can only hope for pharmacological control and eventual cure. However, as bioethicist Stephen Post cautions (2000a), such a technical mindset is contradictory to the needs of the person with dementia for human "caring connectedness" through attention, communication, support, and maximization of the elder's functioning.

While the political economy of care, the care economy within the nursing home, the biomedical model, and the visible impairments of the elders themselves conspire to create a vision of dismal possibilities, some recovery of function is clearly within reach. When positive moments or functional improvements occur, they disturb the sensibilities of caregivers who have been taught to expect less. A caregiver can live with a standard of care, however limited, if she/he believes it is adequate. But when alternative evidence suggests the contrary, it makes the work so much harder. It may be that much of staff burnout results from the nagging sense that one can do so much more.

Muddled Understanding about Quality Care and Quality of Life

There is an unjustified assumption in long-term dementia care that everyone agrees on the parameters of quality caregiving. Nursing home and assisted living facilities often boast about their ability to provide quality dementia care. OBRA and its regulatory agents also operate under guidelines that suggest that there are universally agreed principles of quality care. Quality care, by these guidelines, is measured by the least number of deficiencies detected upon inspection—which has little to do with the actual care experienced by individual residents. The reality is that there is no universally accepted understanding of what quality dementia caregiving should be. Despite their decent intentions, the regulations have instead assured a legacy of care designed around risk aversion, sanction avoidance, and profit (Hyer and Ragan 2002: 199).

Quality of life may be an even more ambiguous concept. In dementia, quality of life may be influenced not only by one's deficits, but by environment, quality of relationships, and perceptions of one's condition. Concepts of life quality have varied from constructs that include measurable psychological, social, and physical dimensions to those that look to the absence of negative caregiver–resident interactions (Kitwood's negative social psychology [1997: 45–49]). As Lawton urges (1999), we must avoid quality of life indicators that rely on standard measures since the very definition of life quality is likely to vary from person to person.[5] Any

---

[5] As cited in Hyer and Ragan (2002: 216).

uncritical assumption that there is a universal understanding about quality of care and quality of life prevents us from trying harder to improve both.

The Need for a Shared Cultural Identity and Script

The lack of social connectedness fostered in contemporary society has served to create many lonely individuals who lack a sense of community with others. Diversity has become a reason to celebrate differences from, rather than to seek commonality with, those who are different from us. Old age may only worsen that sense of aloneness as it imposes a new form of difference that itself evokes feelings of distance from others and even xenophobia (Pipher 2000). The multiple sources of resulting fragmentation impede our ability to find a shared cultural identity and mutual accountability for one another. Ultimately this contemporary cultural condition also erodes our desire to care for each other, especially where the sense of difference dominates.

Given the extreme fragmentation that occurs with individual selves[6] (s^1) as memory is compromised in dementia, a shared cultural identity (i^3) would link elders with caregivers even when they are not familiar with the elder's particular stories or selves (s^2). Philosopher Charles Taylor (1991) argues that it is possible to realize such a cultural identity (i^3) only as part of a larger cultural or spiritual tradition that has been lost in Western society. (It was the recognition of this tradition that, at least in part, motivated Elaine's dedication as a caregiver and reinforced her identity and ultimate sense of belonging.) Taylor believes that a "horizon of meaning" —a new cultural script—about old age, which caregivers and elders would both share,[7] could help to eliminate the fragmentation they both experience, as well as, I might add, the apparent asymmetry of the caregiving relation. This could invoke a common narrative of continuity across the generations that would heal the divides amongst us as we aspire toward something greater.

A director of aging services in a nearby community told me about the exceptional interpersonal involvement of NAs at nursing homes in her rural county with their residents.[8] She speculated that because the

---

[6] Here I refer both to the interior self (s^1), or singular sense of unity, that lasts deep into dementia and to the various social selves (s^2), or stories, that have developed over the life course through social engagement with others. See chapter 2, pp. 50–51, for further discussion.

[7] Charles Taylor, (1991), *The Ethics of Authenticity*, Cambridge: Cambridge University Press.

[8] Personal communication, Barbara Frankenfeld, Commission on Aging, Isabella County, MI, November 17, 2004.

community is so small, the caregivers regularly run into their care receivers' family members in shops, church, and other public places. The charge of moral responsibility, she suggested, is greater when a person shares a common history and feels part of the community of those for whom she cares. Caregiver and care receiver become connected beyond the walls of the nursing home and workplace. The NAs are constantly reminded of the social significance of their work whenever they encounter residents' family members in familiar local settings, and the relationship is one of warmth, commonality, and even intimacy. These relationships and continuing sense of responsibility are of a different order from those of caregivers in a larger urban area where they can be more anonymous. The continuity between private work and public spaces fosters the feeling of membership to a common community that is less apparent in urban areas, but which, as Taylor urges, can be fostered nonetheless.

The historical, political, economic, and cultural conditions of long-term care in the United States have resulted in severe barriers to a more satisfying provision of dementia care for our elders. These barriers, however real, are surmountable. These are the legacy of past legislation, differential power of scientific and corporate interest groups, and the continuing decisions by our legislators. They are also the products of ideologies, choices, values, and powerful cultural scripts. Within the political economy of caregiving (Estes et al. 1991), there are severe limitations about what institutional caregivers can do for our elders even though current knowledge allows for doing much more. However, as we have seen, the barriers—and the responsibility—lie beyond the caregivers.

As a society, we must ask what minimal standard of care we can tolerate. How much mutual effort do we wish to place in improving elder functioning and life quality? How important is it to "prevent the loss of the person to the disease"? Moreover, what is the relative value of demented elders to a society that is occupied with other challenges and a culture that looks to the future? The answers to these questions have major physical, emotional, and moral consequences for our elders, their caregivers, and perhaps all of us.

CHAPTER 10

Conclusion: Toward a New Vision of Dementia Care

A policy researcher recently observed that acute care deals with devastating disease through potentially lethal but "miraculous" cures, while long-term care, though never life-threatening, is unable to deliver dramatic solutions.[1] This study challenges that conclusion. It has shown how instrumental task-centered care that ignores the person can lead to tragic decline that is indeed life threatening. In addition, while relational person preserving caregiving and correcting of disabilities may not produce "miracle" cures, they visibly enhance quality of life and can dramatically improve functioning. Without concerted efforts to improve nursing home caregiving practices, elders with dementia will continue to face unnecessary misery and tragic endings—the "peacetime crimes" of which anthropologist Nancy Scheper-Hughes (2002) so eloquently speaks.

Of the more than 6.5 million people requiring long-term care (Feder,

---

[1] Peter Kemper (2003: 443).

Komisar, and Niefeld 2000), one fourth (about 1.6 million)—80 per cent
of them with behavioral disturbances—reside in the 17,000 nursinghomes
in the United States. The number of those currently in nursing homes is
expected to double by 2030 and triple to almost 5 million by 2050 (Hyer
and Ragan 2002: 200). Long-term care, however, is in the midst of change,
and some experts speculate that the end of the nursing home may be near
(Kane 2004; Thomas 2004). Public dissatisfaction, poor living and working
conditions, nursing shortages, and continual funding cutbacks have boded
ill for the industry. Scandalous abuses by for-profit chains in the late 1990s
have also left their mark.

Families whose relatives need less extensive medical and nursing assistance are turning to *assisted living facilities* as a less costly alternative that
may provide attention that is even more personal. These facilities developed
as a *social* alternative to medically based facilities such as nursing homes. As
such, assisted living facilities promoted the values of resident independence,
individuality, privacy, choice, and dignity in a home-like setting (Carder
2003: 263; Kane and Wilson 1993). They conceptualized medical needs as
simply one of many types of needs, rather than the core of an elder's needs. A
potential limitation of a strongly social model, however, is the eventual exclusion of those with increasing needs for medical attention. If consumer interest
remains strong for this type of residential option, however, they may develop
hybrid models that can accommodate such needs (Carder 2003: 282–83).

Currently, assisted living facilities house about half as many elders
(800,000) as do nursing homes. While some cost only one fourth as much as
nursing homes, others, targeted to the financially secure, may exceed nursing home prices. As assisted living facilities gain popularity and volume of the
long-term care market expands, there are concerns, however, that they may
become subject to standard federal regulation and lose the creative freedom
they have enjoyed in the past (Kylo 2004). Other community-based programs
like the Program of All Inclusive Care for the Elderly (PACE), which provide a
full spectrum of home and community care, are also gaining favor.

The trend toward community options is symptomatic of ongoing dissatisfaction with nursing home care. Since this study ended, many nursing
homes have closed, an unprecedented phenomenon during previous years.
Even the site where I conducted this research was forced to close its doors,
the victim of changed management, fiscal tightening, a series of bankrupt-
cies, severe staff cutbacks, and regulatory problems. As the economic climate
worsened, the quality care it once could provide was no longer possible. This
ended an era at a home that had been on the forefront of innovation and
quality care, but that was already changing by the time of my study.

WINDS OF CHANGE

During the course of my research, I encountered saints like Elaine, but I also saw the darker side of care, the disengaged caregiver understandably worn from years of hard physical toil, under-compensation, and under-appreciation. More disturbing were those caregivers who shamelessly handled and roughly degraded the elder before my eyes. They then expressed disgust and looked to me in vain to empathize with them, rather than with the elder. Of all I witnessed, these recollections have haunted me the most, as they signal that something is very, very wrong. More recently, I visited some marvelous nursing homes, small private places well endowed by church or private communities. I have also seen some publicly funded county homes that exceeded expectations, staffed by local people invested in their community. Both have adopted features of new models currently being embraced in dementia care.

In fact, in the years since this study, the field of dementia care has grown replete with ideas, modalities, and designs calling for "culture change" in long-term care. Many have built on the pioneering work of British psychologist Thomas Kitwood, who demedicalized dementia and challenged notions of behavioral management. He located BDs not in internal brain disease, but in emotional ill-being. More importantly, he brought attention to the person with dementia as a dignified human actor (Capstick 2003: 15). Kitwood and his colleagues at the Bradford Dementia Group developed an intensive observational method called Dementia Care Mapping to evaluate the quality of dementia care services (Innes 2003) based on the specific indicators of the person's quality of life. This method examines such dimensions as the elder's engagement, well- or ill-being, negative interactions with caregivers (negative social psychology), and positive events. Despite the intensity of this method, involving 12 hours of behavioral observation, dementia care centers worldwide, including the United States and China, have adopted it.

Kitwood was not the first writer to focus on the person in dementia care, however. Naomi Feil (2002) introduced her method for validating persons with dementia over 40 years ago. In addition, Quaker facilities,[2] which accept the fundamental divinity in all things—even the most pathetically weak or demented—have long designed care based on the dignity and respect of both care receiver and caregiver. For over 30 years, they have promoted demedicalized settings that forbid both physical and

---

[2] A classic example is Chandler Hall in Newtown, Pennsylvania.

chemical restraints and have been leaders in a national movement to "untie the elderly." Thus, while "person-centered care" has become the buzzword in dementia care today, it is not a new idea, but rather a product of renewed efforts to improve care for our elders.

Organizations like the Robert Wood Johnson Foundation and the Commonwealth Fund have invested in developing innovative caregiving models that will prepare to meet the growing need for long-term care in the future. The Pioneer Network has brought together energetic, passionate, innovative leaders intent on transforming the contemporary culture of dementia caregiving. Nursing home structures are being refashioned to resemble smaller familiar homelike environments with "neighborhoods" of "houses" clustered around large kitchens and pleasant parlors and other common living areas. Innovative models, like the Eden Alternative, which incorporates the natural world into long-term care environments, have also mushroomed throughout the nation as nursing homes have become "Edenized." Many ideas generated by the Pioneer Network encourage changes consonant with those suggested by my study.

"CULTURE CHANGE" THROUGH PIONEERING IDEAS/ APPROACHES TO DEMENTIA CARE

In 1997, a group of *Nursing Home Pioneers*, individuals who had independently been working on ways to humanize nursing home environments, formally convened to consider how to improve the culture of nursing home care. They were concerned about resident loneliness, isolation, and depression as well as high staff turnover (Pioneer Network 2004a). As assisted living facilities came to share some of the same staffing and caregiving problems as nursing homes, they too became included within a larger renamed *Pioneer Network*. Together pioneers attempted to change the culture of long-term care facilities, which they viewed as devaluing both elders and those who cared for them.

They aimed to change this by returning dignity, control, and relationship to those who live and work in long-term care settings. Together they defined holistic person-centered values committed to putting the "person before the task" and reshaping care environments at the spiritual, physical, and organizational levels (Pioneer Network 2004b). They envisioned a culture of aging that would be meaningful and life affirming by building "deep system change" through supportive relationships and community. The pioneers have agreed that knowing each *person* and offering individualized caregiving in a homelike environment is preferable for achieving these goals rather than focusing on a diagnosis and providing task-oriented routines in a medicalized setting (TLC n.d.). They developed a variety of models—Individualized Care, Regenerative Community, Resident-Directed Care, and Eden Alternative (and later the Greenhouse Project)—for achieving this. Below, I outline some features of these models, which support some of my own recommendations for dementia caregiving.

Individualized Care

The Individualized Care Model, developed specifically for dementia care,[3] relies on a permanent group of staff who try to get to know residents and develop caring relationships and mutual feelings of comfort with them. Communication is important in Individualized Care, which encourages the staff to try to understand and be understood by residents. Neither physical nor chemical restraints are permitted, and creative approaches and activities are encouraged for responding to residents with behavioral difficulties. Dignity is promoted by supporting resident choices, risk-taking and autonomy (TLC n.d.), and avoiding limiting paternalistic practices.

Like my research findings, this model recognizes the value of relationship, communication, and the dignity bestowed on every person through respect, even in institutional settings.

Neighborhoods in Resident Directed Care

Resident-Directed Care is a model that features neighborhoods as a structural design to recreate homelike features familiar to the residents. "Neighborhoods,"[4] formerly called "wings" or "units," are structured as small living clusters with about 24 or fewer residents (about 12 per neighborhood). In a typical design, the neighborhood is further divided into two houses (groupings of residents around their own kitchen, den, and formal living room). The attractive nonmedicalized settings minimize

---

[3] The individualized care model was developed by Joanne Rader and her colleagues at the Oregon Health Sciences University.

[4] The neighborhood idea was first developed by Charlene Boyd and the staff of Providence Mount Saint Vincent in Seattle, according to Megan Hannan (2001).

noise and distractions, while maximizing resident freedom of movement in common living areas. Some neighborhoods share a grocery, ice cream parlor, and hairdresser, each clearly marked by symbolic reminders like a barber pole at the entrance; some even have their own mini-theater.[5]

Although not developed specifically for persons with dementia, these familiar design features help prevent confusion and panic that residents often feel in medicalized settings. The pleasant features help to foster an inward peace, and the smaller number of residents in a deliberately calming setting generates minimal noise; both tend to reduce BDs.

Smaller numbers of residents can eat freshly prepared meals, often of their own choosing, from a buffet in the neighborhood kitchen—not fixed meals from a remote institutional kitchen that may be cool by the time they reach the resident. In some settings, food is available from the kitchen all day long, and the smaller number of residents can eat whenever they wish, increasing interest in food and caloric intake, which often suffers in dementia. The flexibility this affords eliminates the need to structure wake-up, care plans, and life around the institutional kitchen. The more flexible schedule also eliminates the need for NAs to speed each feeder (a resident who must be fed by the NA) through the meal in order to move on to the next resident by an "institutional clock," and to come to know their residents well.

The permanent staff, it also advocates, is extremely valuable for dementia care as long as the residents are comfortable and trust the caregiver assigned to them. With relaxing mealtimes, residents are less likely to become agitated. Far more than a superficial design gimmick, the neighborhood concept is structurally revolutionary for its possibilities to rearrange life according to the needs and desires of each resident. This model would be particularly beneficial for residents who value their autonomy and become agitated when it is threatened.

Regenerative Community

While also not specifically designed for persons with dementia, the Regenerative Community model,[6] developed by Debra and Barry Barkan

---

[5] A theater is included, for example, at Towsley Village, an assisted living and nursing home community in Chelsea, Michigan, the descendent of the historic Wesley Hall—a forerunner of innovative dementia care in the 1970s and the brainchild of Nancy Mace and Dorothy Coons.

[6] The idea for Regenerative Community came from Debra and Barry Barkan of the Live Oak Community in California.

of the Live Oak Community, emphasizes wellness and thus discourages the pathologization of behaviors that can be so lethal for people with dementia. The model also encourages the participation of all residents, their families, staff, and volunteers as part of an integrated community, thus enabling the kinds of communications that can both sustain elders and optimize plans of care. Here, "community" is not used to demand conformity to a larger body by elders too confused to understand its rules,[7] but rather to foster support among its members toward a common end of resident well-being. Such communities intend to involve members insofar as possible, thus encouraging the exercise of agency, and with it dignity.

The idea underlying this model is to create smaller groups of staff, residents, and family who together will contribute to the quality of life of elders by attending to their basic needs when they arise, rather than diverting attention to institutionally defined tasks. In the case of dementia and the presentation of BDs, this could mean attentiveness by the entire community to communicative signs from residents that could help determine underlying problems. Daily pleasures, participation within a small group of residents and staff, and enjoyable involvement with one's own family should contribute to life quality and lead to more content, fulfilled, and less agitated elders, with fewer expressions of BDs. Such outcomes in turn should facilitate positive caring attitudes in staff and result in less frustration, guilt, and depression in family members.

The freedom, potential for greater communication, de-emphasis on pathology, and the community support this model could bestow makes it be very promising for persons with dementia.

Eden Alternative

The Eden Alternative has been the most popularized and rapidly growing among these "culture change" models. By 2002, over 300 nursing homes were already officially "Edenized" (Salter 2005–06), and the model has recently spread throughout Europe and Japan. The organization has

---

7 In my research, I discovered the contradictory ways in which nursing home staff appealed to "community" to demand residents to behave "properly" in following institutionally generated rules. In the Regenerative Community model, by contrast, community is generated by the people themselves—something John McKnight would call "true community." See McLean (forthcoming 2006).

trained over 9,000 persons as associates knowledgeable in its tenets, and Edenized facilities are mushrooming across the United States to meet consumer demand. Edenized facilities sign on as paid subscribers to Eden principles, which they gradually implement, and offer training to their staff by the official Eden organization.

Dr. William Thomas, founder of the Eden Alternative, originally piloted the model in 1990 as a way to better serve residents with dementia (Hannan and Shaeffer n.d.). As director of the Chase Memorial Nursing Home in New Berlin, New York, Thomas was struck by the "complexity of suffering" of residents and the lack of respect given direct caregivers. "Loneliness, helplessness, and boredom" were targeted as the source of suffering, and companionship the solution. Thomas worked with the staff to transform the living environment, reorganize and empower caregivers, and restructure the physical design of the nursing home itself.

Thomas and his staff created a nurturing "human habitat" by introducing plants, animals (cf. Savishinsky 1985, 1991), and children for companionship and continuing contact with the noninstitutional world. Thomas also changed the *philosophy* of institutional caregiving (Deaton et al. 2000–01) by reverting decision-making authority from top managers to the caregivers and their peers. He also adopted permanent interdisciplinary teams assigned to the same group of residents. His model adopted neighborhoods, with permanent teams, as a way of creating smaller, more homelike communities within the nursing facility. Returning control to the NAs, who have direct hands-on care, makes sense as long as the caregivers use this control responsibly to better serve those under their care. The consistency afforded by supportive permanent staff and the use of smaller neighborhoods, as described earlier, are also valuable in dementia care.

As a model now adopted in facilities that serve both those with and without dementia, the Eden Alternative demands that all levels of staff be committed to these environmental, organizational, and structural changes. This is of crucial importance in institutional care, given the value of mutual accountability to promote understanding and staff morale that I advocated (R 8.1) in chapter 8.

Because of its wide adoption, various researchers have studied this model. They have found great variations in its implementation, its reception by residents, and its impacts. While some homes have structured regular programs of contact with children, others have limited visitation to the occasional holiday (Deaton et al. 2000–01). Facilities have also varied in their number of cats, dogs, and birds, from only a few animals to over 100! While the spirits of some residents have been dramatically uplifted, others are uncomfortable around pets and even afraid of them. In some facilities, animal litter and food strewn on the floor were potential hazards, and residents were forbidden access to outside areas they used to visit because of animal feces. Furthermore, the Eden organization felt that conformity to specific demands of the Eden model could actually constrain creativity, especially when only some of the concepts were adopted or the facility could not afford adequate training. Moreover, despite evidence to the contrary, some researchers voiced concerns that animals and their "zoolike" effect might over-stimulate and agitate residents (Deaton et al. 2000–01), contributing to BDs. Despite these issues, staff turnover and absenteeism under this model have diminished, as has the use of PRN psychotropic medications in many Eden facilities (Hannan and Schaeffer n.d.).

A major contribution of the Eden Alternative is its recognition of the importance of permanent self-governing teams and the need for the entire staff to accept the new philosophy for delivering care. However, with all the emphasis on habitat change, the model risks appearing gimmicky and misdirecting attention to superficial elements rather than to fundamental transformations in caring *relationships* that this study found to be key to dementia caregiving, and that Thomas himself identifies as basic to good health care (Salter 2005–06: 154). The idea that animals can provide companionship assumes that this will automatically fill a gap for most residents, without adequately theorizing the caregiver–care-receiver relationship. There is also concern that the marketing appeal of Eden may lead many homes to adopt its superficial features to attract consumers without fully accepting its charge to develop genuine culture change—a concern that Thomas himself shares (Stafford 2003: 20).

Green House Project

In contrast to the Eden Alternative, which attempts to improve the quality of life of elders in existing facilities, Thomas's Green House Project aims to virtually abolish institutional structures in an effort to radically transform future long-term care "from scratch." Driven by visions of more humane living environments for frail elders and the impending need of baby boomers, Thomas is set on strategically replacing most of today's 17,000 nursing homes with 100,000 smaller community group homes, geared to the Medicaid-paying population, over the next 20 years! These Green House homes aim to provide skilled nursing care for the "oldest, frailest, most impoverished" (Thomas 2004) people in the United States under the same laws, regulations, and funding mechanisms used for nursing homes.

The Green House Project intends to provide small "intentional communities" in a neighborhood where elders should find "respect, dignity, and a quality of life" less available in a nursing home setting. Fashioned after successful Scandinavian models, Green Houses will be run by community organizations intent on serving elders (Thomas 2004). Green Houses will be small (six to eight people) and provide 36 hours of regular daily staffing to care for the elders and the house. The relatively high resident contact (averaging about six hours per elder per day) is expected to foster intimate relationships with permanent caregivers. The houses will be designed to fit the "character" of neighborhoods where they will be built and to provide a "warm" and pleasant décor for residents (Thomas 2003). They will also be "green," incorporating the living habitat concept of Eden through plants, pets, and contact with children. Finally, they will be "smart," linking Green Houses through information technology to an intricate health care network to provide medical expertise, additional staffing when needed, documentation, and office support.

Thomas insists that this new model will operate on a level equivalent to nursing homes but will be less expensive to build and more economical in the long run because fewer medical costs will be incurred when residents are healthier, happier, and better attended. While acknowledging that existing levels of government funding will be inadequate to fund the project for the upcoming boomer generation, he is attempting to work within existing fiscal structures to promote his innovative model. Thomas is confident that the model will gain currency with a baby boomer constituency unwilling to accept nursing homes for themselves and eager to pressure policy-makers for a model they are willing to embrace.

The era of institutionalized care, according to Thomas, is coming to an end. Green Houses will complement home care as the new standard of long-term care, together with a variety of home and community care options; only a few nursing homes will continue operations over the next couple of decades. The success of models like PACE for providing community services to elders and of the deinstitutionalization of developmentally disabled persons into community homes encourages him that this model should work for elders as well.

The Green House Project contains many laudable elements. The pleasant homelike settings and smaller size should minimize noise and distraction and allow for more relaxed living environments, unencumbered by institutional demands. Green Houses are small and provide the consistent staffing that preliminary studies of *Pioneer* models have found to promote caregiver responsiveness to residents' needs (Adler 2003), which is particularly important for those with dementia. In more recent comparisons between Green Houses and traditional nursing homes, researcher Rosalie Kane found that the Green House staff treated residents with more dignity, and that more residents, families, and staff were satisfied with that model (Baker 2005). Neighborhood locations would allow more potential interaction with others in the community, including children, than is likely at institutional settings in more remote settings. In addition, the six hours contact per day with residents actually exceeds recommended standards that over 90 per cent of nursing homes fail to meet. However, with competing housekeeping duties, including cooking in some settings, it is unclear whether actual resident contact will be as luxurious as the figures suggest. Green Houses provide a very promising self-contained conceptual and structural model that should be seriously entertained as an approach for the future, especially when combined with advantageous features from other community models. It is premature, however, to discard other community models.

I am less sanguine than Thomas is, however, about the evidence of success of the deinstitutionalization of developmentally disabled people into the community as a model for our elders. Psychiatric inpatients who were deinstitutionalized into a "community" that was not equipped to support them have fared poorly. Group homes that are substandard and overcrowded continue to gain licenses and public funding because of their short supply. Psychiatric deinstitutionalization resulted from the combined efforts of liberal humanists who hoped to improve the quality of life of former inmates and fiscal conservatives who were trying to save money. We should not eliminate nursing home options in order to reduce expenses without first establishing preferable alternatives in the community. Already many elders residing in the community are unable to gain the help they need (Feder et al. 2000), and in some areas Medicaid home care grants are hard to obtain and grossly under-funded. If policy-makers use deinstitutionalization as an excuse to reduce future spending for elder care and inadequately fund Green Houses and other desirable community options, dignified community care for persons with dementia will remain a remote ideal, and the problems of institutionalized care could pale in comparison to the unforeseeable problems that might result. In addition, as seen by the Snow units themselves, the utilization of innovative design features may erode as funding streams dry up or residents' abilities decline. That is why therapeutic spaces must go beyond physical spaces to the personal, relational and intersubjective spaces that are so vital for sustaining the person with dementia.

Discussion

What is needed in dementia caregiving is structural and conceptual transformation through broad societal revamping of values and priorities (McLean forthcoming 2006)—the kind of transformation envisioned in these culture change models. These models promote relationship and community by carving out smaller spaces where mutual support and caring can occur. They regard elders as meaningful agents in living communities where they are encouraged to develop relationships. For persons with dementia, meaningful social engagement within a caring community can encourage social well-being and personal healing (Hester 2001: 67–68). In addition, the informality that exists in smaller intentional communities allows caregivers to recapture their innate sense of connectivity with elders, which many of them were trained to ignore in institutions directing them to manage bodies. In Sweden, where similar models have been instituted, caregivers have become very conscious of "letting go" of their need to manage those under their care (Zelkovitz 1997).

Community, however, must not be seen as a "place" or entity in which people are inserted—the mistaken assumption of the psychiatric deinstitutionalization movement—nor simply as a gathering; community entails *deliberate engagement* of its members toward a common end (Hester 2001: 50), the sustaining of persons with dementia. Community theorist John McKnight has cautioned that genuine care must be the product of the "consenting commitment of citizens to one another" (McKnight 1995: x), the defining basis of "community"; anything less is "counterfeit." To McKnight, commodified, managed, curricularized services found in institutions are only artificial substitutes that can never produce care.

Innovative models invested in creating communities hold tremendous promise for transforming dementia caregiving from institutional management to caring relationships, but they are no guarantee. Not everyone is equipped to render care, not even in informal "community" organizations. There is always the risk—even in smaller caregiving settings—that instrumental values will prevail over vulnerable populations under the guise of "community" if caregivers insist on "managing" its members. The "managing" of a community is antithetical to the very values—love, mercy, caring, and covenant (Gadow 1988)—that allow the tender handling of human frailty in communal organizations (Hillery 1978: 29). We must avoid reproducing instrumental values like efficiency, control, and management in the new community models.

Caring for someone with dementia requires a moral commitment from a caregiver who understands his/her own vulnerability and the tragedy of life (McKnight 1995: 172). It entails a covenant of meaning about aging and a shared identity as part of a larger cultural tradition—one that has been eroded in our fast-paced diverse society with its competing traditions. In order to reclaim this tradition, we must embrace a new moral and cultural script of continuity and reciprocity across the generations. Innovators like Thomas hope to accomplish this need for intergenerational connectivity by constructing intentional communities that bring elders into regular contact with children. Despite funding pressures, the Swedes showed considerable success with similar communities that connected intergenerational living complexes with schools and cultural centers (Zelkovitz 1997).[8]

Philosopher Charles Taylor (1991) suggests that only when people of all ages and backgrounds come to share a sense of sameness and a larger "horizon of meaning" about old age, might we realize our identity as part of a larger whole.[9] Only then might we come to accept the obligation *to support fully* the frailest among us. The Oriya Hindu of India practice a "feudal ethics" based on the notion that well-being is interdependent, on the need for taking care of your own, and on the belief that divinity is in all things, even the most pathetically weak (Schweder, Much, Mahapatra, and Park 1998); it is ultimately a concept based on love (Hillery 1978). It yields a world of *intersubjective* community, which stands in dramatic contrast to obligatory or controlling institutional "communities." While we cannot aspire toward such an ethics in an individually oriented consumer economy, the challenge for more constructive dementia caregiving is to find some way to realize such loving communities. The hope for future dementia care comes from the realization of such communities for everyone.

---

8 Subsequent economic pressures and changes in political climate have, however, led them to suspend construction of new complexes, despite their social benefits.

9 Taylor, Charles (1991). *The Ethics of Authenticity*. Cambridge: Cambridge University Press. Cited in ter Meulen (2001: 134–35). Taylor is referring to identity³ (i^3), or cultural identity, as discussed in chapter 2, p. 51.

THE POLITICAL AND MORAL ECONOMY OF LONG-TERM DEMENTIA CARE

Models for transforming the culture of long-term care, however humanistic, are also products of an entrepreneurial fervor. In a country where privately owned industries overwhelmingly dominate long-term care, consumerism is a driving force to innovation. Baby boomers facing their own impending care needs are refusing to settle for traditional institutional care. Speakers at the 2004 Pioneer Network Conference argued that "culture change [is] imperative to staying in business." United States taxpayers have supported a private long-term care industry for 40 years and will no doubt continue to do so to some extent in the future. However, if government funding for long-term care continues to decline, visions of better elder care will reach only the affluent.

These innovations may suggest that a radical transformation of dementia care is soon approaching, but the cultural change movement is still young and overshadowed by the stark reality that more than 90 per cent of current nursing facilities do not meet minimal recommended staffing. Scandalous abuses by for-profit chains have left an indelible mark on the industry. The federal government's gradual devolution of fiscal responsibility to the states has only worsened the situation. In spite of millions of dollars spent annually to regulate the nursing home industry, deficiencies remain grim and will be costly to correct. Whatever their motivations, the cultural changes that are being proposed are long overdue. However, despite the efforts of its enterprising pioneers, the National Citizen's Coalition for Nursing Home Reform (NCCNHR) recently announced that, "deep culture change has not achieved widespread usage in long-term care settings."[10] Among its 2004 resolutions, it urged the Centers for Medicare and Medicaid Services (CMS) and other federal agencies to "incorporate deep culture change as an important component of quality of care and quality of life for individuals in all long-term care settings."

Culture change has been slow because providers have not yet decided whether to rebuild a failing system under increasing regulatory pressures and low government reimbursements or to invest in the new models. As Thomas observes (2004), change in long-term care is inevitable, but it is still uncertain how that change will play out. While consumer demand for innovation is considerable, the federal government, which has been the major funder of long-term care, continues to pull back support. In an

---

[10] This was part of its 2004 Resolution #3 ("Require the Principles and Values of Deep Culture Change in All Long-term Care Settings").

uncertain fiscal environment, providers are reluctant to adopt potentially more costly models.

Long-term dementia care occurs within a *political economy of care* in which economic policies are affected by social and political climates and by the power relations among powerful constituencies. In the United States, where long-term care is overwhelmingly privatized and where universal health coverage is lacking, the most impaired elders must compete with other constituencies for resources and are often hostage to market forces and powerful lobbies that do not represent their best interests (Hess and Markson 1995: 321).

The political economy of long-term care has been at play where nursing home regulations have been inadequate and the federal government (the CMS) has neglected to establish recommended staffing requirements. Recent government reports concerning the survey process for regulating nursing homes have suggested inconsistency in its application among states, a "disturbing understatement of actual harm," and "neglect by many agencies" to take action where deficiencies are found. Reasons cited by the Inspector General's report for some of the problems include "the political climate, the strength of the nursing home lobby, and changing federal and state regulations" (Hedt and Wells 2004).

Several recent studies have strongly corroborated the clinical belief that quality of care is directly related to the number of contact hours of staff with residents. While the CMS accepted the "strong and compelling evidence" from the reports and has admitted that increasing staffing to levels suggested by the studies would improve quality, "it asserts that no action can be taken until there is further analysis of the 'tradeoff' between cost and quality improvement" (Lenhoff 2002). It is concerns for such tradeoffs that have prevented the improvement of quality of care for elders *even when it is possible*. In dementia care in particular, adequate contact between residents and staff is fundamental to the possibility of a strong and supportive caregiving relationship. Meanwhile, despite its acknowledged funding deficiencies to enable adequate staffing for long-term care, the United States Congress is currently contemplating major reductions to the overall Medicaid budget for coming years.[11]

---

[11] Recent Congressional blueprints for cutting $10 billion from the Medicaid budget over the next five years were endorsed (Pear 2005). Earlier there were rumors of that as much as $100 billion in cuts to the Medicaid budget were being planned—double the current Medicaid budget for nursing home care, and one third the entire federal and state outlay for Medicaid. More likely to occur is a shift to giving states fixed block grants, rather than one based on a formula that depends on actual costs and enrollment (Hernandez and Baker 2005). In the current system, the federal expenditures for Medicaid vary from state to state, but are at least 50 per cent of each state's expenses. See Wachino et al. (2004) for the specific formula used in calculations.

The nursing home industry is in crisis because of years of publicly funding privately run institutions whose *ethical* responsibilities to their stockholders out-shadowed their *moral* responsibilities to those whom they contracted to serve. It is the result of an industry in a "free market" protected from the pressure of competition to try harder. It is the legacy of legislators continuing to cave in to the pressures of nursing home lobbies against the safety and happiness of elders and the wishes of citizens for them to remain at home or in communities rather than confined in institutions. It is raising the principle of the free market in the long-term care business enterprise above the covenant of intergenerational responsibility to care for our elders as a moral enterprise. It is government foregoing its responsibilities to its citizenry.

Dementia Care as a Moral Enterprise

As a moral enterprise, long-term care shapes the quality of life of elders in their final years. Thus, *a moral economy* of long-term care is also necessary for addressing the actual impacts of political economies on lived experience, examining assumptions concerning reciprocal obligations among the generations (Minkler and Cole 1999), and articulating the need for policies that will maximize the possibilities for a decent life for persons throughout their entire life course (Hendricks and Leedham 1991).

While we cannot yet cure dementia with *technical* interventions, we can minimize its damage through intensive *human* interventions. Good dementia care, whether at home, in the community, or in an institutional setting, demands profound support and respect for both caregiver and receiver. A caring relationship and labor-intensive person work are the crux of preservative dementia caregiving. My study reaffirmed this, and the Pioneer Network and others are developing models for realizing it. Preserving bodies and supporting persons whose agency can persist deep into their dementia requires patience and energy from caregivers who need time to devote to elders. Such caregiving is costly because the contact hours are high. With inadequate staffing, even the most devoted caregivers—like Elaine—burn out and leave. As long as NA/resident contact is severely restricted because of restricted government support, warehousing and instrumental care will continue to dominate the caregiving of those with dementia, and concerns for their agency and personhood will be put aside. The problem is not the lack of knowledge; it is the lack of moral commitment to support elders in options they prefer, whether at home, the community, or nursing home, at a level and manner that will dignify their remaining years while not impoverishing them or their families.

Although many states have embraced community options, these have received only a fraction of the funding that goes to institutional care. States have slashed innovative programs because of enormous constraints on their budgets, and local agencies for the aged have sometimes donated their own limited resources to cover costs not met by state and federal Medicaid monies.[12] Technicalities in spending under Medicare further limit funding to technical and biomedical care, rather than to the personal care that could keep persons with dementia at home. By regarding our elders "simply as a cost center" (Thomas 2004), we severely limit their possibilities for a better life.

Other nations have managed to order their priorities within a political economy of care that has allowed them to keep precious their covenant with their elders. The Swedes have promised their elders a "middle-way" in which an economic and political order dominated by business interests will be balanced by considerable control by workers and the government (Zelkovitz 1997: 241). Since the early 1980s, they have instituted a national philosophy of integration and dignity for their elders. They have funded elder care in intentional communities that bring them in contact with families and disabled persons, developed group dwellings similar to Thomas's Green Houses, and have promoted caregiving at home or homelike settings rather than in institutions. Families or friends who provide informal care are eligible to receive payment, or if they are already employed, generous paid leaves. Even as the Swedes tackle the forces of privatization, and its government is withdrawing some of its generous social spending (Edwards 2004), the covenant to their elders remains sacrosanct.

Similarly, as women from the Republic of Cyprus have increasingly entered the public work force over the last two decades and become less equipped to provide full-time care to their elders, they have sought ways to retain them at home. The Cypriot government has been committed to keeping elders "in their familiar environment" and to meeting the demand for 24-hour care through financial aid and policies to import needed workers from other countries. It has also provided economic support to local church-based communities to develop homes in familiar localities where elders already know each other. Community members try

---

[12] Personal communication, Barbara Frankenfeld, Commission on Aging, Isabella County, MI, November 17, 2004.

to hire staff already familiar to the elders, and whenever possible, to hire their family members. Whether in the home, the community, or the few existing institutions, the government pays for care that the family cannot provide or afford. Even in its newest highly medicalized institution, family members regularly help serve meals. The chief administrator herself ritually leaves her desk before meal times to participate in the "pleasure" of serving hot food to elders,[13] an example of the mutual accountability[14] that I have advocated.

As a society, we need a collective economic remedy, but local ideas and implementation. Devolution has failed us. Given the enormous regional and cultural variation of the United States, it would be difficult to develop a sense of singular community identity based on common history and cultural homogeneity as exists in Sweden and Cyprus. However, we can develop many local communities where caregivers feel a personal sense of accountability; many private and county homes already do this. The Green Houses proposed by Thomas and culture change concepts of the other pioneers will help us to accomplish this. As Thomas notes (2004), it is now simply an issue of public policy. But that policy can only be implemented if we accept a moral commitment to our elders. Such a pledge is virtually impossible in the absence of a shared cultural script and sense of greater belonging, akin to Taylor's "horizon of meaning" about old age that compels us to accept our moral obligation. In order to achieve this, however, "we" as a concerned citizenry need to demand a "mutual accountability" (Bayer 2004) among all stakeholders involved in formulating, advocating for, implementing, and receiving dementia care policy. As Andrea Capstick of the Bradford Dementia Group makes clear, quality of care and the well-being of our elders does not stop with the caregiver; it "incorporates the *moral actions* of management, organizations, statutory services, and government agencies [italics added]" (2003: 22).

This book has argued that the *person* with dementia can best be supported in an environment that fosters a significant caring relationship between caregiver and receiver that bestows dignity to the elder, no matter how far the dementia advances. Just two years before Medicare and Medicaid were enacted (and long before OBRA), Jules Henry, in *Culture Against Man* (1963), decried the conditions in nursing homes in the United States. Despite this early outcry, many nursing homes remain unsafe places at

---

[13] I observed this during my research in Cyprus, the summer of 2000.
[14] This concept was coined by Professor Trudy Bayer, a communications specialist at the University of Pittsburgh.

the very time that the industry reaps profits and government support lessens. As we face an impending crisis during the next two decades with baby boomers coming of age, we have little time to act. Innovative models of person-centered dementia care are now available, but funding restrictions inhibit our ability to bring them to the majority of elders in need. Of even greater concern are the current calls to re-engineer social welfare toward an individually responsible "ownership society" (Rosenbaum 2005). Such a direction would discourage the very *social* responsibility and intentional communities on which the requisite "horizon of meaning" and visions of culture change are founded.

Instrumental caregiving that denies the validity, and pathologizes the agency, of persons with dementia is devastating to elders. This study showed how, in contrast, elders have thrived under intensive relational caregiving that celebrates their personhood. The measure of a society can be determined by the way it treats its most vulnerable members. We are better equipped today than ever before to treat those with dementia well as new knowledge and humane person-centered models for community care become available. If for political economic or other reasons we choose instead to advance more "cost-saving" instrumental practices, we will subject our elders to continued structural violence and "genocidal-like behaviors" (Scheper-Hughes 2002) which in the past seemed tragically unavoidable. As the proponents of culture change have attuned us to other ways, these practices are no longer acceptable. All of our elders—not only the financially secure or cognitively intact—deserve better treatment, and as a society, we must aspire to a higher moral standard.

FURTHER READING

Kane, Robert, and Wilson, K. (1993). *Assisted Living in the United States: A New Paradigm for Residential Care for Frail Older Persons?* Washington, DC: American Association of Retired Persons.

Thomas, William. (1994). *The Eden Alternative: Nature, Hope and Nursing Homes*. Sherbourne, NY: Eden Alternative Foundation.

Appendices

APPENDIX A:
LINKING NEUROPATHOLOGY TO SPECIFIC DISEASES

Although the neuropathologies underlying AD and VaD have been identified, the particular ways in which they lead to dementia are still being explored by researchers. In addition, there are still questions whether the same neuropathology (disease process) that caused behavioral symptoms in one person are involved in causing those symptoms in another (Dillman 2000: 131). Clinicians have claimed that a definitive diagnosis of AD could only be made following autopsy, when the presence and degree of destructive plaques and tangles could provide the needed evidence. Over the years, that assertion has been challenged by findings of considerable neuronal damage in the brains of persons who showed no clinical signs of AD.[1] Conversely, the absence of characteristic plaques and tangles expected in persons who present with clinical symptoms of AD again leads to questions about the absolute source of the disease in neuronal change. Such findings have led some researchers to regard AD as an elusive concept (Lock 2005) and suggest that there may be much more involved, such as social, psychological, and environmental factors, in the development

---

[1] A discrepancy between dementia in the living patient and the presence and degree of pathology upon autopsy was recognized as early as 1932 (Ballenger 2000: 88) and more recently confirmed by David Snowdon's nun study (1997).

of this disorder rather than purely biological or genetic factors. These findings notwithstanding, AD continues to be viewed as a biological condition resulting in clinical symptoms as the result of brain pathology (Whitehouse 2000: 298).

A major explanation for AD is linked to discoveries made during the 1970s of reduced levels of the neurotransmitter acetylcholine in AD brains. The deficit occurred because of the loss of cholinergic neurons in the forebrain. Previous researchers had found cholinergic systems to be important for learning and memory. Researchers hypothesized that they might be able to treat AD by supplementing the cholinergic system. One approach was to use cholinergic agents that inhibit the degradation of acetylcholine by the enzyme acetylcholinesterase. It took almost three decades, however, before acetylcholinesterase inhibitors, such as tacrine and donepezil (Aricept ®), were approved. These inhibitors proved less effective than similarly developed drugs for Parkinson's disease, perhaps because of more global damage in AD (Turner 2003: 7). According to one researcher, the cholinergic hypothesis was anything but a pure scientific idea. It was also political, given the different camps that placed full or partial faith in it or completely rejected it, as an explanation for cognitive dysfunction (Whitehouse 2000: 297). The controversy continues even as the latest drug trials of acetylcholinesterase inhibitors are under way. The cholinergic hypothesis, however, is but one of many hypotheses attempting to explain the underlying organic mechanisms of dementia.

The most recent medication found to have symptom-reducing effects for AD has been a new class of medication called memantine (and the brand name of Nameda® in the US), approved for sale in the United States beginning 2004. Unlike previous medications, memantine has been found to affect symptoms of persons with moderate to severe symptoms.[2] It also appears to have few side effects. Memantine operates by blocking the transmission of glutamate, which is involved in learning and memory. Scientists speculate by overstimulating the N-methyl-D-aspartate (NMDA) receptor, glutamate has neurodegenerative effects. Memantine blocks this overstimulation. However, like its predecessors, Memantine does not stop or reverse the disease process (O'Boyle 2003).

Much of the scientific focus today has shifted from neuropathology to molecular biology and genetics. After understanding the actual micro-mechanisms involved, the time it will take scientists to successfully develop a cure may be further away than the media had led the public to believe, in spite of warnings from some of the researchers themselves (Bick 2000: 243). In the meantime, elders and their families have continued to cope with the symptoms that dementia imposes on their day-to-day living while they wait for a scientific promise.

---

[2] According to the April 3, 2003, issue of the *New England Journal of Medicine* as cited by Richard O'Boyle, October 17, 2003, *ElderCare Online*.

APPENDIX B: DEMENTIA AS A DEMOGRAPHIC PROBLEM: SOCIAL AND POLICY IMPLICATIONS

Demography refers to the study of the size, composition, and geographical and historical distribution of the population and its future projections. Patterns of fertility (birthrates), mortality (death rates), and migration all affect demography. In the United States, fertility was high in the first quarter of the last century, dropped in the 1930s during the Depression and World War II, and rose once again after the war. This led to a higher birthrate for today's elders who are over 80, a smaller birthrate for those 60 to 80, and a large post-war baby-boomer generation facing retirement by 2010. Improvements in public health during the last century reduced mortality in infants, children, and young adults, enabling many more people to live on to old age than previous generations. The death rate has also dropped for persons 65 to 84 in the last two decades.

As a result of these patterns, there has been a dramatic increase in the number and percentage of persons 65 and older in the population over the last century. In 1870 there were only 1 million people 65 and older, by 1900, 3.1 million (4 per cent of the population), and 35 million (13 per cent of the population) by the end of the century.[1] By 2030, when the baby boomers fully come of age, that figure will more than double to 71.5 million, representing 20 per cent of the nation's population. The oldest old—people 85 and older—the fastest growing segment of the elderly population—will grow from 4.3 million persons (under 2 per cent of the population) in 2000 to at least 9.6 million people by 2030 (*A Profile of Older Americans 2003*). Their number may double again to 19 million (5 per cent of the population) by 2050 when the last of the baby boomers reach 85. This is 190 times their number in 1900 (Moody 2002: 41)!

Debilitating dementia places enormous demands on family caregivers, who may themselves be old and frail, or involved in careers or caring for their own families. Today, more than 20 million families have been directly affected by dementia. The stress of caregiving may endanger the health of the caregivers as well. These factors combine to make senile dementia a major public health problem in North America.

As the elder with dementia declines, the family caregiver may no longer be able to maintain the affected person in the community, given the inadequate services currently available to support home care. Usually with reluctance and often guilt, the caregiver must seek long-term care in a nursing home.

Long-term care options include a range of services to help elders compensate for limitations and to function independently. An independent living facility or

---

[1] The figures in this section were derived and/or extrapolated from the Web sites of the *Centers for Medicare and Medicaid Services, CDC—National Center for Health Statistics– Tables: A Profile of Older Americans: 2001* and *2003, Older Americans 2000: Key Indicators of Well-being,* and *AARP Research,* and from material in Moody (2002).

board and care home will provide meals and medication and varying degrees of help with self-care before the elder requires considerable supervision. If the elder remains at home, the family may try to gain home assistance to help supervise their elder or use the services of adult daycare during the day. However, as the elder comes to require more and more supervision and/or increasingly exhibits disturbed behaviors, such as wandering, agitation, or aggressive behaviors, institutionalization in a 24-hour care facility becomes more likely. Over half of all nursing home residents are cognitively impaired (Sahyoun, Pratt, Lentzner, Dey, and Robinson 2001: 4) and have behavioral problems; the figure is over 90 per cent for those in special care units (Wagner et al. 1995), which are specifically designed for persons with dementia who manifest serious behavioral disturbances.

Nursing home costs, however, are extremely high, beyond the reach of most Americans. By 2000, close to 1.6 million persons resided in nursing homes,[2] at least half of whom had dementia. In 1999, in the United States, the average monthly cost of nursing home care was close to $4000, closer to $5000 in the northeast. At an annual increase in cost of 12 per cent (Moody 2002: 26), this is a significant economic burden. At this rate, care already costs over $70, 000 a year for many elders. With over 85 per cent of elderly households having incomes below $40,000, and few carrying private insurance to cover nursing home care, the public has had to step in to foot the bill.

By 2001, long-term care spending[3] reached $132.1 billion, with nursing homes capturing $98.9 of this amount (Wachino et al. 2004: 13). Government programs covered close to three fifths of these expenses. Medicaid, a joint state and federal program originally designed to provide health care for the poor, is a major payer of nursing home care for middle-class elders who can no longer afford to pay the monthly bills, paying almost half (49 per cent by 2002) of all yearly nursing home costs (Smith et al. 2004: 7). Medicare, a federal program that pays for health care of elders, pays only 12 per cent as it covers nursing home costs only for a limited period following hospitalization. Almost 40 per cent of the economic burden remains with the families of the elders. Taking into account annual cost increases, nursing home costs for 2004 will exceed $100 billion. A good half of that supports elders with dementia. In the US, current costs for annual treatment of all kinds for AD and other dementias, including nursing home expenses, has already exceeded $100 billion (Richter and Richter 2002: 10).

---

[2] The elderly population residing in nursing homes by 2030 is expected to triple to almost five million even though the population itself will only double. This is because more older persons are expected to reside alone rather than with family caregivers, according to the Population Resource Center Web site (2004).

[3] Long-term care costs include expenses for health and social services for elders who have lost the ability to take care of themselves at home, in the community, or in nursing homes (Moody 2002: 3).

Despite these extraordinary costs of nursing home care, it is the only form of long-term care for which payment is assured in the United States health care support system. Although figures vary, an estimate of at least 10 per cent of institutionalized elders could remain in the community if the government helped to pay costs to maintain them there instead. As the number of elders needing long-term care increases, the United States will need to shift some of its support for long-term care from institutional care to more intensive adult daycare and other forms of community care (Moody 2002: 25) that most elders and their families prefer.

Between 1900 and 2030, the percentage of total dependents—the old (65+) and the young (17 and younger) are expected to remain unchanged (about 44 per cent of the population). However, in 1900, the old composed only 4 per cent of the population. By 2030, as 20 per cent of the total population, the percentage of elders will approach that of the young dependents. But while the total number of dependents may not change, the costs of health care are substantially higher for older folks. Since health costs rise with age, the projected growth of the oldest old will place an even greater financial burden on the society. As health care costs in the United States have exceeded the $1 trillion mark,[4] with one tenth of that ($100 billion dollars) due to dementia alone, it is not surprising that ethicists have discussed the idea of rationing care (See Moody 2002: 33–62). In the context of these debates, it is absolutely necessary for clarity about how to define human value in dementia. Otherwise, under tremendous economic pressure, we risk concluding that some lives are just not worth paying to preserve.

Given the high personal and social costs of dementia, it is not surprising that the public has placed considerable faith in science for developing a cure for Alzheimer's disease and providing technological solutions to control it. Since institutionalization accounts for the largest portion of dementia care costs, retarding decline could delay nursing home placement and save billions of dollars. During the late 1960s and 1970s researchers, federal officials, and family members launched a campaign to promote research into finding a cause and cure (Gubrium 1986a; Fox 1989, 2000). Through their efforts, AD succeeded in becoming well entrenched as a disease of aging. However, its success has served the interests of researchers and the pharmaceutical industry better than those suffering from dementia and their families. Magic bullets were held out as the hope to stop the progression of dementia and to save catastrophic expenses of long-term care by 2010; they have not yet delivered. The most promising medications have delayed progression by about six months, but they have not stopped it, making the demographics an even more pressing concern than it was when the research campaign against Alzheimer's disease was initially launched.

---

[4] Total national health spending in fact reached $1.34 trillion by 2002 (Smith et al. 2004: 7).

APPENDIX C:
CONTRIBUTIONS OF PREVIOUS ETHNOGRAPHIC STUDIES
TO NURSING HOME RESEARCH

Two influential studies about the dehumanizing character of institutional settings were conducted during the mid 1950s (Goffman 1961; Henry 1963). Sociologist Erving Goffman's now classic, *Asylums: Essays on the Social Situation of Mental Patients and Other Inmates* (1961), based on ethnographic research conducted at St. Elizabeth's hospital in Washington, DC, was written when unsatisfactory conditions of psychiatric hospitals propelled a deinstitutionalization movement. Goffman spent a year among the inmates of St. Elizabeth to learn firsthand about their world. His resulting structural analysis of "total institutions,"[1] which demoralized those they intended to serve, has been valuable in understanding the workings of nursing homes as well, despite some differences between the types of these institutions (Shield 1988: 101–04).

In *Culture Against Man* (1963), anthropologist Jules Henry offers a "passionate ethnography" (p. 3) in which he criticizes various aspects of his contemporary American culture and its impacts on people across the life cycle. His compelling volume was based on research conducted in three nursing homes during a period of nursing home shortages, government encouragement for hospital-based care, and a virtual absence of regulation. While conditions varied from site to site, he poignantly describes how the worst greed of the management, the orderliness of the facility, the demoralization of the staff, and a demeaning view of elders as "child-animals" (p. 440) conspired to assault the bodies and minds of the residents. He describes how even within the best home, "the mind of the patients gets in the way of the real business of the institution, which is medical care, feeding, and asepsis" (p. 474). Thus by the early 1960s—even before the massive expansion of nursing homes afforded by the Medicare Act—two influential ethnographies had paved the way for studying the impact of nursing home culture on the lives of elders.

The first major ethnography on nursing home life, *Living and Dying in Murray Manor* by Jaber Gubrium (1975), eloquently describes how residents were encouraged to conform to a routinized care industry that thrives on efficiency of "bed and body work" at the cost of "person work." The consequent depersonalization was documented from within by anthropologist Carobeth Laird. *Limbo: A Memoir about Life in a Nursing Home by a Survivor* (1979) is the product of participant-observation by an actual resident, struggling to preserve her sense of self through her writing.

---

[1]   A total institution, as defined by Goffman is "a place of residence and work where a large number of like-situated individuals, cut off from the wider society for an appreciable period of time, together lead an enclosed, formally administered round of life" (1961: xiii–xiv).

Jennie Kayser-Jones in *Old, Alone and Neglected* (1981) provides an ethnographic study comparing care in a nursing home in the United States with one in Scotland. It points out various ways in which depersonalization (pp. 43–45) and dehumanization (pp. 46–51) erode the human soul in the United States home, in contrast to the very person-oriented practices in Scotland. Her analysis goes beyond a description of the differences to a historical and structural explanation of their causes.

Several additional ethnographies were published by the late 1980s and early 1990s, when steps to implement OBRA legislation were just beginning. In *Uneasy Endings* (1988), Renée Rose Shield states that she does not want to bash nursing homes. After studying a "quite good" nursing home in the United States, she tries to understand the cultural and structural reasons that help explain why life in nursing homes can be so difficult for their residents. Using Arnold van Gennep's analysis of rites of passage (1990) together with Victor Turner's notion of liminality, a period in-between two life stages or rites of passage (1974), Shield explains some of the difficulties elders face in nursing homes as a result of the absence of rituals that accompany this period of liminality, while waiting for the next stage of life (or death). She argues that without shared rituals to facilitate their transition to the rite of passage to the nursing home elders become isolated and increasingly dependent on others. Joel Savishinsky's prizewinning ethnography, *The Ends of Time: Life and Work in a Nursing Home* (1991), describes the power that nursing staff have over residents. In spite of their loss of control over their person and things, however, many residents find creative ways to preserve the little power they have. Vesperi (1983) astutely describes how the effort to assert control over some aspect of their lives in an overly controlled setting often translates into residents' "acting out" behaviors, such as incontinence or refusal to eat.

Sociologist Timothy Diamond, like anthropologists Maria Vesperi and Neil Henderson, conducted nursing home research while working as an NA (nursing assistant). Thus his *Making Gray Gold* (1992) can provide not only an in-depth view of nursing home life for residents, but also an insider's view of the institutional pressures and rules that make an NA's work so difficult. He highlights how these pressures transform caregiving from an interpersonal process to an act performed by the NA on an acontextualized object (pp. 201–10)—the basis for instrumental caregiving.

Nancy Foner directs attention to other victims of the nursing home structure—NAs, who are the primary caregivers of residents. Underpaid and overworked, they also lack considerable autonomy over their work and their breaks. Even though they have the most amount of contact with the residents, they are rarely asked for their input about them. Those who resent their poor working conditions and minimal control over their labor tend to impose excessive control over the residents under their charge (1994: 227). In addition, Foner found that

NAs suffer the same abuses of racial and class inequalities from residents and their families that they may experience outside the nursing home.

The Culture of Long-term Care (1995), edited by Neil Henderson and Maria Vesperi, is a collection of articles from nursing home ethnographers throughout the United States. It provides a variety of perspectives about the structure of nursing home care and nursing home life from the viewpoints of the staff and residents. In addition, the ethnographers describe the actual processes by which they maneuver among the many actors in the nursing home to successfully conduct their research, and some of the challenges they face. A sequel to this work, *Gray Areas: Ethnographic Encounters with Nursing Home Culture* edited by Philip Stafford (2003), whose contributions I site throughout this book, is important both for its micro-level examination of relationships among residents, families, and staff, and its macro-level analyses of the political economy of the long-term care industry. Except for some selections in the two edited volumes, most of these ethnographies occurred in nursing homes or units that housed elders with a variety of conditions rather than dementia alone.

Karen Lyman's ethnography, *Day In, Day Out With Alzheimer's* (1993), however, focuses on caregiving within Alzheimer's daycare centers. Like many nursing home ethnographers, she examines how the organization of work contributes to the stress on workers, which in turn affects the quality of care they can offer. She also provides a critical account and excellent analysis of the limitations of a biomedical approach to dementia caregiving. Her analysis, however, is restricted to daycare centers, rather than institutional settings.

APPENDIX D: THIS ETHNOGRAPHY AS A JOURNEY

Ethnography is not a uniform method with uniform results. As many ethnographers indicate in their writing, it is a journey. As I think back to the years when I conducted my fieldwork, I recall how totally unfamiliar, foreign really, the nursing home and its residents first appeared to me. This is how ethnographic fieldwork, which developed through the now controversial study of "the other,"[1] is expected to be; in fact, in the past, ethnographic research that appeared too familiar was not seen as credible. My study did not occur in a remote setting, but in the familiar urban area where I resided.[2] Maria Vesperi recalls how, as foreign as the nursing home was to her, the residents themselves were disconcertingly familiar (Vesperi 1995: 9). This was not my experience, however, perhaps because the residents I studied manifested so many behavioral impairments.

Such unfamiliarity can be disconcerting. One nurse told me, for example, how a research psychologist who came to study Unit 1 quit after just two weeks, not able to "take it" anymore. Some researchers indeed have cautioned about the dangers of entering the exotic world of "the other" too intimately. Estroff, for example, in her research with psychiatric patients, notes, "The more time one spends amid confusion, fear, anxiety, and unhappiness, the more it is highlighted in oneself" (1981: xvi). In my own work, that did not happen. In fact I found greater certainty, greater clarity, and greater comfort the closer I came to understanding, even identifying with the elders on my unit (See McLean, forthcoming). It may also be that ethnographers of nursing homes must necessarily embrace the aging process, since they inevitably come face to face with it daily in their research (cf. Vesperi 1995: 10).

But my comfort only developed in steps. My first impression of the elders, embarrassingly, was as an undifferentiable conglomerate of marginalized ancient beings. This, however, changed over time until each and every one of them assumed a unique, unquestionable identity. Drawing from my field notes, I will highlight some of the elements of that journey and my evolving impressions.

To the newcomer, a sense of undifferentiated sameness may actually be a defense against the overwhelming unfamiliarity that one finds in one's own backyard.[3]

---

[1] This "otherness," many have argued, is the product of anthropology's origins in colonialism. For various discussions about this problem, see Diamond (1974: 401–29), Asad (1979), Said (1979), Pandian (1985), and Trouillot (1991). For a feminist take on this issue also see Abu-Lughod (1991).

[2] As anthropologists increasingly began to study at "home" during the late 1970s and 1980s, many issues were raised. See Jackson (1987) and Messerchmidt (1981) concerning those issues.

[3] Several ethnographies in a recent collection (Hume and Mulcock 2004) address some of the issues raised when anthropologists confront the unfamiliar in familiar places.

Looking from the safe side of the locked gate during my first visit to Unit 1, I watched with caution and reserve, even mild fear, as the old people congregated together with a staff that seemed anesthetized to their presence. I write:

> How strange those on the other side appeared to my naïve eyes. Their frail, contorted bodies set them apart from me. But the noise and mutterings they produced forced an even more profound rupture from the rest of humanity.

My field notes later read:

> My musings were broken by a jolly man who directed his wheelchair in my direction. He said with calm assurance, "It's better out there; you don't want to come here; some strange people are inside; stay away before it's too late." He then chuckled to himself.

This encounter helped me regain my bearings. If this man (Jim) could show an awareness of my presence and hesitation, address it directly, and extend his humanity with a friendly warning, the place he occupied and its residents could not be as alien as I had imagined.

This was the most extreme unit in the nursing home—"the late-stage Alzheimer's unit," as one nurse described it—and housed the most difficult, intractable residents/patients in the home. But Jim didn't seem like that. In fact, something about Jim drew me to this place.

During my graduate training, I remember learning that first impressions, acquired when an ethnographer is still new to a setting, are the most valuable, because the researcher is assaulted by so many new stimuli to which she may become desensitized the longer she spends in the environment. I was also told of the importance of returning to those notes later in the research when the unfamiliar had lost its freshness. Because of the striking contrast between the new world one enters and that with which one is most familiar, early observations, due to their innocence, are rich with insights. I found this to hold true in my work on these units. It was during an orientation by Jeannie, an astute young nursing assistant (NA) on the unit, that various elders defined their identities as distinct from the undignified heap I initially perceived.

My notes recall:

> What impressed me was that she talked about them as persons with real wants, particular ways of expressing themselves

and various idiosyncrasies. By so doing, she immediately transformed them from bizarre human material to individual persons with feelings, intentionality, and purpose. This alone elevated them in my eyes to a dramatically different status.

This was a crucial early step in my journey, and a step to appreciating the vital importance of personhood as a relational construct. With Jeannie's guidance, the elders were transformed to persons, something I expect would have happened with time. However, I recognize with some embarrassment that it also revealed how susceptible I was to my own cultural values, by which I denied them their human due until they were acknowledged by others.

As we moved from one elder to the next, I came to learn, that despite their visible impairments, there was much more to them than what I saw from the other side of the gate:

> One man, who was seated apart from the others, looked ordinary and pleasant enough and seemed vaguely aware of my presence. He had a peculiar way of calling out "Baba, Baba," repeatedly. When I came by to greet him, however, he waved me away. "He takes time before he trusts new faces," explained Jeannie. "You have to wait until he's ready to accept you; if you don't, he'll spit at you."

This comment presented this man as being somewhat in charge of his environment, while also capable of terribly uncivil behavior to offenders.

As our walk continued, I later observe:

> One woman, who appeared extremely agitated in countenance, was occupied with pulling threads from her blouse, which she had removed. "She is one of our strippers," Jeannie explained, identifying her, I felt, by her pathology. But then she assigned meaning—whether historically accurate or not—to her apparently aberrant behavior: "She used to be a seamstress, and she still looks like she wants to be sewing."
>
> As we continued on our walk, it was impossible to ignore the harsh calling out of one man: "Get the hell out of here, nigger!" Jeannie explained "that he is racist, probably always was, but now can no longer control—or doesn't care to control—his expression of it." Jeannie, who was African-American, stated this directly, as a matter of fact, without disgust or apparent

concern. She walked up to him again gently, provoking a similar outburst. "He says similar things to others who are not black," she added, extending a different quality to his remarks. "He's just very angry—doesn't want to be here."[4]

We then came upon a pair of women whose catatonic bodies had been placed together, each peacefully reclined in her chair, apparently oblivious to her surroundings. I was struck by the smooth, clear, pearlescent, if delicate, condition of their faces—something surprising, but not uncommon among the women I observed.

"Where are all the wrinkles?" I wondered. "What will I look like when/if I get to be this old?" I even wondered if something about dementia softens or defies wrinkles. And yet, as clear and smooth as their faces were, they possessed thin arms, discolored, marred, bruised, apparently easily by rough, awkward, or simply hurried hands. The very translucence and fineness of their facial skin were set in alarming contrast to their damaged arms and bodies, full of sores and bruises, still healing, leaving a very different impression.

As I observed them more keenly and reflected on my reactions, it became clear to me that my journey was only beginning:

> With affection, as well as a tinge of disrespect, one NA called them the "Bobbsey Twins." They indeed looked remarkably alike with their long oval faces, long hair pulled back tightly, further exposing the sharp bony lines of their fine smooth faces. The languor of this twosome and its expression of declining life somehow overwhelmed me, and I quickly entered their room to hide my incipient tears. Just why this affected me so, I was unsure. Perhaps it was the presence in duplicate of fragility that intensified the significance of their dimming existence, so cruelly drawn out over years and reduced to their disdainful label. And yet, as I noted above, they appeared peaceful. What was it that they represented in their current state of being that I found so powerfully difficult to take? What

---

[4] Sometime later, when I got to talk with his wife, she insisted, with embarrassment, that he had never been racist, but admitted that he was indeed furious with having been placed at the home; his anger permeated his interactions with everyone, including herself.

did it say about my own estimation about the value and po-
tency of existence? Perhaps it was their impotence and dependence that I found, as one conditioned in Western notions
of human worth, measured by power and productivity, that
threatened my own possible future, terrifying and saddening
me that I, too, could come to this unworthy end. But did that
mean I accepted the Western construction of their unworthi-
ness, or simply the inevitability of escaping it?

Interestingly, several months later, a nurse on the 3 p.m. to 11 p.m. afternoon shift happened to mention that one of these women actually talks. I
looked at her in amazement as she explained that during the 7:00 a.m. to 3:00
p.m. morning shift the woman is silent, and so is treated as such, but during
the 3:00 p.m to 11:00 p.m. afternoon shift, she actually makes requests. A
couple of weeks later I learned this to be true firsthand, and observe in my
notes:

As I walked by her on my way to observing a noisier resident, I heard her whisper something. I stopped and listened
again. "I'm cold," she declared. "May I have a blanket?" I
quickly went to find one. When I covered her, she thanked
me. Her desire, intentionality, and ability to request were
still there; only her ability to satisfy it was gone. Just then
I realized how I was no different—even worse—than the
caregivers of whom I was growing critical, who must to
some degree attend to all. I, like them, had allowed elders
like her to become invisible as my attention was being
drawn elsewhere.

With all they have to do, it is not surprising that NAs give little attention to
those who are quiet. As Foner describes, NAs learn to cut corners any way they
can to complete their work. They even come to expect the help of family members who typically provide care when they visit, and resent them when they don't
(1995: 172). But what was my excuse? Clearly I was studying those whose behaviors were considered problematic, because it had become a significant concern
in dementia, and was costly of NA time in nursing homes. Even though I was
studying those with behavioral "disturbances" as potentially meaningful communication, less behaviorally disturbed elders, some even more advanced in their
dementia, could also lay claim to communicating, if only someone were available
to decode their efforts.

The response of this woman made me ponder more about her silent life and of the little we know of elders who in settings like this become "invisible" because they don't pose problems to the staff. As one man who visited his catatonic wife later complained about the research, "Why not study my wife? You spend too much time on the squeaky wheels. There is much to be learned as well from people who don't make trouble." This well-preserved man in his 90s, who visited his wife diligently every day to help feed her, remarked how his wife, though silent, signals him in various ways to communicate hunger, pain, or the need to have her diaper changed. It made me wonder if we should be expanding our gaze beyond those with disturbed behaviors.

Returning to my tour with Jeannie, a final visit afforded me some profound lessons. I write:

> As we walked around the floor, we were drawn to the activities room where Tim, a musician and the single male NA on the unit, was playing some soft jazz tapes. About 10-12 people were arranged in chairs and wheelchairs, listening. The generally noisy unit was remarkably quiet. I walked up to one reclining woman and gently asked, "Do you like this music?" wondering if she would be able to answer. "I like it, but I don't understand it," she responded to my utter amazement! This musically untrained, supposedly demented woman (as I determined from later conversations with the staff) showed an exceptional recognition of music not only as pleasurable event, but as communication! She, like so many others I had encountered, had emerged from the dregs of a formless, aged humanity as a person with complexity, depth, and intelligence.

After talking with the nurse in charge of the unit, I added these comments to my field notes:

> The nurse explained that this woman spontaneously calls out every now and then, and that this would not be "tolerated" on other units. (The willingness of this unit to tolerate such bothersome behavior distinguishes it as a "special care unit.") Later today I heard her outbursts myself. They were anguished, desperate repeated calls, "I want to go home." The medical chart indicates the woman is retarded. I don't believe it. This does explain, though, the content of her other cry, "I'm not a dummy!" articulated with tearful insistence. I couldn't agree more.

The tour with Jeannie helped me penetrate the chaotic veneer of undifferenti-ated bodies to persons with agency, history, and identity. Even among those few who remained silent and invisible to me, as I later pursued the paths of those who were visibly and vocally behaviorally disruptive, their humanity was no longer an issue for me. This was an important lesson to acquire early on and clearly shaped my subsequent investigations, albeit, never facilely. I did not have to struggle to find some inkling of a "lost self." While I began with a genuine inability to dis-tinguish among their collective selves, over time, they themselves—some sooner than others—revealed their identities to me.

While Jeannie's tour and observations helped me to appreciate the individual-ity of several elders we encountered, I did not simply accept her interpretations about them at face value as "truths." What most struck me though, and what was important to me at the time, was not what she said but the fact that she had come over time to see distinct, individual selves and persons that were sadly not visible to me at first.

APPENDIX E: METHODOLOGICAL DETAILS

Before beginning research on each unit, I sent out letters to family members identified by the administration as the "responsible party" for each resident. The letters described the research and gave information for contacting me about questions. After later selecting each of seven or eight residents on each unit for intensive study, I contacted the responsible family member to discuss my intentions and request their signed permission to include their relative. I also described the study in simple terms to the few residents who seemed able to understand, and I requested their verbal consent.

I spent nine consecutive months on each of the two units. While I immediately began my observations and informal interviews with staff, residents, and families, I waited about one month to get better acquainted with everyone and to get a better "feel" for the unit before selecting residents for intensive study. At that point I elicited the help of all nurses and NAs from the unit to select the seven or eight residents they deemed most behaviorally disturbed or difficult. On both units, staff initially had difficulty selecting particular individuals. When pushed a bit to identify those who were the most difficult to care for however, there was surprising consistency within a shift, but not necessarily between shifts. This was not surprising since residents often varied in their moods and behaviors during different times of the day. In addition, because of the variability that occurs with dementia over time, I eliminated some residents from the list whose disturbed behaviors had improved and added others whose behaviors came to be viewed as more problematic. Thus, with my tentative list, I began intensively observing the selected residents one by one (changing the list as warranted) for one-month periods, while continuing to carry out my general floor-wide observations.

The bulk of my research occurred during the day shift (7:00 a.m. to 3:00 p.m.) and several hours into the evening shift (3:00 p.m. to 11:00 p.m.). However, I spent considerable time on every shift, including the 11:00 p.m. to 7:00 a.m. shift. For several weeks I arrived on the unit well before 7:00 a.m. to shadow the NAs as they carried out their early morning care routines—a time when disturbed behaviors were prominent. I also observed the transitional "shift meeting" between the two charge nurses, in which they discussed special problems or concerns. On a couple of occasions I stayed on the units for 24 consecutive hours to gain a better sense of what life must be like for the residents who were confined there day and night. I did not, however, experience the unit during weekends, when the unit could be staffed by nonregular staff.

During my stay on each unit, I interacted with the entire staff (from housekeepers to physicians) as well as with companions who had been hired privately

by families of particular residents. I also spent considerable time talking informally with the residents and their families, trying to get a sense of them as persons and their behaviors on the unit in light of their past history. On any given
day I moved from place to place, talking with different people while observing
a particular occurrence or paying attention to an activity (a fight between two
residents, a musical activity, or the entrance of a family member).[1] I tried to
learn about the various views of both staff members and residents' families
about each resident, dementia in general, and proper dementia care. I also inquired about the institution and how it operated, how care was organized on
the unit, families' and residents' perceptions, complaints and concerns about
care, and the constraints the caregiving staff faced in conducting their work.

In addition to moving about the unit, I spent parts of my day behind the nurses'
station, where the head nurse stayed most of the time, completing what seemed
like endless documentation. There I reviewed medical records and asked questions
about something I had observed, nursing home policy or regulations, or a person
I had not seen before. During this time, I also inquired about the nurse's views on
dementia, her caregiving philosophy, and priorities she set for staff; these supple-
mented my own observations of other statements she may have made or actions
suggestive of her philosophy.

The weekly care conferences where several residents were discussed on a
rotating basis provided yet additional information on the residents from the
perspective of the social worker, activities therapist, nutritionist, and medical
professional. By attending these, I came to know different professionals who periodically would offer me information on someone they knew I was studying. I also
attended regular meetings held with the NAs, or occasional meetings involving
administrators or families.

I kept two sets of field notes: general daily journal field notes and a separate set of intensive documentation about 15 selected residents. The general
notes documented all my conversations with residents (even those I planned
to later follow more intensively), the staff, and family members whom I
encountered daily, as well as my in-depth observations about life on the
unit, caregiving, and interactions among various persons. Whenever possible, I wrote my notes immediately after a conversation or observation to
retainfull details. When that was impossible, I would write a short outline of
topics that I would later elaborate on in my written field notes. I attempted

---

[1] To some theorists, the ethnographer at her best *must* engage in a range of "position,
place, and identity" (Coffey 1999: 36). To them, the high degree of activity I assumed in
my fieldwork and the diverse positions and roles I assumed in each, as I spoke with elders,
their families, and various categories of staff, served to enhance my ethnography.

to write from the perspective of a naïve observer who assumed nothing and to note every detail and impression.[2] This was done to preserve the freshness of my original insights as I later tried to make sense of my data. Such elaboration prevents important details from getting lost or marred in memory (Atkinson 1990: 471). As I wrote my daily field notes, I continuously reflected on my data, considering current observations in light of previous ones.

I reserved the more intensive log for in-depth study of behaviors of each of the 15 residents for a one-month period. This log included my daily observations of the resident during their care routines, quiet time, and interactions with others. I anticipated particular times when the elder was said to be most agitated (such as morning wake-up and grooming, late afternoon, bedtime, or when they were with a particular family member) and focused, but did not restrict myself, to activity and BDs (behavioral disturbances) that occurred during those times. I attempted to examine the entire course of a BD from the context of its emergence through its development and suppression, exacerbation, or resolution as the elder responded to various interventions. In this log I documented discussions with nurses and NAs from all shifts about the interventions and strategies they had tried. I also included informal discussions with family visitors and more elaborate interviews with at least one family member about the resident, the BDs, and the facility and staff. Finally, I included data from medical records that tracked the staff's impressions about the resident and her/his BDs over time. During my first few months, I dictated and audio-recorded my daily journal entries for later transcription. After that, funding ran out, and I had to rely strictly on handwritten or typed notes.

Data analysis was ongoing and reflexive, demanding continual review and cross-confirmation among multiple data sources of thematic findings and apparent consistencies. I pursued questions about my formative conclusions by ongoing questioning of the data and further discussion with the key and other informants. (See also McLean and Perkinson 1995.)

SOME RESEARCH GLITCHES

As Foner (1995) describes, the family/nursing home–staff relationship can be adversarial. Given this knowledge, I tried to avoid competitive tensions between staff and families. From the beginning, I explained to everyone involved in the research that all their comments were strictly confidential and that

---

2   These details, of course, are necessarily selective, and those that capture the imagination of each researcher will vary (McLean, forthcoming).

I would be talking with as many people as possible involved in the life of the elder to gain a comprehensive picture about her behaviors in the context of nursing home life; this might entail asking questions that didn't seem directly related to the behavior. I further explained that, while my research focused on disturbed behaviors, I needed to understand the situation in which the troubled behavior occurred, the persons who were present, and events that preceded and followed it.

Despite this preparation, some of the staff on the first unit suspected at first that I was a spy for the administration because they were not accustomed to the ongoing nature of ethnographic research. In the past they had encountered researchers who conducted short periodic observations over a year or had filled out brief research questionnaires. However, all my note taking, questions about difficult residents, and observations of their caregiving made them wonder if I was reporting to the administration. At one point, a care manager asked me what anthropologists "really do," and I did my best once again to explain. Despite my efforts to explain my need to gain many perspectives, the head nurse started asking why I bothered to talk to families—particularly those who had voiced dissatisfaction with care—and why, if I were interested in residents' behaviors, my questions were about apparently unrelated things like administrative procedures for replacing lost dentures. While she was willing from the start to answer questions about residents and the operations of the home, it took several months before she seemed to appreciate my inquiries and independence from the administration and freely offered her views on various administrators and their policies.

My relationships with NAs on the first unit were cemented during a strike when I decided (after gaining their support following considerable discussion with them) to help those who remained on the unit to care for the residents. This offered me a chance to put myself in their "shoes" and get a taste of their work experience. My successful efforts to finally change the diaper of one resistant resident were met with unexpected cheers from the unit's few remaining NAs. This signaled a newfound sense of camaraderie and a turning point in our relationship. From then on, they seemed very trusting and open.

At the second unit, I did not undergo a similar warming-up period with the head nurse, perhaps because staff from the previous unit had told her I was "safe" and perhaps because she was very secure in her position. While nurses on the other shifts on this unit were also very helpful, most of the NAs remained guarded or elusive with me and seemed less able or willing to find time to meet with me; I came to understand their reluctance as the research proceeded.

Works Cited and Recommended Reading

Abu-Lughod, Lila. (1991). Writing against culture. In Richard Fox (Ed.), *Recapturing Anthropology* (pp. 137–62). Santa Fe, NM: School of American Research Press.

Adams, Trevor. (1996). Kitwood's approach to dementia and dementia care: A critical but appreciative review. *Journal of Advanced Nursing, 23*, 948–953.

Adler, Jane. (2003). Pioneer concept: Focus on resident. *Chicago Tribune Online Edition.* June 29, 2003. <http://www.chicagotribune.com>. Retrieved January 23, 2004.

Agich, George. (1993). *Autonomy and Long-term Care.* Oxford, ENG and New York: Oxford University Press.

Aroskar, M. (1990). Bathing: On the boundaries of health treatment. In Rosalie Kane and Arthur Caplan (Eds.), *Everyday Ethics: Resolving Dilemmas in Nursing Home Life* (pp. 178–89). New York: Springer Press.

Arras, John. (1987). A philosopher's view. *Generations, 11*(4), 65–66.

Asad, Talal. (1979). Anthropology and the colonial encounter. In Gerrit Huizer and Bruce Mannheim (Eds.), *The Politics of Anthropology: From Colonialism and Sexism Toward a View from Below* (pp.85–94). The Hague and Paris: Mouton.

Atkinson, Paul. (1990). *The Ethnographic Imagination: Textual Constructions of Reality.* London: Routledge Press.

Au, Derrick K.S. (2000). Brain injury, brain degeneration, and loss of personhood. In Gerhold K. Becker (Ed.), *The Moral Status of Persons: Perspectives on Bioethics* (pp. 209–17). Amsterdam and Atlanta, GA: Rodopi Press.

Baker, Beth. (2005). Small World. *AARP Bulletin, 46*(9), 29, 39.

Ballenger, Jesse. (2000). Beyond the characteristic plaques and tangles. In Peter J. Whitehouse, Konrad Maurer, and Jesse Ballenger (Eds.), *Concepts of Alzheimer's disease: Biological, Clinical and Cultural Perspectives* (pp. 83–103). Baltimore: The Johns Hopkins University Press.

Barker, Judith, Linda Mitteness, and Connie Wolfsen. (1994). Smoking and adulthood: Risky business in a nursing home. *Journal of Aging Studies Special Issue: Threats to Adult Status in Late Life, 8*(3), 309–26.

Bartol, Mari Anne. (1979). Nonverbal communication in patients with Alzheimer's disease. *Journal of Gerontological Nursing, 5*, 21–31.

Basler, Barbara. (2004). Battle of the banned: Couple fights court order limiting visits to nursing home. *AARP Bulletin, 45*(10), 28–29.

Bates, Eric. (1999). The shame of our nursing homes: Privatization has produced millions for investors and misery for the elderly. *The Nation, 269*(12), 11–19.

Battaglia, Debbora. (1995). Problematizing the self: A thematic introduction. In Debbora Battaglia (Ed.), *The Rhetorics of Self-Making* (pp.1–15). Berkeley, CA: University of California Press.

Bayer, Trudy. (2004). Personal communication regarding "mutual accountability." July, 2004.

Beard, Renée. (2005). Advocating voice; organizational, historical and social milieux of the Alzheimer's disease movement. In Phil Brown and Steven Zavetoski (Eds.), *Social Movements in Health* (chapter 7). Malden, MA and Oxford: Blackwell Press.

Beauchamp, Tom L. (2001). The failure of theories of personhood. In David Thomasma, David Weisstub, and Christian Hervé (Eds.), *Personhood and Health Care* (pp. 59–69). Dordrecht, NLD: Kluwer.

Becker, Gerhold. (2000). The moral status of persons: introduction. In *The Moral Status of Persons: perspectives on bioethics* (pp. 4-11). Amsterdam, NLD: Rodopi B.V.

Beghi, Ettore, Grancalo Logroscino, and Amos Korczyn. (2004). Alzheimer's disease and other dementias. In Patrick du Souich, Michael Orme, and Sergio Erill (Eds.), *The IUPHAR Compendium of Basic Principles for Pharmacological Research in Humans* (pp. 212-27). Irvine, CA: IUPHAR.

Bernard, Jean. (2001). The person. In David Thomasma, David Weisstub, and Christian Hervé (Eds.), *Personhood and Health Care* (pp. 55–58). Dordrecht, NLD: Kluwer Academic.

Bick, Katherine. (2000). The history of the Alzheimer's Association: Future public policy implications. In Peter Whitehouse, Konrad Maurer, and

Jesse Ballenger (Eds.). *Concepts of Alzheimer's Disease: Biological, Clinical and Cultural Perspectives* (pp. 234-44). Baltimore: Johns Hopkins University Press.

Binney, Elizabeth, and James Swan. (1991). The political economy of mental health care for the elderly. In M. Minker and C. Estes (Eds.), *Critical Perspectives on Aging: The Political and Moral Economy of Growing Old* (pp. 165–88). Amityville, NY: Baywood.

Binstock, Robert. (1993). Plaques and tangles in approaching dementia. *The Gerontologist, 28*(3), 133–35.

Blackmun, Susie. (1998). Is it depression or is it dementia? *Psychiatric Times, 15*(2). <http://psychiatrictimes.com/p980267.html>. Retrieved October 7, 2005.

Bochner, Arthur, and Carolyn Ellis (Eds.). (2001). *Ethnographically Speaking.* Walnut Creek, CA: Altimira Press.

Bohannan, Paul, and Dirk van der Elst. (1998). *Asking and Listening: Ethnography as Personal Adaptation.* Prospect Heights, IL: Waveland Press.

Boomers and aging. *Maclean's.* (23 June 1997). *110*(25), 47.

Bowers, Barbara. (1988). Family perceptions of care in a nursing home. *The Gerontologist, 28*(3), 361–67.

Brody, Elaine, M. Powell Lawton, and Bernard Liebowitz. (1984). Commentary. Senile dementia: Public police and adequate institutional care. *American Journal of Public Health, 74*(12), 1381–83.

Butler, Robert. (1975). *Why Survive? Being Old in America.* New York: Harper and Row.

Caplan, Arthur. (1990). The morality of the mundane: Ethical issues arising in the daily lives of nursing home residents. In Rosalie Kane and Arthur Caplan (Eds.), *Everyday Ethics: Resolving Dilemmas in Nursing Home Life* (pp. 37–50). New York: Springer Press.

Capstick, Andrea. (2003). Theoretical origins of dementia care mapping. In Anthea Innes (Ed.), *Dementia Care Mapping* (pp. 11–22). Baltimore: Health Professions Press.

Capstick, Andrea. (2004). Reviews: Trevor Adams and Jill Manthorpe (Eds.), *Dementia Care*, Arnold, London, 2003. *Ageing and Society, 24,* 131–32.

Carder, Paula. (2003). The social world of assisted living. In Philip Stafford (Ed.), *Gray Areas: Ethnographic Encounters with Nursing Home Culture* (pp. 263–84). Santa Fe, NM: School of American Research Press.

Caro, Francis, and Robert Morris. (2002). Devolution and aging policy. *Journal of Aging and Social Policy, 14*(3/4), 1–14.

Clifford, James. (1986). Introduction: Partial truths. In James Clifford and George Marcus (Eds.), *Writing Culture: The Poetics And Politics of Ethnography* (pp. 1–26). Berkeley, CA: University of California Press.

Clifford, James, and George Marcus (Eds.). (1986). *Writing Culture: The Poetics and Politics of Ethnography*. Berkeley, CA: University of California Press.

Coffey, Amanda. (1999). *The Ethnographic Self*. London: Sage.

Cohen, Donna, and Carl Eisdorfer. (1986). *The Loss of Self*. New York: W.W. Norton.

Cohen, Lawrence. (1999). *No Aging in India*. Berkeley, CA: University of California Press.

Cohen, Uriel, and Kristen Day. (1992). *Contemporary Environments for People with Dementia*. Baltimore: Johns Hopkins University Press.

Cohen-Mansfield, Jiska. (2000). Approaches to the management of disruptive behaviors. In M. Powell Lawton and Robert L. Rubinstein (Eds.), *Interventions in Dementia Care* (pp. 39–64). New York: Springer.

Collopy, Bart. (1990). Ethical dimensions of autonomy in long-term care. *Generations*, Supplement, 9–12.

Cotrell, Victoria, and Richard Schulz. (1993). The perspective of the patient with Alzheimer's disease: A neglected dimension of dementia research. *The Gerontologist*, 33(2), 205–11.

Crapanzano, Vincent. (1986). Hermes' dilemma: The masking of subversion in ethnographic description. In James Clifford and George Marcus (Eds.), *Writing Culture: The Poetics and Politics of Ethnography* (pp. 51–76). Berkeley, CA: University of California Press.

Culture Change. (2001). Communities. <http://www.culturechangenow.com/community/index.htm>. Retrieved January 23, 2004.

Daar, Abdallah, and Binsumeit Khitamy. (2001). Bioethics for clinicians: 21. Islamic bioethics. *Canadian Medical Association Journal*, 164(1), 60–63.

Davis, Daniel. (2004). Dementia: Sociological and philosophical constructions. *Social Science and Medicine*, 58, 369–78.

Deaton, Gail, Christopher Johnson, Roxanna Johnson, and Peter Winn. (2000–01). The Eden alternative: An evolving paradigm for long-term care. Article 37. In Harold Cox (Ed.), *Annual Editions: Aging 2000–01* (pp. 209–12). Sluice Dock, Guilford, CN: Dushkin/McGraw-Hill.

Delumeau, Jean. (2001). The development of the concept of the person. In David Thomasma, David Weisstub, and Christian Hervé (Eds.), *Personhood and Health Care* (pp. 13–18). Dordrecht, NLD: Kluwer Academic.

Diamond, Stanley. (1974). Anthropology in question. In Dell Hymes (Ed.), *Reinventing Anthropology* (pp. 401–29). New York: Vintage Books.

Diamond, Timothy. (1992). *Making Gray Gold*. Chicago: The University of Chicago Press.

Dillman, Rob. (2000). Alzheimer's disease: Epistemological lessons from history? In Peter J. Whitehouse, Konrad Maurer, and Jesse Ballenger (Eds.), *Concepts of Alzheimer's Disease: Biological, Clinical and Cultural Perspectives* (pp. 129–57). Baltimore: Johns Hopkins University Press.

Doucet, Hubert. (2001). The concept of person in bioethics. In David Thomasma, David Weisstub, and Christian Hervé (Eds.), *Personhood and Health Care* (pp. 121–28). Dordrecht, NLD: Kluwer Academic.

Downs, Murna. (1997). Progress report: The emergence of the person in dementia research. *Ageing and Society, 17,* 597–607.

Downs, Murna. (2000). Ageing update: Dementia in a socio-cultural context: an idea whose time has come. *Ageing and Society, 20,* 360–75.

Dreyfus, H., and P. Rabinow. (1983). *Michel Foucault: Beyond Structuralism and Hermeneutics,* 2nd ed. Chicago: University of Chicago Press.

Edwards, Mike. (2004, November/December). The world's best place to live. *AARP The Magazine, 47*(6a), 42–45, 46–49, 90.

Emerson, Robert M., Jan Fritz, and Linda Shaw. (1995). *Writing Ethnographic Field Notes.* Chicago: University of Chicago Press.

Erde, Edmund. (1999). Paradigms and personhood: A deepening of the dilemmas in ethics and medical ethics. *Theoretical Medicine and Bioethics, 20,* 141–60.

Estes, Carroll, and Elizabeth Binney. (1991). The biomedicalization of aging: Dangers and dilemmas. In M. Minker and C. Estes (Eds.), *Critical Perspectives on Aging: The Political and Moral Economy of Growing Old* (pp. 117–34). Amityville, NY: Baywood.

Estroff, Sue. (1981). *Making It Crazy.* Berkeley, CA: University of California Press.

Estroff, Sue. (1993). Identity, disability, and schizophrenia: The problem of chronicity. In Shirley Lindenbaum and Margaret Lock (Eds.), *Knowledge, Power and Practice: The Anthropology of Everyday Life* (pp. 247–86). Berkeley, CA: University of California Press.

Ewing, Katherine. (1990). The illusion of wholeness: "Culture," "self," and the experience of inconsistency. *Ethos, 18*(3), 251–78.

Fabian, Johannes. (2001). *Anthropology with an Attitude: Critical Essays.* Stanford, CA: Stanford University Press.

Farmer, Paul. (1999). *Infections and Inequalities.* Berkeley, CA: University of California Press.

Feder, Judith, Harriet Komisar, and Marlene Niefeld. (2000). Long-term care in the United States: an overview. *Health Affairs, 19*(3), 40–56.

Feil, Naomi. (2002). *The Validation Breakthrough,* 2nd ed. Baltimore: Health Professions Press.

Feldt, Karen. (1999). Hello in there: Understanding the success of person-centered care. *The Gerontologist, 39*(2), 249–50.

Fleischer, Theodore. (1999). Review article: Personhood wars. *Theoretical Medicine and Bioethics, 20,* 309–18.

Foldes, Stephen. (1990). Life in an institution: A sociological and anthropological view. In R. Kane and A. Kaplan (Eds.), *Everyday Ethics: Resolving Dilemmas in Nursing Home Life* (pp. 21–36). New York: Springer Press.

Foner, Nancy. (1994). *The Caregiving Dilemma: Work in an American Nursing Home.* Berkeley, CA: University of California Press.

Foner, Nancy. (1995). Relatives as trouble: Nursing home aides and patients' families. In J. Neil Henderson and Maria Vesperi (Eds.), *The Culture of Long-term Care* (pp. 165–78). Westport, CT: Bervin and Garvey.

Foucault, Michel. (1977 [1975]). *Discipline and Punish: The Birth of the Prison.* Alan Sheridan, trans. New York: Random House.

Fox, Patrick. (1989). From senility to Alzheimer's disease: The rise of the Alzheimer's disease movement. *The Milbank Quarterly, 67*(1), 58–102.

Fox, Patrick. (2000). The role of the concept of Alzheimer's disease in the development of the Alzheimer's Association in the United States. In Peter J. Whitehouse, Konrad Maurer, and Jesse Ballenger (Eds.), *Concepts of Alzheimer's Disease: Biological, Clinical and Cultural Perspectives* (pp. 209–33). Baltimore: Johns Hopkins University Press.

Frankenberg, Ronald. (1980). Medical anthropology and development: a theoretical perspective, *Social Science and Medicine, 14B,* 187–207

Freund, Peter, and Meredith McGuire. (1995). *Health, Illness, and the Social Body,* 2nd ed. Englewood Cliffs, NJ: Prentice-Hall.

Gadow, Sally. (1988). Covenant without cure. Letting go and holding on in chronic illness. In J. Watson and M. Ray (Eds.), *The Ethics of Care and the Ethics of Cure: Synthesis in Chronicity* (pp. 5–14). New York: National League of Nursing.

Gimzal, A., and C. Yazgan. (2004). Abstract. Mild cognitive impairment. *Turk Psikiyatri Derg,* 15(4), 309–16. <http://www.ncbi.nlm.nih.gov/entrez/query.fcgi?cmd=Retrieve&db=PubMed&list_uids= 15622511&dopt=Citation>. Retrieved October 7, 2005.

Ginsburg, Faye. (1995). Production values: Indigenous media and the rhetoric of self-determination. In Debbora Battaglia (Ed.), *The Rhetorics of Self-Making* (pp.121–38). Berkeley, CA: University of California Press.

Glass, C., R. Mustian, and L. Carter. (1986). Knowledge and attitudes of health care providers toward sexuality in the institutionalized elderly. *Educational Gerontology, 12,* 465–75.

Goffman, Erving. (1961). *Asylums: Essays on the Social Situation of Mental Patients and Other Inmates.* Chicago: Aldine.

Goodman, Lenn. (2001). Persons. In David Thomasma, David Weisstub, and Christian Hervé (Eds.), *Personhood and Health Care.* (pp.19-42). Dordrecht, NLD: Kluwer Academic.

Grabowski, David, Zhanlian Feng, Orna Intrator, and Vincent Mor. (2004 June). Recent trends in state nursing home payment policies. *Health Affairs*, 363–73.

Graf, Frederick-Wilhelm. (2000). "The worth of a person": A speciesist prejudice? Theological comments on the current controversy over bioethical concepts. In Gerhold Becker (Ed.), *The Moral Status of Persons: Perspectives on Bioethics* (pp. 169–78). Amsterdam, NLD: Rodopi.

Graneheim, Ulla, Astrid Norberg, and Lilian Jansson. (2001). Interaction relating to privacy, identity, autonomy and security: An observational study focusing on a woman with dementia and "behavioural disturbances," and on her care providers. *Journal of Advanced Nursing, 36*, 256–65.

Gubrium, Jaber. (1975). *Living and Dying in Murray Manor.* New York: St. Martin's Press.

Gubrium, Jaber. (1986a). *Oldtimers and Alzheimer's: The Descriptive Organization of Senility.* Greenwich, CT: JAI Press.

Gubrium, Jaber. (1986b). The social preservation of mind: the Alzheimer's disease experience. *Symbolic Interaction, 9*(1), 37–51.

Gubrium, Jaber. (1987). Structuring and destructuring the course of illness. *Sociology of Health and Illness, 9*, 1–24.

Habermas, J. (1984). *The Theory of Communicative Action, Vol.1, Reason and the Rationalization of Society.* Boston: Beacon Press.

Habermas, J. (1987). *The Theory of Communicative Action, Vol.2, The Critique of Functionalist Reason.* Boston: Beacon Press.

Hammersley, Martyn. (1992). *What's Wrong with Ethnography?* London and New York: Routledge Press.

Hannan, Megan. (2001). *Nursing Home Culture Change.* <http://www.culturechange-now.com/culture_change/pioneers.htm>. Retrieved January 23, 2004.

Hannan, Megan, and Keith Shaeffer. (n.d.). *The Eden Alternative: More Than Just Fuzzy Props and Potted Plants.* <http://www.edinmidwest.com/about_eden.html>. Retrieved November 30, 2004.

Harrington, C., C. Kovner, M. Mezney, J. Kayser-Jones, S. Burger, M. Mohler, R. Burke, and D. Zimmerman. (2000). Experts recommend minimum nurse staffing standards for nursing facilities in the United States. *Gerontologist* 40(1), 5-16.

Harrington, C., D. Zimmerman, S.L. Karon, J. Robinson, and P. Beutel. (2000). Nursing home staffing and its relationship to deficiencies. *Journal of Gerontology: Social Sciences,* 55B(5), S278-87.

Harris, John. (2001). The concept of the person and the value of life. In David Thomasma, David Weisstub, and Christian Hervé (Eds.), *Personhood and Health Care* (pp. 99–111). Dordrecht, NLD: Kluwer Academic.

Harrison, Christine. (1993). Personhood, dementia and the integrity of a life. *Canadian Journal of Aging, 12*(4), 428–40.

Hastrup, Kirsten. (1995). *A Passage to Anthropology: Between Experience and Theory.* London and New York: Routledge Press.

Hedt, Alice, and Janet Wells. (2004). Letter to Mark McClellan, Administrator of CMS, DHHS, July 29, 2004. <www.nccnhr.org>. Retrieved November 20, 2004.

Henderson, J. Neil. (1995). The culture of care in a nursing home: Effects of a medicalized model of long-term care. In J. Neil Henderson and Maria Vesperi (Eds.), *The Culture of Long-term Care* (pp. 37–54). Westport, CT: Bervin and Garvey.

Henderson, J. Neil. (2003). Alzheimer's units and special care: A soteriological fantasy. In Philip Stafford (Ed.), *Gray Areas: Ethnographic Encounters with Nursing Home Culture* (pp. 153–72). Santa Fe, NM: School of American Research Press.

Henderson, J. Neil, and Maria Vesperi (Eds.). (1995). *The Culture of Long-term Care.* Westport, CT: Bervin and Garvey.

Hendricks, Jon, and Cynthia Leedham. (1991). Dependency or empowerment: Toward a moral and political economy of aging. In M. Minker and C. Estes (Eds.), *Critical Perspectives on Aging: The Political and Moral Economy of Growing Old* (pp. 51–66). Amityville, NY: Baywood.

Hengstebeck, Barbara. (2004). Closing remarks, Barbara Hengstebeck, President, National Citizens' Coalition of Nursing Home Reform, at the annual meeting, October 17–20, 2004, Arlington, VA. <http://nursinghomeaction.org/public/245_1269_9910.cfm>. Retrieved December 3, 2004.

Henry, Jules. (1963). *Culture Against Man.* New York: Vintage Books.

Hernandez, Raymond, and Al Baker. (2005). Bush's Medicaid proposals could lead to overhaul of New York's system. *The New York Times, 154,* Sunday, January 9, 2005, Section 1, p. 24.

Herskovits, Elizabeth. (1995). Struggling over subjectivity: Debates about the "self" and Alzheimer's disease. *Medical Anthropology Quarterly,* 9(2), 146–64.

Hess, Beth, and Elizabeth Markson. (1995). *Growing Old in America,* 4th ed. New Brunswick, NJ: Transaction.

Hester, D.M. (2001). *Community as Healing.* Lanham, MD: Rowman & Littlefield.

Hewitt, Martin. (1991). Bio-politics and social policy: Foucault's account of welfare. In M. Featherstone, M. Hepworth, and B. Turner (Eds.), *The Body: Social Process and Cultural Theory* (pp. 225–255). London: Sage.

Hillery, George. 1978. Freedom, love and community. *Society,* 15(4), 24–31.

Hindess, Barry. (1996). *Discourses of Power: From Hobbes to Foucault.* Oxford: Blackwell.

Holahan, John, Alan Weil, and Joshua Wiener. (2003). Which way for federalism and health policy? *Health Affairs—Web Exclusive,* July 16, 317–33.

Holahan, John, Joshua Wiener, and Westpfahl Lutzky. (2002 May). Health policy for low-income people: States' responses to new challenges. *Health Affairs—Web Exclusive,* May 22, 187–218.

Hughes, Julian. (2001). Views of the person with dementia. *Journal of Medical Ethics*, 27(2), 86–91.

Hume, Lynne, and Jane Mulcock (Eds.). (2004). *Anthropologists in the Field: Cases in Participant Observation.* New York: Columbia University Press.

Hyer, Lee, and Amie Ragan. (2002). Training in long-term care facilities: Critical issues. *Clinical Gerontologist*, 25(3/4), 197–237.

Innes, Anthea (Ed.). (2003). *Dementia Care Mapping.* Baltimore: Health Professions Press.

Jackson, Andrew (Ed.). (1987). *Anthropology at Home.* London: Tavistock.

Kane, Robert. (2004). Commentary. Nursing home staffing: More is necessary but not necessarily sufficient. *Health Services Research*, 39(2), 251–55.

Kane, Robert, and K. Wilson. (1993). *Assisted Living in the United States: A New Paradigm for Residential Care for Frail Older Persons?* Washington, DC: American Association of Retired Persons.

Kaufman, Sharon. (2000). In the shadow of "Death with Dignity": Medicine and cultural quandaries of the vegetative state. *American Anthropologist*, 102(1), 69–83.

Kayser-Jones, Jeanie Schmit. (1981). *Old, Alone, and Neglected: Care of the Aged in Scotland and the United States.* Berkeley, CA: University of California Press.

Kayser-Jones, Jeanie. (2003). The treatment of acute illness in nursing homes. In Philip Stafford (Ed.), *Gray Areas: Ethnographic Encounters with Nursing Home Culture* (pp. 23–67). Santa Fe, NM: School of American Research Press.

Kemper, Peter. (2003). Long-term care research and policy. *The Gerontologist*, 43, 436–446.

Kidder, Tracy. (1993). *Old Friends.* Boston: Houghton Mifflin.

Kitwood, Tom. (1989). Brain, mind and dementia: With particular reference to Alzheimer's disease. *Ageing and Society*, 9, 1–15.

Kitwood, Tom. (1990). The dialectics of dementia: With particular reference to Alzheimer's disease. *Ageing and Society*, 10, 177–96.

Kitwood, Tom. (1997). *Dementia Reconsidered: The Person Comes First.* Buckingham: Open University Press.

Kitwood, Tom, and Kathleen Bredin. (1992). Towards a theory of dementia care. *Ageing and Society*, 12, 269–87.

Knuf, Joachim. (2000). The margins of communication: Coping with adult dementia. In Dawn Braithwaite and Teresa Thompson (Eds.), *Handbook of Communication and People with Disabilities: Research and Application* (pp. 485–503). Mahwah, NJ and London: Lawrence Erlbaum.

Kovach, Christine. (1997). Behaviors associated with late-stage dementia. In Christine Kovach (Ed.), *Late-Stage Dementia Care: A Basic Guide* (pp. 127–41). Washington, DC: Taylor & Francis.

Kral, Vojtech. (1962). Senescent forgetfulness: Benign and malignant. *Canadian Medical Association Journal, 86,* 257–60.

Kramer, A.M., and R. Fish (2001). The relationship between nurse staffing levels and the quality of nursing home care. In *Appropriateness of Minimum Nurse Staffing Ratios in Nursing Homes.* Report to Congress, Phase 2 final, chapter 2 (pp. 1—26). Washington, DC: U.S. Department of Health and Human Services, Health Care Financing Administration.

Kunin, J. (2003). Withholding artificial feeding from the severely demented: Merciful or immoral? Contrasts between secular and Jewish perspectives. *Journal of Medical Ethics, 29,* 208–12.

Kutsche, Paul. (1998). *Field Ethnography: A Manual for Doing Cultural Anthropology.* Upper Saddle River, NJ: Prentice-Hall.

Kylo, David (2004). Expert Opinion, David Kylo, Executive Director, National Center for Assisted Living. *Snalfnews.com,* posted 06/07/2004. <http://www.snalfnews.com/ExpertOpinion.cfm?id=5317>. Retrieved December 2, 2004.

Lacey, Debra. (1999). The evolution of care: A 100-year history of institutionalization of people with Alzheimer's disease. *Journal of Gerontological Social Work, 32*(3/4), 101–31.

Laird, Carobeth. (1979). *Limbo: A Memoir about Life in a Nursing Home by a Survivor.* Novato, CA: Chandler and Sharp.

Lawton, M. Powell. (1999). Measuring quality of life in nursing homes: The search continues. Invited address, divisions 34, 5, & 20, annual meeting of the American Psychological Association, August 23, 1999, Boston.

Lawton, M. Powell, and Robert L. Rubinstein. (2000). Introduction. In M. Powell Lawton and Robert L. Rubinstein (Eds.), *Interventions in Dementia Care* (pp. xiii–xx). New York: Springer.

Leibing, Annette. (2006). Divided gazes: Alzheimer's diseases, the person within and death in life. In Annette Leibing and Lawrence Cohen (Eds.), *Thinking About Dementia: Culture, Loss and the Anthropology of Senility* (pp. 240–68). New Brunswick, NJ: Rutgers University Press.

Lenhoff, Donna. (2002). *Government Study Provides "Compelling Evidence" For Nurse Staffing Standards In Nursing Homes.* National Citizens' Coalition for Nursing Home Reform, February 18, 2002. <http://nccnhr.newc.com/govpolicy/51_162_2852.CFM>. Retrieved December 3, 2004.

Lerner, Alan, and Robert Friedland. (1996). The evolution of Alzheimer's disease. *Gerontologist, 36*(5), 713–14.

Lichtenberg, P., and D. Strezpek (1990). Assessments of institutionalized dementia patients' competencies to participate in intimate relationships. *The Gerontologist, 30*(1), 117–20.

Lidz, Chuck, and R.W. Arnold. (1990). Institutional constraints on autonomy. *Generations* 14, special supplement, 65–68.

Liebowitz, Bernard. (1976). Administrative and economic aspects of an innovative treatment setting. Presented at the Symposium on the Weiss Institute. 29th annual scientific meeting of the Gerontological Society. New York.

Liebowitz, Bernard, M. Powell Lawton, and Arthur Waldman. (1979). Evaluation: Designing for impaired elderly people. *American Institute of Architects Journal, 68,* 59–61. (*A Prosthetically Designed Nursing Home,* title of original manuscript.)

Lindeman, David, and Rhonda Montgomery. (1994). Special care unit research challenges and opportunities. *Alzheimer's Disease and Associated Disorders, 8,* Supplement 1, S375–88.

Litwak, E. (1985). *Helping the Elderly: The Complementary Roles of Informal Networks and Formal Structures.* New York: Guildford Press.

Lock, Margaret. (1993). Cultivating the body: Anthropology and epistemologies of bodily practice and knowledge. *Annual Review of Anthropology, 22,* 133–55.

Lock, Margaret. (2005). Alzheimer's disease: A tangled concept. In Susan McKinnon and Sydel Silverman (Eds.), *Complexities: Beyond Nature and Nurture* (pp. 196–222). Chicago: University of Chicago Press.

Lock, Margaret, and Nancy Scheper-Hughes. (1996). A critical interpretive approach in medical anthropology: Rituals and routines of discipline and dissent. In Carolyn Sargent and Thomas Johnson (Eds.), *Medical Anthropology: Contemporary Theory and Method* (pp. 41–70). Westport, CN: Praeger Press.

Longino, Charles, and John Murphy. (1995). *The Old Challenge to the Biomedical Model.* Amityville, NY: Baywood.

Lyman, Karen. (1989). Bringing the social back in: A critique of the biomedicalization of dementia. *The Gerontologist, 29*(5), 597–605.

Lyman, Karen. (1993). *Day In, Day Out with Alzheimer's.* Philadelphia: Temple University Press.

Lynch, Marty, and Carroll Estes. (2001). The underdevelopment of community-based services in the U.S. long-term care system: A structural analysis. In Carroll Estes and Associates, *Social Policy and Aging: A Critical Perspective* (pp. 201–15). Thousand Oaks, CA: Sage.

Mace, Nancy. (1990). The management of problem behaviors. In N. Mace (Ed.), *Dementia Care: Patient, Family, and Community* (pp. 74–112). Baltimore: Johns Hopkins University Press.

Mace, Nancy, and Peter Rabins. (2001). *The 36-Hour Day.* Baltimore: Johns Hopkins University Press.

MacIntyre, Alisdair. (1981). *After Virtue.* Notre Dame, IN: University of Notre Dame Press.

Macklin, Ruth. (1990). Good citizen, bad citizen. In Rosalie Kane and Arthur Caplan (Eds.), *Everyday Ethics: Resolving Dilemmas in Nursing Home Life* (pp. 58–70). New York: Springer Press.

Marcus, George. (1995). On eccentricity. In Debbora Battaglia (Ed.), *The Rhetorics of Self-Making* (pp. 43–58). Berkeley, CA: University of California Press.

Marcus, George, and Michael Fischer. (1986). *Anthropology as Cultural Critique.* Chicago: The University of Chicago Press.

Marshall, Patricia. (1992). Anthropology and bioethics. *Medical Anthropology Quarterly,* 6(1), 49–73.

Martin, Richard, and Stephen Post. (1992). Human dignity, dementia and the moral basis of care giving. In Robert Binstock, Stephen Post, and Peter Whitehouse (Eds.), *Dementia and Aging: Ethics, Values, and Policy Choices* (pp. 55–68). Baltimore: Johns Hopkins University Press.

Maslow, K. (1994). Current knowledge about special care units: Findings of a study by the US Office of Technology Assessment. *Alzheimer's Disease and Associated Disorders,* 8, Supplement 1, S14–40.

McCann, Dennis. (2000). The concept of the person in Catholic social teaching. In Gerhold Becker (Ed.), *The Moral Status of Persons: Perspectives on Bioethics* (pp. 151–67). Amsterdam: Rodopi.

McEntee, William, and Glenn Larrabee. (2000). Age-associated memory impairment. *Current Treatment Options in Neurology,* 2, 73–80.

McKnight, John. (1995). *The Careless Society: Community and Its Counterfeits.* New York: Basic.

McLean, Athena. (1990). Contradictions in the social production of medical knowledge: The case of schizophrenia. *Social Science and Medicine,* 30(9), 969–85.

McLean, Athena. (1993). Limits to Sexuality and Personhood: Elderly residents in a Nursing Home. The annual meeting of the American Anthropological Association, Washington, DC, November 20, 1993.

McLean, Athena. (1994). What kind of love is this? *The Sciences,* 34(5), 36–40.

Mclean, Athena. (2001). Power in the nursing home: The case of a special care unit. *Medical Anthropology,* 19, 223–57.

McLean, Athena. (2006). Coherence without facticity in dementia: The curious case of Mrs. Fine. In Annette Leibing and Lawrence Cohen (Eds.), *Thinking About Dementia: Culture, Loss and the Anthropology of Senility* (pp. 157–70). New Brunswick, NJ: Rutgers University Press.

McLean, Athena. (forthcoming 2006). From commodity to community: An impossibility? A Forum piece. *Ageing and Society.*

McLean, Athena. (forthcoming). When the border of research and personal life become blurred: Thorny issues in conducting dementia research. In Athena McLean and Annette Leibing (Eds.), *The Shadow Side of Field Work: Theorizing the Borders Between Ethnography and Life*. Malden, MA: Blackwell Press.

McLean, Athena, and Margaret Perkinson. (1995). The head nurse as key informant: How beliefs and institutional pressures can structure dementia care. In J. Neil Henderson and Maria Vesperi (Eds.), *The Culture of Long-term Care* (pp. 126–48). Westport, CT: Bergin and Garvey.

Messerschmidt, Donald. (1981). *Anthropologists at Home in North America: Methods and Issues in the Study of One's Own Society*. Cambridge: Cambridge University Press.

Miller, Edward. (2002). State discretion and Medicaid program variation in long-term care: When is enough, enough? *Journal of Aging and Social Policy*, 14(3/4), 15–35.

Minkler, Meredith, and Thomas Cole. (1999). Political and moral economy: Getting to know one another. In M. Minkler and C. Estes (Eds.), *Critical Gerontology: Perspectives from Political and Moral Economy* (pp. 37–53). Amityville, NY: Baywood.

Minkler, Meredith, and Carroll Estes (Eds.). (1991). *Critical Perspectives on Aging: The Political and Moral Economy of Growing Old*. Amityville, NY: Baywood.

Montgomery, Rhonda. (1983). Staff-family relations and institutional care policies. *Journal of Gerontological Social Work*, 6(1), 25–37.

Montgomery, Rhonda, Tracy Karner, and Karl Kosloski. (2002). Weighing the success of a national Alzheimer's disease service demonstration. *Journal of Aging and Social Policy*, 14(3/4), 119–38.

Moody, Harry. (1988). Toward a critical gerontology: The contribution of the humanities to theories of aging. In James Birren and Vern Bengston (Eds.), *Emergent Theories of Aging* (pp. 19–39). New York: Springfield.

Moody, Harry. (1992). A critical view of ethical dilemmas in dementia. In Robert Binstock, Stephen Post, and Peter Whitehouse (Eds.), *Dementia and Aging* (pp. 86–100). Baltimore: Johns Hopkins University Press.

Moody, Harry. (2002). *Aging: Concepts and Controversies*, 4th ed. Pp. xxi–xxviii, 1–50. Thousand Oaks, CA: Pine Forge Press.

Mukamel, Dana, and William Spector. (2003). Quality report cards and nursing home quality. *The Gerontologist*, 43, 58–66.

Murray, D.W. (1993). What is the Western concept of the self? On forgetting David Hume. *Ethos, 21*(1), 3–23.

National Center for Assisted Living (NCAL). (2001a). Assisted Living: Independence, Choice and Dignity. http://www.ncal.org/about/alicd.pdf.. Retrieved December 2, 2004.

National Institute on Aging (NIA). (2003). *Alzheimer's: Unraveling the Mystery, Part 1*. USDHHS, NIH Publication #02-3782. <www.nia.nih.gov/Alzheimers/

Publications/Unraveling the Mystery/Part1/Hallmarks.htm>. Retrieved April 17, 2006.

Norris, Margaret, Susan MacNeil, and Mary Haines. (2003). Psychological and neuropsychological aspects of vascular and mixed dementia. In Peter A. Lichtenberg, Daniel Murman, and Alan Mellow (Eds.), *Handbook of Dementia: Psychological, Neurological, and Psychiatric Perspectives* (pp. 173–95). Hoboken, NJ: John Wiley & Sons.

Novak, David. (2001). The human person as the image of God. In David Thomasma, David Weisstub, and Christian Hervé (Eds.), *Personhood and Health Care* (pp. 43–54). Dordrecht, NLD: Kluwer Academic.

O'Boyle, Rich. (2002). *Medicare Coverage for Dementia Patients Clarified. ElderCare Online.* <http://www.ec-online.net/Knowledge/Articles/medicaredementia.html>. Retrieved November 30, 2004.

O'Boyle, Rich. (2003). *Memantine Officially Approved for Use in U.S. ElderCare Online.* <http://www.ec-online.net/Knowledge/Articles/memantine.html>. Retrieved November 30, 2004.

Office of Technology Assessment (OTA). Congress of the United States. (1992). *Special Care Units for People with Alzheimer's and Other Dementias: Consumer Education, Research, Regulatory, and Reimbursement Issues.* Washington, DC: U.S. Government Printing Office.

Ory, Marcia. (1994). Dementia special care: The development of a national research initiative. *Alzheimer's Disease and Associated Disorders, 8,* Supplement 1, S389–394.

Pandian, Jacob. (1985). *Anthropology and the Western Tradition.* Prospect Heights, IL: Waveland Press.

Parker, Jonathan. (2001). Interrogating person-centered dementia care in social work and social care practice. *Journal of Social Work, 1*(3), 329–45.

Pear, Robert. (2005). States propose sweeping changes to trim Medicaid by billions. *New York Times,* 154, May 29, 2005. Late Edition, Final, Section 1, p. 1.

Perkinson, Margaret. (2003). Defining family roles within a nursing home setting. In Philip Stafford (Ed.), *Gray Areas: Ethnographic Encounters with Nursing Home Culture* (pp. 235–61). Santa Fe, NM: School of American Research Press.

Pioneer Network. (2004a). *Pioneer History.* <http://www.pioneernetwork.net/index.cfm/fuseaction/showHistory.cfm>. Retrieved January 23, 2004.

Pioneer Network. (2004b). *Values, Vision, Mission.* <http://www.pioneernetwork.org/index.cfm/fuseaction/showValues.cfm>. Retrieved January 23, 2004.

Pipher, Mary. (2000). Another country, and xenophobia: Our fears divide us. In Olivia J. Smith (Ed.), *Aging in America* (pp. 140–52). *The Reference Shelf, 72*(3). New York: H.W. Wilson.

Plourde, Simonne. (2001). A key term in ethics. In David Thomasma, David Weisstub, and Christian Hervé (Eds.), *Personhood and Health Care* (pp. 137–48). Dordrecht, NLD: Kluwer.

Post, Stephen. (2000a). Alzheimer's disease in a hypercognitive society. In Peter J. Whitehouse, Konrad Maurer, and Jesse Ballenger (Eds.), *Concepts of Alzheimer's Disease: Biological, Clinical and Cultural Perspectives*, (pp. 245–59). Baltimore: Johns Hopkins University Press.

Post, Stephen. (2000b). *The Moral Challenge of Alzheimer's disease*, 2nd ed. Baltimore: Johns Hopkins University Press.

Potter, Van Rensselaer. (1999). On dying with personhood. *Perspective in Biology and Medicine*, 43(1), 1–5.

Quadagno, Jill. (1999). *Aging and the Life Course*. Boston: McGraw Hill College.

Rabins, Peter. (2003–04). *Communicating with the Alzheimer Patient*. Videotape 3 in a 3-tape series, *The Guide for Providing Quality of Life for Alzheimer Patients*. Baltimore: Video Press, University of Maryland, School of Medicine.

Rabins, Peter. (2004). Research update: Mild cognitive impairment (MCI): Definition, diagnosis, and treatment possibilities. *Advanced Studies in Medicine*, 4(6), 290–96.

Ramsey, Paul. (1970). *The Patient as Person: Explorations in Medical Ethics*. New Haven, CN: Yale University Press.

Reisburg, Barry, and Jeffrey Borenstein. (1986). Clinical diagnosis and assessment. *Drug Therapy*, 16(10), 43–59.

Reverby, Susan. (1997). A caring dilemma: Womanhood and nursing in historical perspective. In P. Conrad (Ed.), *The Sociology of Health and Illness: Critical Perspectives*, 5th ed. (pp. 215–25.). New York: St. Martin's Press.

Rhodes, Lorna A. (1992). The subject of power in medical/ psychiatric anthropology. In Atwood Gaines (Ed.), *The Cultural Construction of Professional and Folk Psychiatries* (pp. 51–65). Albany, NY: SUNY Press.

Richter, Ralph, and Brigette Richter. (2002). *Alzheimer's Disease*. London: Mosby Press.

Robertson, Ann. (1991). The politics of Alzheimer's disease: A case in apocalyptic demography. In *Critical Perspectives on Aging: The Political and Moral Economy of Growing Old* (pp. 135–52). Amityville, NY: Baywood.

Robertson, Russell, and Marcos Montagnini. (2004). Geriatric failure to thrive. *American Family Physician*, 70(2), 343–50.

Román, Gustavo. (2003). Neurological aspects of vascular dementia; basic concepts, diagnosis, and management. In Peter A. Lichtenberg, Daniel Murman, and Alan Mellow (Eds.), *Handbook of Dementia: Psychological, Neurological, and Psychiatric Perspectives* (pp. 149–72). Hoboken, NJ: John Wiley & Sons.

Rosenbaum, David. (2005). Bush to return to "Ownership Society" theme in push for social security changes. *The New York Times*, 154 (53,096), Sunday, January 16, 2005, Late national edition, Section 1, p. 17.

Sabat, Steven, and Rom Harré. (1992). The construction and deconstruction of self in Alzheimer's disease. *Ageing and Society*, 12, 443–61.

Said, Edward. (1979). *Orientalism*. New York: Vintage Books.

Salter, Chuck. (2005–06). (Not) the same old story. Article 31. In Harold Cox (Ed.), *Annual Editions: Aging 05/06*, 17th ed. (pp. 152–56). Dubuque, IA: McGraw-Hill/Dushkin. Reprinted from *Fast Company*, 76–86, February 6, 2002.

Sanjek, Roger. (1990). On ethnographic validity. In Sanjek R. (Ed.), *Fieldnotes: The Makings of Anthropology*. Ithaca, NY: Cornell University Press.

Sano, Mary, and Christine Weber. (2003). Psychological evaluation and non-pharmacologic treatment and management of Alzheimer's disease. In Peter A. Lichtenberg, Daniel Murman, and Alan Mellow (Eds.), *Handbook of Dementia: Psychological, Neurological, and Psychiatric Perspectives* (pp. 25–47). Hoboken, NJ: John Wiley & Sons.

Savishinsky, Joel (1985). Pets and family relationship among nursing home residents. *Marriage and Family Review*, 8(3/4), 109–34.

Savishinsky, Joel (1991). *The Ends of Time: Life and Work in a Nursing Home*. New York: Bergin and Garvey.

Sayhoun, Nadine, Laura Pratt, Harold Lentzner, Achintya Dey, and Kristen Robinson. (2001). The changing profile of nursing home residents: 1985–1997. *Aging Trends*, No. 4. Hyattesville, MD: National Center for Health Statistics.

Scheibe, Karl. (1989). Memory, identity, history and the understanding of dementia. In L. Eugene Thomas (Ed.), *Research in Adulthood and Aging: The Human Science Approach* (pp. 140–59). Albany, NY: SUNY Press.

Scheper-Hughes, Nancy. (2002). The genocidal continuum: Peace-time crimes. In Jeannette Mageo (Ed.), *Power and the Self* (pp. 29–47). Cambridge: Cambridge University Press.

Schnelle, John, Sandra Simmons, and S. Cretin. (2001). Minimum nurse aide staffing required to implement best practice care in nursing facilities. In *Appropriateness of Minimum Nurse Staffing Ratios in Nursing Homes*, Report to Congress, Phase 2 final, chapter 3. (pp. 1–40). Washington, DC: U.S. Department of Health and Human Services, Health Care Financing Administration.

Schnelle, John, Sandra Simmons, Charlene Harrington, Mary Cadogan, Emily Garcia, and Barbara Bates-Jensen. (2004). Relationship of nursing home staffing to quality of care. *Health Services Research*, 39(2), 225–50.

Schwartz, H., P. de Wolf, and J. Skipper. (1994). Gender, professionalization and occupational anomie: The case of nursing. In H. Schwartz (Ed.), *Dominant Issues in Medical Sociology*, 3rd ed. (pp. 266–76). New York: McGraw-Hill.

Schweder, R., N. Much, M. Mahapatra, and L. Park. (1998). The "Big Three" of morality (autonomy, community, divinity) and the "Big Three" explanations of suffering. In A. Brandt and P. Rozin (Eds.), *Morality and Health* (pp. 119–69). London and New York: Routledge.

Shield, Renée Rose. (1988). *Uneasy Endings*. Ithaca, NY: Cornell University Press.

Shield, Renée Rose. (2003). Wary partners. Defining family roles within a nursing home setting. In Philip Stafford (Ed.), *Gray Areas: Ethnographic Encounters with Nursing Home Culture* (pp. 203–33). Santa Fe, NM: School of American Research Press.

Shomaker, Dianna. (1987). Problematic behavior and the Alzheimer patient: Retrospection as a method of understanding and counseling. *The Gerontologist, 27*(3), 370–75.

Silberfeld, Michel. (2001). Vulnerable persons. In David Thomasma, David Weisstub, and Christian Hervé (Eds.), *Personhood and Health Care* (pp. 299–316). Dordrecht, NLD and Boston: Kluwer.

Smith, David. (1992). Seeing and knowing dementia. In Robert Binstock, Stephen Post, and Peter Whitehouse (Eds.), *Dementia and Aging* (pp. 44–54). Baltimore: Johns Hopkins University Press.

Smith, V., R. Ramesh, K. Gifford, E. Ellis, R. Rudowitz, and M. O'Malley. (2004). *The Continuing Medicaid Budget Challenge: State Medicaid Spending Growth and Cost Containment in Fiscal Years 2004 and 2005*. Results from a 50-state survey. The Henry Kaiser Commission on Medicaid and the Uninsured. October 2004. <http://www.kff.org/medicaid/7190.cfu>. Retrieved January 23, 2005.

Snowdon, David. (1997). Aging and Alzheimer's disease: lessons from the Nun Study. *The Gerontologist, 37*(2), 150–56.

Stafford, Philip. (1995). Foreword. In J. Neil Henderson and Maria Vesperi (Eds.), *The Culture of Long-term Care* (pp. ix–x). Westport, CT: Bergin and Garvey.

Stafford, Philip (Ed.). (2003a). *Gray Areas: Ethnographic Encounters with Nursing Home Culture*. Santa Fe, NM: School of American Research Press.

Stafford, Philip (2003b). Introduction. *Gray Areas: Ethnographic Encounters with Nursing Home Culture* (pp. 3–22). Santa Fe, NM: School of American Research Press.

Stone, Deborah. (2004). Shopping for long-term care. *Health Affairs, 23*(4), 191–96.

Takala, Tuija. (2001). Genetic knowledge and our conception of ourselves as persons. In David Thomasma, David Weisstub, and Christian Hervé (Eds.), *Personhood and Health Care* (pp. 91–97). Dordrecht, NLD: Kluwer.

Tancredi, Laurence (1987). The mental status exam. *Generations*, Summer 1987, 24–30.

Taylor, Charles. (1991). *The Ethics of Authenticity*. Cambridge: Cambridge University Press.

ter Meulen, Ruud. (2001). Toward a social concept of the person. In David Thomasma, David Weisstub, and Christian Hervé (Eds.), *Personhood and Health Care* (pp. 129–35). Dordrecht, NLD: Kluwer.

Thomas, William. (1994). *The Eden Alternative: Nature, Hope and Nursing Homes.* Sherbourne, NY: Eden Alternative Foundation.

Thomas, William. (2003). *The Green House Project: A Radically New Approach to Long-term Care.* <http://thegreenhouseproject.com/the%20idea.htm>. Retrieved January 23, 2004.

Thomas, William. (2004). *Expert Opinion,* William Thomas, M.D., Founder, The Green House Project. *Snalfnews.com.* Posted 08/09/2004 <http://www.snalfnews. com/ExpertOpinion.cfm?id=5823>. Retrieved December 2, 2004.

TLC (n.d.). *A Closer Look at Pioneer Practices.* <http://www.tlcinltc.org/ pioneerpractices/pioneerpractices.htm>. Retrieved December 3, 2004.

Trouillot, Michel-Rolph. (1991). Anthropology and the savage slot: The poetics and politics of otherness. In Richard Fox (Ed.), Recapturing Anthropology (pp. 18–44). Santa Fe, NM: SAR Press.

Turner, Bryan. (1984). *The Body and Society.* Oxford: Basil Blackwell.

Turner, Scott. (2003). Neurological aspects of Alzheimer's disease. In Peter A. Lichtenber, Daniel Murman, and Alan Mellow (Eds.), *Handbook of Dementia: Psychological, Neurological, and Psychiatric Perspectives* (pp. 1–24). Hoboken, NJ: John Wiley & Sons.

Turner, Victor. (1974). *The Ritual Process.* Harmondsworth: Penguin Press.

van Gennep, Arnold. (1960). *The Rites of Passage.* Chicago: University of Chicago Press.

Vesperi, Maria. (1983). The reluctant consumer: Nursing home residents in the post-Bergman Era. In Jay Sokolovsky (Ed.), *Growing Old in Different Societies: Cross Cultural Perspectives* (pp. 225–37). Belmont, CA: Wadsworth Press.

Vesperi, Maria. (1995). Nursing home research comes of age: Toward an ethnological perspective on long-term care. In J. Neil Henderson and Maria Vesperi (Eds.), *The Culture of Long-term Care* (pp. 7–21). Westport, CT: Bervin and Garvey.

Vesperi, Maria and Neil J. Henderson. (1995). Introduction. In J. Neil Henderson and Maria Vesperi (Eds.), *The Culture of Long-term Care* (pp. 1–4). Westport, CT: Bervin and Garvey.

Wachino, Victoria, Andy Schneider, and David Rousseau. (2004). *Financing the Medicaid Program: The Many Roles of Federal and State Matching Funds.* January 2004. The Henry Kaiser Commission on Medicaid and the Uninsured. October 2004. <http://www.kff.org/medicaid/7190.cfu>. Retrieved January 23, 2005.

Wagner, A., L. Terio, N. Orr-Rainey. (1995). Behavioral problems of residents with dementia in special care units. *Alzheimer's Disease and Associated Disorders,* 9(3), 121–27.

Walshe, Kieran. (2001). Regulating U.S. nursing homes: Are we learning from experience? *Health Affairs, 20*(6), 128–44.

Walshe, Kieran, and Charlene Harrington. (2002). Regulation of nursing facilities in the United States: An analysis of resources and performance of state survey agencies. *The Gerontologist, 42*(4), 475–87.

Ware, Tricia, Tihana Matosevic, Brian Hardy, Martin Knapp, Jeremy Kendall, and Julien Forder. (2003). Commissioning care services for older people in England: The view from care managers, users and carers. *Ageing and Society, 23*, 411–28.

Weisstub, David, and David Thomasma. (2001). Human dignity, vulnerability, personhood. In David Thomasma, David Weisstub, and Christian Hervé (Eds.), *Personhood and Health Care* (pp. 317–32). Dordrecht, NLD: Kluwer.

Weitz, Rose (1996). *The Sociology of Health, Illness, and Health Care: A Critical Approach*. Belmont, CA: Wadsworth.

Whitehouse, Peter. (2000). History and the future of Alzheimer's disease. In Peter Whitehouse, Konrad Maurer, and Jesse Ballenger (Eds.), *Concepts of Alzheimer's Disease: Biological, Clinical and Cultural Perspectives* (pp. 291–306). Baltimore: Johns Hopkins University Press.

Whitehouse, Peter J., Konrad Maurer, and Jesse Ballenger (Eds.). (2000). *Concepts of Alzheimer's Disease: Biological, Clinical and Cultural Perspectives*. Baltimore: Johns Hopkins University Press.

Whitehouse, Peter, and Harry Moody. (2006). Mild cognitive impairment: A "hardening of the categories"? *Dementia, 5*(1), 11–26.

Wiener, Joshua, and David Stevenson. (1998). State policy on long-term care for the elderly. *Health Affairs*, May/June, 81–100.

Williams, C.C. (1990). Long-term care and the human spirit. *Generations* (Fall), 25–28.

Winzelberg, Gary. (2003). The quest for nursing home quality. *Archives of Internal Medicine, 163*, 2552–56.

Wunderlich, Gooloo, and Peter Kohler (Eds.). (2001). *Improving the Quality of Long-term Care*. Committee on Improving Quality Care, Division of Health Care Services. Washington, DC: Institute of Medicine.

Wysocki, Bernard. (2002). As details slip, one man battles a loss of memory. *The Wall Street Journal, 240*(109), 1, A16, December 3, 2002.

Young, Allan. (1992). The anthropologies of illness and sickness. *Annual Review of Anthropology, 11*, 257–85.

Zarit, Steven, and Murna Downs. (1999). State of the art for practice with dementia. *Generations, 23*(3), 6–8.

Zeisel, John, and Paul Raia. (2000). Nonpharmacological treatment for Alzheimer's disease: A mind-brain approach. *American Journal of Alzheimer's disease and Other Dementias, 15*(6), 331–45.

Zelkovitz, Bruce. (1997). Transforming the "Middle Way": A political economy of aging policy in Sweden. In Jay Sokolovsky (Ed.), *The Cultural Context of Aging*, 2nd ed. (pp. 239–52). Westport, CN: Bergin & Garvey.

Zhang, Xinzi, and David Grabowski. (2004). Nursing home staffing and quality under the nursing home reform act. *The Gerontologist*, 44, 13–23.

Zucker, A. (1981). Holism and reductionism: A view from genetics. *Journal of Medicine and Philosophy*, 6(2), 145–63.

Zwillich, Todd. (2005). White house panel warns of aging crisis: Nation is unprepared to deal with care of elderly, President's council says. *WebMD Medical News*, September 29, 2005. <http://www.my.webmd.com/content/Article/112/110554.htm>. Retrieved, October 5, 2005.

INTERNET RESOURCES AND WEB SITES USED

AARP Research: <http://research.aarp.org/health/fs10r_nursing.html>.

AARP Research/Nursing Homes: <http://resarch.aarp.org/health/fs10r_nursing.html>

American Health Care Association: <http://www.ahca.org/news/nr030108.htm>

CDC-National Center for Health Statistics: Tables: <http://www.cdc.gov/nchs/data/hus/tables/2003/03hus>.

Center for Medicare and Medicaid Services: Charts and Statistics: <http://www.cms.hhs.gov/charts/series/sec3-b-c>; <http://www.cms.hhs.gov/statistics/nhe/historical/highlights.asp>.

ElderCare Online: <http://www.ec-online.net>.

Long-term Care: <http://ltc-usa.com/LTC/nursing_homes.htm>.

National Center for Assisted Living (NCAL): <http://www.ncal.org>.

National Pace Association: <http://www.npaonline.org/content/rsearch/what_pace.asp>.

Older Americans 2000: Key Indicators of Well-being, Updated Detailed Tables: <http://www.agingstats.gov/chartbook2000/population.html>.

The Older Population: A Profile of Older Americans: 2001: <www.aoa.gov/aoa/stats/profile/2001/1.html>.

Population Resource Center: <http://www.prcdc.org/summaries/aging/aging/html>.

A Profile of Older Americans: 2003, AoA: Statistics: <www.aoa.dhhs.gov/prof/Statistics/profile/2003/6_pf.asp>.

Rock Ethics Institute. Conference: Islam and Bioethics, March 27–28, 2006: <http://rockethics.psu.edu/islam_bioethics/cfp.htm>.

Index